MURDERERS AMONG US

A jealous husband opens fire at a wedding party, leaving a beautiful young woman dead. He then flees to Mexico ... A nine-year-old girl is the victim of a brutal and relentless sex killer ... A heated argument between two men on a highway leaves one dead and the other on the loose ... a deranged serial murderer leaves as his signature a bizarre kind of sexual mutilation. ... These, along with more than forty other intriguing cases are profiled in depth in this latest triumph by the authors of *The Only Living Witness*. A nerve-shattering portrait of crime in America, this compelling book will hold you in thrall with some of the most horrific murders ever to shock even the police.

With an Introduction by Roger L. Depue, Former chief of the FBI's Behavioral Science Unit, the Bureau's expert team of criminal personality profilers.

MURDERERS AMONG US:

Unsolved Homicides, Mysterious Deaths and Killers at Large

Stephen G. Michaud
and
Hugh Aynesworth

A SIGNET BOOK

SIGNET
Published by the Penguin Group
Penguin Books USA Inc., 375 Hudson Street,
New York, New York 10014, U.S.A.
Penguin Books Ltd, 27 Wrights Lane,
London W8 5TZ, England
Penguin Books Australia Ltd, Ringwood,
Victoria, Australia
Penguin Books Canada Ltd, 10 Alcorn Avenue,
Toronto, Ontario, Canada M4V 3B2
Penguin Books (N.Z.) Ltd, 182–190 Wairau Road,
Auckland 10, New Zealand

Penguin Books Ltd, Registered Offices:
Harmondsworth, Middlesex, England

First published by Signet, an imprint of New American Library,
a division of Penguin Books USA Inc.

First Printing, December, 1991
10 9 8 7 6 5 4 3 2 1

REGISTERED TRADEMARK—MARCA REGISTRADA

Printed in the United States of America

BOOKS ARE AVAILABLE AT QUANTITY DISCOUNTS WHEN USED TO PRO-
MOTE PRODUCTS OR SERVICES. FOR INFORMATION PLEASE WRITE TO PRE-
MIUM MARKETING DIVISION, PENGUIN BOOKS USA INC., 375 HUDSON
STREET, NEW YORK, NEW YORK 10014.

ACKNOWLEDGMENTS

This book would have been impossible to complete without the active assistance of the police. We gratefully acknowledge our indebtedness to the scores of officers, detectives, inspectors, and agents from 65 law enforcement jurisdictions in 17 states and Canada who were both patient and generous with their help.

We were ably assisted by our associates, Avery Hunt and Larry Sutherland. Their persistent and innovative reporting was much appreciated.

Thanks once more to Kathy Robbins, aka Agent Orange, and her professional staff at The Robbins Office: Stephen Bromage, Elizabeth Mackey, Lauren Marino, and Julia Null.

Finally, we owe Ms. Macabre, Michaela Hamilton, for her steadfastness and deft guidance.

CONTENTS

SECTION TWO: CENTRAL

SECTION THREE: EAST AND SOUTHEAST

INTRODUCTION

by Roger L. Depue

In 1962, when I was a young police officer in Clare, Michigan, just beginning my career in law enforcement, 8,404 persons were reported murdered in the United States. I remember seeing that figure in the FBI's Uniform Crime Report (UCR) and reflecting on its sheer size; the annual number of murders in the United States exceeded Clare's entire population at the time. However, to paraphrase the old music hall line, I hadn't seen nuthin' yet. In 1990, the UCR figure for reported homicides in the United States was a staggering 23,438.

A police homicide squad's effectiveness customarily is measured by the percentage of murders that detectives clear by arrest in any calendar year. The national clearance rate in 1962 was 93 percent, meaning that fewer than 600 homicides that year remained open cases on December 31. It wasn't easy to get away with murder in those days.

At present, by contrast, the clearance rate has plummeted to below 70 percent, meaning that about 7,000 cases were officially unsolved at year's end. Not only have we seen a significant increase in murders since the early 1960s, but the cleared-by-arrest record has deteriorated alarmingly. Since I first came on the job, the number of people being killed each year has risen 280 percent, while at the same time the number of murderers who aren't even arrested, much less tried, convicted, or sentenced for their crimes, has exploded by more than 1200 percent.

How can we explain the increasing violence in our communities, large and small? Why has there been this bold emergence of cold-blooded homicide by criminals as diverse as the knife-wielding murderer-emasculator whose story is found in "A Serial Killer" in Section One of _Murderers Among Us_, or the drug-trade hitman Mario Coto "Risita" in Section Three or the psychologically troubled Vietnam vet, Ron Miranda "Demons" in Section One, for whom alcohol was a deadly stimulant to mayhem? These are deeply troubling mysteries that interweave every story in _Murderers Among Us_, a fearsome and sobering portrait of murder in modern America.

Perhaps the answers to some of these questions are to be found in the very fabric of our society. As a people, we have undergone a transformation, creating physical and emotional distance among us. In the early 1900s, the majority of Americans lived and worked on family farms. Today, a scant 3 percent of us live on farms and work in agribusiness, as it is now known. This mass migration from the countryside and small-town America to the cities and their suburbs wrought important changes in how we live and how we relate to one another.

For the first time, the majority of fathers weren't home-based and self-employed. They became wage earners and left their homes—and families—for 10, 12, 14 hours or more each day. One result of this paternal void at home was a dilution of positive fatherly influence on their sons. Many young men were denied their caring mentors, or role models, and thus failed to receive much needed adult guidance in their often turbulent years of transition from dependence to independence; there was no proper initiation into their own manhood.

Rebellion, of course, is natural to youth. Nor is it a recent phenomenon. "The youth of today no longer listen to the wise counsel of the elders," complained Socrates more than two millennia ago. "They make light of the wisdom of the past. They make jest of their teachers."

The difference, of course, is that 2,400 years ago Socrates was worried about willful ignorance, impertinence, and sass among the young. Today, alienated or antisocial young males commit 9 out of every 10 crimes of violence.

The family itself has been dislocated. From the old communities of extended families living in physical proximity to friends and close acquaintances, we now constantly move among strangers. The transience of American society is astounding. Today, an average family will move 12 times before the children are grown. Each year, about 36 million Americans relocate; that is more than a tenth of the population establishing new addresses every 52 weeks! In this sort of world, the cohesion and supportive socialization traditionally fostered by family, religion, neighborhood, and school are seriously—fatally—undermined. In a transient, fast-paced assembly-line environment, the weekly paycheck and television have supplanted the old customs and influences as focal points of life.

There are also subtler clues to the type of society we have become, physical changes that reflect our psychological isolation from one another. Consider the evolving design and structure of the average American home. In the 1930s and 1940s, the average house offered about 800 square feet of interior living space, whereas today's residential structures are far roomier, more than 2,000 square feet, on average.

Families of 50 years ago could abide their houses' comparatively cramped interiors because most also were outfitted with magnificent front porches, sometimes huge covered spaces with room for chairs, tables, couches, a glider, or possibly even a small swing. Weather permitting, on weekday evenings and all through the weekend these spacious, often gracious, informal family pavilions beckoned to neighbors and passersby to come up the steps to sit and visit awhile. Every sort of social intercourse, from checker games to luncheons to courtship, occurred on the nation's front porches.

In the 1950s and early 1960s, the front porch began to shrink. Wooden construction gave way to utilitarian concrete and a black wrought-iron railing. There was maybe enough room for two chairs.

Then, in the late 1960s and 1970s, the front

porch disappeared altogether. Today, the front door of most new homes opens onto a modest concrete slab and that's about it. In most modern subdivisions, neighbors would think it eccentric for a person, or a couple, or a family to sit together around their front door.

So what happened to the front porch? It migrated around to the rear of the house and today is called the deck, or patio. As a rule, it looks out over a backyard enclosed by a fence or hedges. An unannounced, early-evening drop-in visit from a neighbor is one of the last things a modern breadwinner wishes to encourage after a long and hectic working day. Instead, he or she hopes for peace and tranquility in which to savor a can of beer or a cocktail in the nightly effort to relax before dinner. Privacy, isolation, and insulation are our critically important tools for coping with an increasingly stressful existence.

Naturally, criminals see new opportunities in this world of strangers. Felons, too, are adaptive. They modify their techniques and adjust their behavior patterns to take advantage of the changing environment.

Serial killers, for example, spread their depredations from jurisdiction to jurisdiction, knowing that separate police departments have difficulty coordinating their investigations of such crimes. Similarly, the modern hitman moves from place to place, executing his targets in comfortable anonymity. Even on crowded urban streets, the outrageous effrontery of a drive-by slaying can be committed with relative impunity. Ghetto witnesses too often have very poor recall for the identities of those who wreak havoc in their neighborhoods. It's safer to keep one's mouth shut.

Law enforcement agencies wage an uneven struggle with this cresting wave of violent lawlessness. They are hobbled, in my view, by a cultural lag, a general unwillingness on the part of the public to be alert and responsive to the human predators in their midst. Neighborhood Watch programs are one effective way of recruiting the public in the fight for their own safety. In the past few years, television programs such as *America's Most Wanted* and *Unsolved Mysteries* have given local law enforcement a welcome boost in the never-ending hunt for fugitives or clues to their identity. New community policing initiatives are useful attempts at bringing officers and civilians together, reminding both of their shared interests and common humanity. Books such as this one, as well as the authors' previous volume, *Wanted for Murder*, help to educate society about its criminals, and encourage readers to get involved responsibly. To date, however, the criminals remain the clear winners.

Yet the good guys can adapt, too. One of the most innovative and potent new weapons for fighting violent crime is a program I was pleased and honored to lead. In 1985, the FBI established at its academy in Quantico, Virginia, the National Center for the Analysis of Violent Crime (NCVAC), and with it, the Bureau's Violent Criminal Apprehension Program (VICAP).

We founded NCVAC and VICAP as a behavioral science and data processing resource center to provide assistance for local law enforcement agencies confronted with unusual, bizarre, vicious, and repetitive crimes of violence. Many of those 7,000 unsolved homicides each year now are submitted to the FBI by police departments and are entered into VICAP's computers where each case, described in detail, can be compared with all other unsolved homicides within the system.

In the past, officers such as Stevan Ridge in Utah "A Serial Killer" and Trooper Stephen Toboz in Pennsylvania might have learned of each other's similar homicides by luck, if at all. Now, VICAP can make the linkages as it did in this case, plus the computers are programmed to identify trends and patterns. Later, profiles of the unknown offenders can be developed, leading to strategies for the swifter apprehension of these perpetrators. This is an important benefit, because if law enforcement can put a timely stop to a serial killer, not only will open cases be solved, but future murders will be prevented, too.

Elsewhere at NCVAC, original research conducted by members of the FBI's Behavioral Science Unit has lead to important new knowledge of violent criminals such as assassins, sexually oriented serial killers, serial rapists, and child abductors. Intensive interviews with the most sophisticated of representative offenders in each group, together with careful analysis of their crimes by experienced agents and officers with behavioral science degrees, have yielded insights into the criminals' motives, patterns of development, techniques for targeting and attacking victims, and their methods for evading detection and apprehension. This information, in turn, has been made available to local police via criminal justice publications and advanced training courses conducted for police officers by the FBI at Quantico.

I would like to see a reaffirmation of that bond that people once felt with their police. Because more than 90 percent of all crimes cleared by arrest have that outcome as a result of information furnished to police by interested citizens, a return to trust and respect between the public and the police would certainly expedite the return of peace and civility to our beleaguered communities. As you, the reader, make your way through *Murderers Among Us*, take time to reflect on persons you may have seen who resemble these criminals. If you think you know where one of the killers might be, call the number provided with each story, or any FBI office.

In the end, responsibility for dealing with the evil is ours. Toward the close of the eighteenth century, the political philospher, Edmund Burke, expressed this truth best: "The only thing necessary for evil to triumph," Burke wrote, "is for good men to do nothing."

Dr. Depue, a noted authority on criminal behavior, holds a Ph.D. in counseling and development from American University in Washington, D.C. In 1967, he resigned as chief of the Clare, Michigan, police force to join the FBI, where he became a member of the Bureau's first SWAT (Special Weapons and Tactics) team, "Spider One." From 1974 until his retirement in 1989, Depue was assigned to the FBI's Behavioral Science Unit at Quantico. He was named chief of the unit in 1980. Dr. Depue currently is president of The Academy Group, Inc., of Manassas, Virginia, a company of mental health professionals and former FBI, CIA, and Secret Service agents with behavioral science expertise, who consult with private industry on a range of problems and issues from "avenger" employees to sabotage, kidnapping, extortion, product tampering, and violence in the workplace.

It was the surety of it, the inevitability that during every single day that dawned man could be depended upon to prove again that even after thousands of years of progressing civilization, he was utterly incapable of controlling his earliest criminal impulse. In this one thing man was frighteningly consistent, and incorrigible.

—David L. Lindsey
Spiral

SECTION ONE

WEST AND SOUTHWEST

Suspect

Breckenridge, Colorado

Is Jeffrey Oberholtzer of Alma, Colorado, indeed the anguished widower he claims to be, still mourning his murdered wife Bobbie, and angry that after nearly a decade of investigation the authorities have yet to identify her brutal killer, let alone arrest him? Or, as his younger brother Jamie suspects, is Jeff Oberholtzer himself the killer—a double killer—and an amazingly durable dissembler who so far has betrayed not a trace of guilt for the merciless crimes he committed on a bitter-cold Epiphany night, January 6, 1982?

"I can't prove it," says Jamie Oberholtzer. "All the evidence is what you call circumstantial. But I do believe he killed her."

Jeff responds that his brother may be blinded by his own unrequited love for Bobbie. "She was a very lovable gal," says Jeff. "He had a crush on her, and I married her. I love my brother dearly, but he's messed up my life real bad."

Here are the background and details of the

3

bloody night, together with the puzzling, contradictory evidence that tends both to implicate Jeffrey Oberholtzer, and to exonerate him, in the January 6, 1982, gunshot murders of his wife and another female of his acquaintance, 21-year-old Annette Kay Schnee.

Barbara Jo Burns was born on Christmas Day, 1952. She spent her girlhood in Racine, Wisconsin, where she matured into a spirited young woman, about five feet three inches tall, 110 pounds, with blue eyes and blond hair. Bobbie became pregnant while still in high school and left before graduation in order to have her baby girl, whom she named Jackie. She subsequently married the child's father. They were amicably divorced in 1974.

That same year, Bobbie, then 22, and another Racine youth, 19-year-old Jeff Oberholtzer, moved together to the Mt. Snow vicinity of southern Vermont, then back to Wisconsin where they were married in 1978. Bobbie's ex-husband meanwhile took custody of their daughter.

Jeff worked as a machinist, fabricating garbage disposal systems in the local In-Sink-Erator plant while he learned home appliance repair from Bobbie's father. After belatedly finishing high school, Bobbie was employed as a waitress, a chambermaid, and as a clerk in a Racine pet store. She loved animals.

In May of 1980, after several visits to Colorado, the couple decided to quit their native northern plains for a new life up in the Rockies. They settled in Alma, an old mining town on State Route 9, south of the Continental Divide and steep Hoosier Pass from Breckenridge, the more affluent vacation ski village 17 miles away.

Jeff Oberholtzer opened a repair business, "Alpine Appliances," which he operated out of their rented duplex in Alma, right on Route 9. Bobbie took a secretarial job at a local real estate firm, as well as part-time work tending bar at Alma's Only Bar, also known as the A-O-B. In January of 1981 she landed a more lucrative position at Cal-Colorado, a real estate investment company up the road and over the pass in Breckenridge.

Their combined incomes allowed the Oberholtzers to just get by, week to week. Yet though they were chronically short of cash, the couple did manage to buy Bobbie a horse, a $75 mustang she called Nakoosa, and to make a down payment on a 2-acre potential homesite in neighboring Park County. Jeff Oberholtzer secured the loan for the land with his Ford pickup and a coin collection.

Brother Jamie Oberholtzer, who followed Jeff out to Alma from Racine, and Jamie's wife, Cindy, whom he met and married in Colorado, both allege that there were significant strains in the Oberholtzer marriage, problems stemming in part from Jeff's drug use. Although Jeff concedes that he did consume controlled substances, he insists that his marriage to Bobbie was solid. According to Richard Eaton, an investigator for the Summit County Sheriff's Department, police inquiries uncovered no inordinate stresses in the Oberholtzer marriage.

Jeff wrote poetry. Bobbie raised birds: finches and a cedar waxwing that she had discovered injured in Wisconsin and had nursed

Bobbie
Oberholtzer.

Bobbie with
Jeff on their
wedding day.

to health. Sometimes Jeff and Bobbie fought. On Monday night, January 4, 1982, for example, Bobbie was supposed to come home with a hot pizza for dinner. She was late. The pizza was cold. Jeff lost his temper. Jamie Oberholtzer claims Jeff was so irate that he took a swing at Bobbie, missed, and put his fist through a wall. The argument spilled over into the next day and evening at a bar and, later, was duly recounted by witnesses to the police. "The cops just blew it all out of proportion at the time," says Jeff. "We had a fight over cold pizza and so I murdered her?"

Another point of contention: Jeff says Bobbie was ready to have another child, and that she stopped taking her birth-control pills on January 2, 1982. Jamie and Cindy deny this was so. They insist that later, in the Oberholtzers' house, they found a note—unsigned and undated but clearly written in Bobbie's hand—which read, in their paraphrase, "If you kill me today, how can I ever have your child tomorrow? You don't know what I just found out." Jamie and Cindy say that the note was handed over to the police and what Bobbie had "just found out" probably was an instance of philandering: They accuse Jeff of chronic womanizing. Investigator Richard Eaton reports that he never has seen this note and has no knowledge of the alleged message.

The last day of Bobbie Oberholtzer's life, January 6, a Wednesday, began as most weekdays did with a 5:30 alarm. According to Jeff, Bobbie readied herself for work as usual, then asked if he had a little money to help buy some golden raisins; her finicky waxwing would eat nothing else. Oberholtzer recounted to police that he was able to scrounge up a few quarters.

Since Jeff needed his Ford pickup for his business, Bobbie was obliged to hitchhike to work, which she did not particularly relish. However reasonable her distaste for bumming transportation may have been, Bobbie's husband insists the practice was common in their group at that time, and that hitching in the Breckenridge area was not particularly inconvenient or dangerous, even for a young woman. Bobbie never rode with someone she didn't know. "You stood out at a certain spot in front of the house or in Breckenridge," he says, "and people who knew you would pull right over. You didn't have to stick your thumb out. It was like a community carpool-bus stop."

A cup of coffee in hand, Oberholtzer watched from a window that morning as his wife stood in front of their house, waiting for a lift. He remembers seeing a car stop for her, and remembers that he didn't recognize the vehicle, which bore out-of-state plates. Whoever the driver was, he or she delivered Bobbie safely to work at the Cal-Colorado offices on time at 8:30. Mrs. Oberholtzer spent an uneventful day at her desk.

Annette Kay Schnee of Blue River, Colorado, on the north side of Hoosier Pass, was a willowy native Iowan, an inch or two taller than Bobbie Oberholtzer. She weighed just 95 pounds. Her eyes were brown as was her hair, which Annette streaked with a blond rinse. According to her mother, Eileen Franklin, Annette had been a member of her high school drill team in Sioux City, and later studied modeling in Omaha. Before moving to the Breck-

Annette Schnee.

enridge area, where she had many friends, Annette often had talked of becoming an airline stewardess.

In contrast to the assertive and high-spirited Bobbie Oberholtzer (with whom she may have had a nodding familiarity), Annette Kay Schnee was normally docile and sometimes given to moods. In her diary, she often complained that her personal life was unfulfilling, and that men seemed to take her for granted. "I feel I need to get my act together here real soon," she wrote on January 2. "I'm not sure what's in store for me . . . this year, but it should be interesting."

At 3:30 on the frigid, clear afternoon of January 6, Annette Schnee finished her shift as a chambermaid at the Holiday Inn in the town of Frisco, about 10 miles north of Breckenridge along Route 9. She had five hours off before she was scheduled for work at her second job as a cocktail waitress at a Breckenridge nightspot known as The Flipside.

Like Bobbie, Annette hitched almost everywhere she went. Her first stop that afternoon was the Summit County Medical Center, also in Frisco, where she was treated for a yeast infection. Next, Annette headed south down Route 9 for Breckenridge and a pharmacy, The Drug Store, where she would get her infection prescription filled. A local man later informed police that he picked up Annette after her medical appointment and drove her half the distance south to Breckenridge. It is at present unknown how she covered the rest of the way.

In Breckenridge, Drug Store pharmacist Bob Beitcher would remember filling Annette Schnee's prescription and that she walked out the pharmacy door at some time around 4:30. Beitcher's only other relevant recollection was of another white female, unfamiliar to him, dark-headed and probably in her early twenties, about five feet three inches tall and of medium build, who appeared to be with Annette that afternoon. As Summit County sheriff's detective Eaton tells the story, Schnee was overheard reminding the unidentified other female that she'd mentioned she needed cigarettes. "Oh, yeah," the woman answered, and bought a pack of Marlboros. To this day, her identity is not known.

Annette's next destination was the house she shared with five other single people about a half-mile off Route 9 in Blue River, another small mountain community 6 miles south of Breckenridge. She was due home to change into her night uniform, the cowboy hat and hotpants Annette wore when waitressing at The Flipside.

She never made it.

A full darkness had descended over Breckenridge by late afternoon on the sixth, and with the sun gone the ambient temperature began plummeting to an overnight low of around 30 below zero. People bundled themselves in several layers of clothing wherever they went.

At a little past 5, according to Detective Eaton, Bobbie reportedly called home to tell her husband Jeff that she was going to have a drink with friends at a bar called The Pub in the Bell Tower Mall, a short walk from the Cal-Colorado office. There was no answer down in Alma.

At 6:20 she called Jeff again from a pay phone at The Pub. This time he answered. According to Jeff Oberholtzer, he and his wife discussed what they would eat for dinner—pot roast, probably—and Bobbie informed him that her friends Char McKesson and Dan Carey would be driving her home.

An hour passed. "Supposedly," says Detective Eaton, "she started getting upset with these people because they didn't want to go home. She told the bartender that she was going to call home. She grabbed some change and went into the hall and came back a few minutes later, grabbed her coat, and told the bartender, 'I'm gonna leave. Don't tell them I've gone for a while. Just tell 'em I'm going to hitchhike home, thanks anyway.' Then she left."

According to this version of the story, Bobbie had a short walk to a convenience-store parking lot where she and other hitchers customarily waited for rides south on Route 9 over Hoosier Pass to Alma. At approximately 7:50 that night, a local resident stopped his truck at the store to offer a ride to a hitcher who fit her description; the man later was able to describe the clothes Bobbie wore that day. He told investigators that she declined to get in his truck because he wasn't going all the way south to Alma. This man is the last person to report seeing Bobbie Oberholtzer alive.

Jeff Oberholtzer discounts both the bartender and the truckdriver's recollections. He says he told his wife by telephone that if she wanted a ride she need only call home. "I told her, 'If you want me to come get you, I'll come get you.' She said, 'Don't worry about it. I'll see you when I get home.'

"I believe that she walked back to the telephones and saw someone she knew and they went out the door together. That's why she didn't go back in the bar. It was 30 below that night, with the wind blowing. There was no way she was going to go outside and hitchhike home when she could have made a telephone call to me."

Down at their rented house in Alma, Jeff Oberholtzer seems to have received a steady stream of visitors that afternoon. Only in mid-1991 have most of them finally been located by the authorities and thoroughly questioned as to their recollections of that afternoon and early evening. According to Detective Eaton, it appears that Jeff Oberholtzer could not have been away from the Alma residence for more than just a couple minutes from around 4:00 or 4:30 until some time after 6. Telephone company records support Jeff's memory of answering Bobbie's 6:20 P.M. call from The Pub. Still later visitors to his house place Jeffrey there, watching television, at least until eight o'clock.

Alone in the house, as he explained to investigators, Oberholtzer put away the uneaten dinner—including the chocolate pudding he'd made for dessert—and continued watching television as he grew increasingly upset with his wife for not arriving home, or calling. He dressed for bed and was able to sleep, he says, until 12:10 A.M. when Oberholtzer was startled awake by a police or ambulance siren, wailing south on Route 9 toward the town of Fairplay, 6 miles away, where Route 9 intersects with Route 285, the main road to Denver, which lies about 50 miles to the northeast. Worried anew, he says, Oberholtzer dressed himself and moved to the couch where he dropped off again until approximately 2:10 A.M. At this point, Jeff told police, he was "extremely anxious."

It was too late to call The Pub, so Jeff jumped in his pickup and drove over to his brother's house. "He was having a screaming fit," Jamie recalls. 'Bobbie's dead! Bobbie's dead!' And I said, 'What are you talking about?'

" 'Oh, she's dead! She's not home. If she was alive she'd be home! She's dead!' " Jamie also remembers that his brother seemed freshly showered, which seemed odd for the hour and circumstance.

Jeff borrowed $5 from Jamie, and then drove to Char McKesson and Dan Carey's house, awakened them, and asked what they knew about his missing wife. His friends replied that Bobbie had consumed about three rum-and-

Cokes with them, and then, according to what bartender Gus Garbounoff told them, she'd left on her own at about 7:30 to hitch a ride home.

"Again," he says, "that didn't make sense to me. She *knew* I was at home. The thing that sticks in my craw is that *no* locals hitchhiked over to Alma at that time of night, especially in that kind of weather."

Jeff drove north to the Cal-Colorado office in Breckenridge. He says he jumped up on the garbage dumpsters so he could peer down through a window into Bobbie's office: Possibly, he remembers thinking, she had drunk a little too much at The Pub and, for some reason, had gone back to her desk and dozed off. He saw no sign of her, however, and all he got the several times he dialed her office number was Bobbie's recorded voice.

"Afterward it was eerie, thinking about that," he says.

Oberholtzer's next stop was the Breckenridge police department, where he reported his wife missing. It was now about 3:30 A.M. According to Jeff, he spent the balance of the night driving around the area, searching for Bobbie.

By nine o'clock that morning, Jeff Oberholtzer had returned home where he took a call from rancher Donald Hamilton, of Como, Colorado, a community 10 or 11 miles northeast of Fairplay on Route 285, the Denver road. Hamilton reported to Oberholtzer that he had just found Bobbie's driver's license in his yard. Subsequent searches would reveal that the license and the rest of the contents of Bobbie's wallet apparently had been flung onto Hamil-

ton's property from Route 285. The wallet itself was not recovered.

Jeff dispatched Jamie to retrieve the license,
and then joined friends as they searched Route 9
and 285 between Alma and Como, hoping to
find more evidence of Bobbie. About 4 miles
southwest of Como, on the right, or southeast,
side of Route 285, they recovered Bobbie's distinctive blue backpack. Nearby was one of her
gloves, stained with what lab tests would show
was human blood, type unknown, and a facial
tissue also smeared with human blood. A Kool
filter cigarette butt lay there, too.

Some hours later, a snowplow operator working the east side of Route 9 came upon Bobbie's
leather cosmetic pouch. It was resting on the
roadside berm, or snowbank, between Alma and
Fairplay. Based on this and the other discover-
ies that morning, it seemed that someone had
driven south in the night on Route 9 to Fairplay, and then northeast on 285, tossing Bobbie's property out of their car as they drove
along, possibly bound for Denver. On the other
hand, the apparent trail might have been a de-
liberate deception, a red herring designed to
lead detectives away from their quarry.

Jeffrey Oberholtzer and his friends took Bobbie's recovered belongings to the sheriff's office in Fairplay, and once again reported her
missing. The sheriff made no immediate move
to join in the hunt for Mrs. Oberholtzer. In fact,
the deputy Oberholtzer talked to suggested
Bobbie had simply decided to split. As it turned
out, the search for her didn't take long.

At three o'clock on the afternoon of the seventh, fewer than 20 hours after she was last
seen alive, a party of searchers on skis discov-

ered Bobbie Oberholtzer's frozen corpse, with
two bullet holes in it, lying in deep snow at the
top of Hoosier Pass, about 65 feet to the west
of the Route 9 centerline. She was fully clothed.

From interviews with her husband and
friends, subsequent searches and forensic processing of the crime scene, as well as the
nearby Hoosier Pass parking lot—and with
what could be established at autopsy—the police have pieced together the following probable scenario of Bobbie Oberholtzer's final
minutes and murder.

She was so adamant about never hitching
with strangers that it seemed likely that Bobbie knew her killer, or perhaps killers; more
than one person may have been responsible for
the crime. Else she was coerced into his, or
their, vehicle, perhaps at gunpoint. A nylon
wire restraint, similar to the plastic "flex
cuffs" that many police departments now use
in place of metal handcuffs, was attached to
her left wrist. Through it was looped a second
such flat wire, clearly intended for her right
wrist. Investigators speculate that Bobbie, who
was very strong for her size, successfully
fought off all attempts to secure both cuffs.
Also, she sustained abrasions on her right
hand, injuries consistent with a fistfight in
which the victim managed to land a few
punches. Since her heavy brass keyring (a defensive weapon Jeff had made for Bobbie's
protection) was found in the Hoosier Pass
parking lot, at least a portion of the struggle
probably occurred there.

If the attack's intent was rape, it was foiled.
The coroner reported that Bobbie had not been
sexually abused. Instead, judging from the bul-

let wounds and blood and footprint patterns at the crime scene, it appeared that she broke loose from the abduction vehicle in the parking lot and took off, running south along the crest of Hoosier Pass on Route 9.

She made it about 100 yards, says Detective Eaton. Bobbie then must have clambered to her right up the 3- to 4-foot high roadside snowbank where she turned around, perhaps to plead for her life.

She was shot, twice. One bullet grazed Bobbie Jo's right breast. The other slug, the fatal one, pierced her right lung.

Blood splatters and her footprints preserved in the otherwise undisturbed snow suggested that she tumbled down the other side of the berm, away from her attacker, who did not try to follow her. Mortally wounded, Bobbie Jo stumbled south through the snow until she hit deep drifts, then willed herself back north along the berm, rapidly losing strength. Her scarlet trail then veered wildly to the west, away from the road, to a point where she collapsed and bled to death.

One day later, on January 8, one of Annette Schnee's coworkers at the Holiday Inn in Frisco reported her missing to the Summit County sheriff, whose investigators soon established that pharmacist Bob Beitcher at The Drug Store in Breckenridge was the last known person to see Annette alive as she left the store with her prescription—and possibly the dark-haired woman—at 4:30 on the afternoon of the sixth. From then until the next summer, neither the sheriff nor detectives for the Colorado Bureau of Investigation (CBI) were able to make any appreciable progress in either case.

In the late morning of July 3, 1982, vaca-
tioner Arthur S. Davison of Denver called the
Park County Sheriff's Office to report that his
13-year-old son, Allen, had just discovered a
dead woman lying facedown in Sacramento
Creek. Annette Kay Schnee had been found.

The first fact of interest was her body's location. To reach the creek site, Annette's killer,
or killers, had turned west off Route 9 onto
County Road 14 about a mile and a half north
of Fairplay. He, or they, then drove approximately 3 miles to a spot just short of where
County Road 14 ended in a cul-de-sac barely
wide enough for an average-size vehicle to
make a U-turn. County Road 14, although it
was serviced through the winter by snow-
plows, was little more than a gravel track.
Most motorists along Route 9 wouldn't even
notice the turnoff. It was the near-universal assumption among the cops working the case
that whoever murdered Annette Schnee knew
beforehand about County Route 14. The detectives would be looking for someone local.

Equally important clues emerged at Annette's
autopsy—some of them forensic, others inferen-
tial. Her body was far too decomposed for the
medical examiner to find evidence of sexual assault. As Annette's clothes were being removed,
however, it was discovered that one of her knee-
length socks (which she wore over her long un-
derwear) was stuffed in her sweatshirt pocket.
She also was missing one of the orange footies
that she wore over her knee socks.

The footie's mate had been discovered
months earlier on Hoosier Pass, about 100
yards from where Bobbie Oberholtzer was

found. This strongly suggested that the same person, or persons, murdered both women.

The knee sock in her sweatshirt pocket also was a strong clue. According to her mother, Annette was a meticulous dresser, unlikely ever to have an article of clothing, no matter how trivial, out of place. Furthermore, she had had the opportunity at her doctor's to clothe herself carefully against the afternoon chill. The most logical explanation of the sock in the pocket is that Annette had been forced to disrobe, no doubt was sexually assaulted, and then, in shock and/or hysteria over the physical violation, she redressed herself in haste.

This interference, in conjunction with the scientific evidence, enabled detectives to posit a likely sequence of events. There was a single sign of violence to her body, a ¼-inch-wide gunshot wound in her back from a firearm of unknown caliber, but not dissimilar from the gun used to kill Bobbie Oberholtzer. Like Bobbie, Annette's right lung was perforated. Also like Bobbie, she probably bled to death.

It seemed plausible to the police that she acceded without physical resistance to whatever sexual demands were made of her; her clothing was not torn and there were no indications of a struggle. Afterward, once she was dressed, Annette may have threatened to turn her attacker in to the police, or perhaps he threatened her life for some other reason. Whatever the case, she probably jumped or was pushed from the vehicle and, much like Bobbie, was running through the snow for her life when she was shot in the back and left to die.

To date, no arrests have been made in either the Oberholtzer or the Schnee murder. And after

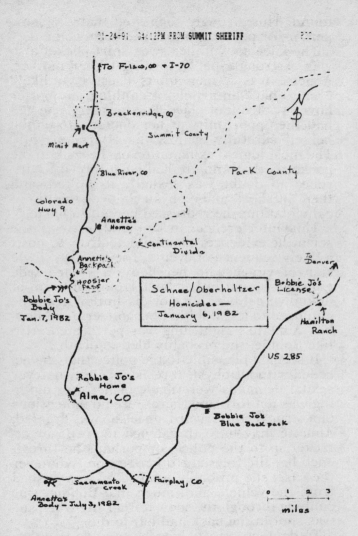

Sheriff's map of the Oberholtzer-Schnee crime scenes.

years of focusing their interest mainly upon Jeffrey Oberholtzer, the police now have only a longshot hope of finally solving the grisly crimes.

The theory that an area resident was responsible for both slayings only intensified the heat of suspicion directed toward Jeffrey Oberholtzer. The discovery of one of his business cards in a pocket of Annette Schnee's ski jacket seemed further to confirm what most investigators felt.

Oberholtzer also created problems for himself by at first denying he knew Annette Schnee, and then, after her picture appeared in the newspaper, remembering that they *had* met when he once gave her a ride. But his greatest difficulty—aside from being an obvious target under any circumstance—was the complete absence of any other suspects. According to James Hardtke, a former CBI investigator who worked the Oberholtzer-Schnee cases until 1988, the investigation did not identify a single other credible suspect in the case.

Jeff Oberholtzer maintains that he was harassed unremittingly. The police, he says, would show up to ask questions when he was out working on customers' appliances. That practice soon dried up his business (he's now a plumber). Similarly, he alleges, the cops contacted any female he saw after Bobbie's death. "I lost friends," Oberholtzer explains. "This has blown a lot of good things for me. It's all been downhill."

Even after he volunteered for, and passed, both a polygraph and a hypnotic exam, Oberholtzer remained the prime suspect in the cases. "On paper," says former CBI man James Hardtke, "he is the most logical suspect. In reality, I don't think he did it. And if he did, he planned it really well.

He's psyched himself into thinking he didn't do it, or that it was totally justified."

Then there is brother Jamie, who denies that his own suspicions stem from any lingering jealousy that Jeff, and not he, married Bobbie. Lacking hard physical evidence of Jeff's guilt, or any witnesses to either murder, Jamie and his wife Cindy nevertheless sound very certain of themselves. One of the determining factors in this certitude, they say, is the entity known to them, and to Jeff, as Mr. Death, or sometimes Mr. Darkness.

After Bobbie's murder, Jeff moved to a new house which, he says, harbored an evil spirit that sat at nights at the end of his bed. The being also revealed itself one night to Cindy as she slept in the house with Jamie.

"It's not occult," she explains. "It's just karma. I just happen to see spirits. I always have. Whenever they're around they usually come over and say, 'hi.' "

On the night in question, at least a year after Bobbie's murder, Cindy recalls having a dream shattered. "It was like a hammer hit it," she says. "Like glass. I jolted up and faced the doorway to his bedroom and this thing just sort of materialized. It was huge, black, very dense, like a cloud. Really dense. It was about seven feet tall. I figure it woke me up coming after me, and I just stared it down. For some reason, I knew it wanted Jamie. But I stayed up all night staring it down. As soon as dawn hit, it just dissipated, right?"

Cindy Oberholtzer believes the apparition she saw is a spirit of vengeance out to find justice for the slain Bobbie Oberholtzer. Jeff argues that Mr. Death is a site-specific spook—he only saw the thing while he lived in the house, which he long since has left—and might be some mournful old miner lost between heaven and hell. He vehemently denies that Mr. Death has anything to do with guilt for Bobbie's murder, or the suicides he occasionally contemplated in the darker times following the crimes.

Detective Eaton, who says he has heard all of Jamie and Cindy's allegations, can't see what they add up to. "There's a lot of supposition and theory," he says. "There's nothing in there based on fact."

After many years of thinking otherwise, Eaton now agrees with Jim Hardtke that Jeff Oberholtzer really is as innocent as he insists he is. "We've pretty well eliminated him," says Eaton. "For the last nine years, most of the emphasis has been on putting together enough to prove Jeff did it. Now we're trying to see if we can eliminate him, and it looks like we can."

Unfortunately, this movement of suspicion away from Oberholtzer has not been accompanied by a movement of suspicion *toward* anyone else—although Jeff himself has suggested that maybe his little brother's possible role in the killings deserves more attention than it has received. Richard Eaton, who now is laboriously reinterviewing everyone even remotely connected with the case, does allow that he's developed some new ideas that he'll pursue as he can. They don't include Jamie. As for Jeff Oberholtzer, "the main idea is to find out who did it," says Eaton. "If he's not involved, I don't want him."

Demons

RONALD GERALD MIRANDA
Los Banos, California

DATE OF BIRTH: October 17, 1947
HEIGHT: Five feet six inches
WEIGHT: 150 pounds
HAIR: Brown
EYES: Hazel
DISTINGUISHING MARKS: Multiple gunshot and shrapnel wounds covering back, arms, and thighs
OTHER: Small arms expert
CONTACT: Any FBI office
　　　　　(I.O. #5133)

Ronald Miranda was outgoing, friendly, and a generally likable young man—when he was sober. Alcohol summoned up the other Ron, an ugly, violent creature with lethal impulses. He once told his wife Debra that as a child he'd been physically abused. If so, such boyhood trauma would help to explain his seemingly polar-opposite natures, as well as the rowdiness of his youth and the spiraling emotional disintegration of his later years: alcoholism, wartime heroics, then thwarted ambition, failure, and—almost inevitably it now appears—a brutal murder committed in a drunken jealous fury.

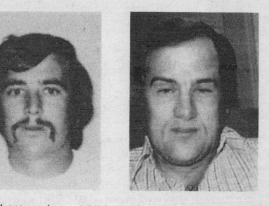

Ronald Miranda in 1976, and in a computer-aged image.

Miranda, the son of a prominent Los Banos, California, dairy farmer, was born and raised in the agricultural community of some 20,000 residents (many of them Portuguese-Americans, like the Miranda family) in California's fertile northern San Joaquin Valley, about 10 miles east of Interstate 5 and midway between San Jose and Fresno. His FBI file shows he did time in a state-run reform school in 1963, and was arrested at least twice "for offenses relating to public drunkenness," before his twentieth birthday in 1967. After high school graduation in 1965, Miranda enrolled at Fresno City College, where he studied business administration with poor results. Three years later, in the autumn of 1968, he was drafted into the Army and shipped to Vietnam as a grunt in Delta Company, 2nd Battalion, lst Infantry Division, 196th Infantry Brigade.

On June 28, 1969, in the midst of the Army's

so-called Tet counteroffensive, Ron Miranda achieved his single, shining moment of personal triumph. As his Silver Star citation reads:

> A platoon from the company had left its night laager position near landing zone Baldy when it encountered a well-entrenched North Vietnamese Army force. In the initial contact, the element sustained several casualties, and Private Miranda immediately rushed forward to aid his wounded comrades. At this time, he spotted a strategic hostile emplacement that was placing effective fire on the entire platoon. With complete disregard for his personal safety, Private Miranda, armed only with a pistol, assaulted the bunker. Despite receiving rifle and fragmentation wounds, he continued his attack and silenced one enemy soldier with fire from his personal weapon. Upon closing with the position, Private Miranda ran out of ammunition, but threw two hand grenades into the bunker and completely neutralized the emplacement. His courageous actions enabled the casualties to be swiftly evacuated and were instrumental in the overall success of the mission.

The citation, according to Ron's older brother Mark, erred as to certain details and omitted other facts of interest. Mark Miranda explains that Ron later told him that he was armed with an M-16 and a shotgun that day, not just his sidearm. Ron claimed to his brother that 38 dead North Vietnamese soldiers were found in the bunker, and that his own bullet and shrapnel wounds were so extensive that "they thought he was dead," says Mark.

Not just battle, but military life in all its phases seemed to agree with Ron Miranda. In November of 1969 he was promoted to Specialist 4th Class and became a weapons instructor at the Army's Advanced Infantry Training School at Fort Ord, California, next door to the seaside town of Monterey. A year later, he reenlisted, made sergeant, and was sent to air traffic control school. He then served for three years as a military air traffic controller at Fort Leonard Wood in Missouri.

In view of ensuing events, it seems a mistake for Ron Miranda to have left the routine and discipline of Army life. But he did in 1974, and returned home to Los Banos where Miranda made application to become a civilian air traffic controller with the Federal Aviation Administration. The FAA turned him down, probably because evidence of Miranda's drinking problems surfaced in the agency's preemployment investigation. Whatever the FAA's reason for rejecting Miranda, the experience shattered him, according to his friends, who later told investigators that this is when Ron began hitting the bottle most seriously.

For a time he found work as a sheepherder, which at least kept him out of harm's way, but then Miranda took a job as a bartender at Carlo's restaurant in Los Banos, which placed the outwardly affable but dangerously unsteady Vietnam vet under influences and among people with whom his damaged psyche ultimately could not cope. "He got along very well with the customers," says Inez Colzani, Carlo's wife. "He did have a temper, but the customers liked him." It was in the course of this work that Ron Miranda met his future wife, Debra, who tended bar at another restaurant, Chalet Basque, in Los Banos. "She was a very cute girl," remembers Colzani.

Debra and a stable family life might have dispelled Ron's demons if he somehow could have stayed away from liquor. He and Debra married in early 1980, and he adopted her toddler son, Mike, from a previous marriage. But Ron Miranda apparently had sunk too deeply into his intermittent despondency, and continued to drink too much, too often, when he should not have drunk at all. "In July of 1980," reports the FBI case précis, "Miranda became separated from his wife. The two had numerous marriage problems which appeared to relate, at least in part, to his propensity for alcohol and staying out late at night at the local bars."

Mrs. Miranda, who was then 24, began dating another man after the separation. He was 45-year-old Mitchel Martin Arambel, an American of Basque descent who operated a chemical fertilizer business. Arambel's father was a sheep rancher who, like Ron's father, Willie, enjoyed great public respect in and around Los Banos. Ron Miranda and Mitchel Arambel knew one another slightly.

In the weeks following the estrangement, Ron did his best to reform himself and thus possibly win back his bride and her child. It isn't known what sort of threat Mitchel Arambel posed to this possible reconciliation, but there seems to be little doubt that Miranda thought he had a chance to patch things up. This certainly was on his mind early on November 19, 1980, a Wednesday. Debra had agreed to go out on a date with him that night, a very positive sign, or so Miranda thought. However, early in the evening Mrs. Miranda called to cancel "in order to spend the evening with Arambel," according to the FBI.

Debra's decision ignited something primal and deadly within Ron Miranda. Witnesses report that he started drinking at 9 that night and didn't stop drinking until 1:30 A.M. Then he went home for his 870 Remington shotgun, a 12-gauge model, loaded it with double-aught shot, and headed for the house he once shared with Debra.

Once there, according to her later statement to police, Miranda broke down the front door and struggled briefly with Debra before he stomped into the living room where Mitchel Arambel had fallen asleep on the sofa. Miranda's shotgun roared twice, tearing a huge hole in Arambel. An enraged Debra attacked him with her fists as he fled out the door and into the night, drunk and confused and suddenly a fugitive killer. Ron Miranda has not been seen, or heard from, since.

A Serial Killer

Wasatch County, Utah

Utah State Route 40, a major two-lane east-west arterial between Salt Lake City and Denver, plunges down 13-mile-long Daniels Canyon, alongside Daniels Creek, about 65 miles due west of Salt Lake in Wasatch County. Daniels Canyon is remote and rugged. The countryside is wild.

"Yeah," says Wasatch County sheriff's detective Stevan Ridge. "It's the tules."

At about 7:00 P.M. on Monday, June 14, 1982, Detective Ridge was on duty at the sheriff's office in Heber City when he received a report that a corpse had just been discovered on the banks of Daniels Creek near a wide spot on Route 40 in Daniels Canyon. Half an hour later, Ridge was at the crime scene.

He learned that a fly fisherman, Lee Valdez, had found the body that afternoon. It lay among some willows, about 3 feet from the creek. The victim, a white male, was nude except for his socks. Ridge described him in his report as approximately 23 or 24 years old.

HAS ABOUT SHOULDER LENGTH RED-
DISH BROWN HAIR, the detective's report
continued. A THIN SCRAGGLY BEARD
AND MUSTACHE. ON FIRST OBSERVATION
THERE IS A FAIR AMOUNT OF BLOOD ON
THE VICTIMS [sic] FACE AND HEAD. SUB-
JECT IS LYING ON HIS BACK, WITH KNEES
PULLED SLIGHTLY UP, AS IF HE HAD BEEN
PICKED UP AND DROPPED INTO THE WIL-
LOWS AT THE EDGE OF THE CREEK.

The victim, who had been dead for a day at
most, was not very large; he weighed about 125
pounds and stood approximately five feet five
inches tall. There was a bullet hole in the back
of his head. At autopsy it was determined that
a single gunshot, probably .38 caliber, had
been fired from about 1 foot away. After pen-
etrating the skull, the bullet traveled slightly
upward, right to left, and lodged behind the
victim's left forehead. From these forensic indications, it seemed a good guess that the killer
was right-handed and of about the same height
as the deceased.

It required about two hours to process the
crime scene before the body could be removed.
Only then did Detective Ridge learn the full
truth of what had been done to his unidentified
victim, provisionally known as John Doe.
UPON MOVING THE BODY FROM THE
POINT OF REST IT WAS DISCOVERED
THAT THE SUBJECT HAD BEEN CAS-
TRATED, Ridge recorded. GENITALIA WERE/
ARE COMPLETELY ABSENT. A SUBSE-
QUENT SEARCH OF THE AREA DID NOT
PRODUCE SAID GENITALIA.

"I think the person got between his legs, bent
down, and just sawed it off," Ridge elaborates.

"And when I say saw off, that's what I mean. It looked like you would slice back and forth on raw meat. *Everything* was gone. The only thing that remained of his genital area was a small, narrow band of pubic hair at the top. Everything else was *gone!*"

At autopsy the next morning in Salt Lake City, it was established that the mutilation was postmortem; John Doe at least had been spared the agony and horror of experiencing his own sexual mutilation. The examination further revealed superficial abrasions on his face and hands, injuries consistent with a brief struggle before the murder. "I think he realized what was coming," says Ridge, "and tried to do what he could do."

The medical examiner also found two distinctive tattoos. One, on Doe's upper right arm, was a lightning bolt with the word "crash" inscribed through it. The second tattoo, above the nipple on the left side of his chest, was a black spider on a red background.

The murder was front-page news in Utah for several weeks. Ridge fielded a barrage of phone calls and tips, and showed Doe's body to at least four prospective witnesses. None could identify Doe. None had any idea who might have killed the young man. When nothing of substance developed, the media coverage flagged and the flow of new leads dried up. On July 8, the medical examiner removed and preserved John Doe's jaws for future identification purposes, and then released the body to be buried in the potter's field section of the Heber City cemetery. Wasatch County sheriff Mike Spanos, a Mormon bishop, conducted the graveside ceremony. Members of his department acted as pallbearers.

Detective Stevan Ridge made absolutely no progress on the case until October 6, 1983, when he received a telephone call from a Mike Kelly, who identified himself as a missing and unidentified persons investigator for the California state Department of Justice. Kelly wanted to discuss the multistate bulletin that Detective Ridge had prepared and disseminated to western law enforcement agencies almost 16 months earlier.

"I've been cleaning off my desk and I found this flier," Ridge recalls Kelly telling him. "I don't normally keep them. I don't know how it stayed on my desk, but it did."

Still according to Ridge, Kelly recounted how he'd glanced at the flier and noticed the description of the black-on-red spider tattoo. "It caught my eye," Kelly explained. "I took a missing persons report last year sometime from a lady in Truckee whose son had this same tattoo. Can you send me some print cards?"

The fingerprints left Heber City for California at 4:00 that afternoon. Five days later, at 12:40 P.M. on the eleventh of October, Kelly called Stevan Ridge again. He had a positive identification: John Doe was Marty James Shook of Truckee, California, in the Sierra Nevadas not far from Lake Tahoe and Reno.

"We had a few minutes of ecstasy," remembers Stevan Ridge. "We thought, 'Jeez! Now we know who he is. We're gonna get somewhere on this.' But it just didn't happen."

Ridge flew out to Reno, and then drove up to Truckee to interview Marty Shook's mother. As

Marty Shook.

the detective describes the meeting, she told him her 21-year-old son had left the area on Saturday night, June 12 (fewer than 48 hours before he was found dead in Utah), intending to hitchhike to Colorado where he hope to find summer work on an oil-exploration seismology crew.

She said her boy had a chip on his shoulder about his size, and that his temper sometimes got him into fights. But Marty's mother could think of no other habit, trait, or sexual preference that would necessarily put him in such harm's way. Nothing except the everyday risk of hitchhiking.

"We kinda thought it might be a biker or doper problem," explains Ridge, "because the mutilation says that someone was *really* upset with him. But she said, 'No, he probably smoked weed now and then, but that was it.' No real ties to any biker group or anything like that. This is a gut feeling, but I honestly think Marty just was in the wrong place at the wrong time. He was hitchhiking and the wrong person picked him up."

Marty Shook's parents, who were divorced, came together to Heber City to visit their son's grave and to place a headstone over it. Meanwhile, the hunt for Marty's killer again fell into limbo. "I worked on it off and on as time permitted," says Stevan Ridge. "Nothing much came of it."

Several years passed. Then in 1988 Ridge happened to discuss the Shook murder with Jim Bell, a Salt Lake City homicide detective familiar with serial murder cases. Both Ridge and Bell knew that the circumstances of the crime indicated a strong chance that the killer was a traveler, perhaps a truck driver. Also, the mutilation had a practiced look to it. "We thought that the instant we saw what had happened to the body," says Ridge. "There weren't any other cuts or stab wounds or anything. It just appeared that the suspect had shot Marty in the head and grabbed his genitals and whacked them off. It was real matter of fact like, 'Oh, I gotta finish this job, so here we go!'"

Taken together, these conjectures raised the possibility that a serial killer, or killers, had murdered Marty Shook. Perhaps there were similar cases elsewhere in the country. To find out, Jim Bell suggested that Stevan Ridge report the Shook murder to VICAP—for Violent

Criminal Apprehension Program—at the FBI academy in Quantico, Virginia.

VICAP is a computerized database containing the details of thousands of unsolved murders across the United States. It provides local law enforcement officials with access to an accurate and comprehensive look at killings in other jurisdictions. VICAP primarily was designed to aid in the detection and capture of serial murderers. If Marty Shook's killing was part of a serial pattern—and if the cops in other jurisdictions had taken the time to report their cases—then the VICAP computer should come up with a match, somewhere. On May 13, 1988, Stevan Ridge submitted his VICAP questionnaire to the Bureau.

Another sixteen months elapsed before Ridge received a call from Pennsylvania. State Trooper Stephen Toboz was on the line with the news that he, too, had an unsolved castration case, this one dating from 1981. Toboz, who had sent his information to VICAP in May of 1989, informed Ridge that the FBI computer had found significant similarities between their two murders.

Toboz' victim, also a white male, was discovered August 19, 1981, by a forestry worker cutting grass along a dirt road about 6 miles north of Interstate 80 in Crawford Township, not far from Williamsport, in the north-central part of Pennsylvania. The victim was nude, had been shot in the back of the head, and then was completely castrated. As was true of Marty Shook, neither the victim's genitalia nor any of his missing clothing ever were recovered.

The similarities were striking. What is more, Stephen Toboz also had a slug recovered from his victim's skull. Detective Ridge immediately sent Toboz the bullet recovered from Marty Shook. Laboratory examination indicated that the spent bullets bore identical markings. The same weapon, probably a .38 handgun, had been used to kill both men.

Stephen Toboz, who had headed the original Pennsylvania investigation, told Ridge that his victim was about two days' dead when found, and that the dead man appeared to have been killed elsewhere and then dumped over a slight embankment a few feet from the road. Like the Utah case, the disposal seemed to be neither hurried nor sloppy. On the other hand, the killer made no special effort to conceal his victim.

A fingerprint submission to the FBI resulted in a relatively quick identification. On September 27, 1981, eight days after the body was discovered, the FBI reported that the dead man was Wayne Rifendifer, a 30-year-old drifter from Bridgeport, Connecticut. Rifendifer was spare framed, similar to Marty Shook. He stood five feet nine inches tall, weighed 136 pounds, and had black hair and green eyes. He had been arrested once, for minor larceny in Raleigh, North Carolina, and at that time had listed his occupation as house painter.

Rifendifer had no ties to the north-central Pennsylvania area. Doubtlessly he had been passing through, by thumb, when he, like Marty Shook, met his murderer. One significant difference between the two victims was that Rifendifer, as far as Trooper Toboz' investigation could determine, was not a strict heterosexual. If the chance arose and the price was right, it seemed, Rifendifer wasn't averse to a bit of hustling.

Besides the bullet match, easily the most provocative new evidence was contained in a telephone call received by the Pennsylvania state police the day that Wayne Rifendifer was identified, but hours before his name was released to the public.

The caller, a male, knew Rifendifer's name, claimed that he had a sexual liaison with Rifendifer just before the murder, and that he had some of the dead man's possessions. It was a long-distance call, made from a public telephone booth. "He said he would come forth," explains Trooper Toboz. "He indicated that he was at a truck stop and that this guy [Rifendifer] left the truck stop with another individual. And that's where [the call] ended. I believe the caller was the culprit."

At the news from Pennsylvania, Stevan Ridge once again felt a momentary exhilaration. "For a few minutes it was really neat," he says. "Everybody was excited, jumping up and down. Then reality set in. We knew it was the same guy, but it was obvious that we weren't any closer than we were before."

Perhaps not, but the match, together with what Trooper Toboz was able to share about his crime, provided a much clearer picture of motive and modus operandi. Also, there are indistinct indications of possibly similar murders in several other states, including Wyoming and Georgia. Although it is at present impossible to positively link these crimes to the Shook and Rifendifer cases, it definitely would be in character for their killer to have continued on throughout the 1980s, moving from town to town and refining his technique.

This is the mark of the successful serial killer, and a main reason why a November 1986, case in Connecticut has been of special interest to the Utah and Pennsylvania detectives. There have been no arrests in the case. And the murder weapon is unknown. But the evidence is appallingly evocative of what befell Marty Shook and Wayne Rifendifer.

At a rest stop on north-south State Route 8 near Litchfield in western Connecticut, another sexually mutilated male was found. He was Jack Andrews, 26, originally from Oklahoma. Like Marty Shook and Wayne Rifendifer, Jack Andrews was small: five feet nine inches and 135 pounds. Like Rifendifer, Andrews had a criminal record. He may have occasionally hustled his body. Andrews is thought to have been hitching at the time of his death.

He was discovered nude in a blanket at the rest stop; apparently he had been killed elsewhere. Andrews's genitals were completely cut away. His nipples had been excised. His legs were severed between his hips and knees. And his head was missing. None of his missing body parts or clothing were ever recovered. There still are no suspects in the case.

Could the same person who killed Marty Shook and Wayne Rifendifer have progressed to the later murder-mutilation of Jack Andrews? "I wouldn't say it's our best bet," observes Detective Tim Palmbach of the Connecticut State Police's Western District Major Crimes Squad. "But we can't rule it out. It's certainly possible."

What Her Brother Knew

Dallas County, Texas

Dallas County sheriff's detective Larry Forsyth remembers Wednesday, December 23, 1981, began ordinarily enough at the Seagoville substation in the extreme eastern end of the county. The north-central Texas winter sky was pale blue, the temperature mild, and a Christmas party was scheduled for that afternoon. Sgt. Forsyth had been appointed the substation's official turkey carver for the occasion. Looking forward to the big meal, Forsyth ate very little that morning.

Then the substation radio crackled with the ghastly news that a young mother and her child had just been found slain nearby. So much for the Christmas party—and Christmas itself—for Larry Forsyth.

"The first 72 hours after such a murder are *so* important," says the detective, now a lieutenant. "You don't get much sleep trying to get all the leads before they're cold. As a personal note, I also didn't get a chance to eat until ten o'clock that night. We were all awful hungry folks by then.''

The bodies were discovered at about 11:45 that morning by Deputy Roy L. Baird. While on routine patrol in a semirural area of truck farms scattered among woodlots, creek beds, and the occasional small hill, Baird spotted an empty 1978 tan-and-blue Ford Thunderbird parked with its driver's side door open on Holloman Rd., a narrow dirt lane, three tenths of a mile east of the nearest paved arterial, Lawson Rd.

The car was registered to 30-year-old Roxann Jo Jeeves, an attractive divorcée who had moved to Texas from Oklahoma in April of the previous year. She lived with her son, Kristopher, in a second-story apartment, No. 234, at a complex called The Sussex Place on Larmanda St. in northeast Dallas.

Deputy Baird approached the Thunderbird and noted a woman's purse and gloves on the front seat. In the backseat he saw wrapped Christmas presents, some personal papers, and a blue canvas bag with white trim.

Sensing that something was very wrong, Baird began a general search of the vicinity. In a wooded area 137 feet directly north of Holloman Rd., he found 5-year-old Kristopher lying on his left side. The boy had been slain with a single .38 caliber bullet to his forehead. He was clad in blue pants and a blue coat. A yard or so away was his mother, shot once in the cheek and again in her temple.

Roy Baird discovered Roxann Jo Jeeves on her back, covered from her toes to her shoulders with a green blanket. From the general appearance of the crime scene, Detective For-

Roxann Jo Jeeves with Kristopher.

syth suspects Roxann Jeeves was forced to watch her son's execution before being murdered herself. At autopsy, Dallas County chief medical examiner Charles S. Petty would find bruises around her neck and stomach, and an inordinate quantity of blood, 100 cubic centimeters, pooled in her abdominal cavity. From this evidence, investigators would infer that her killer may have throttled Roxann Jeeves into submission, then pinned the woman to the ground with his knee as he shot her.

Ms. Jeeves, like her son, was fully clothed. The keys to the Thunderbird were found in one of her pockets. Neither victim had been sexually assaulted. Neither had been dead for more than an hour, nor had the car been parked on

12-23-81 Murder (two offenses) Victims: Jeeves, Roxann J.   ♀ 9-23-51 SER #81-18030
Holloman Rd, 3/10 m. West of Lawson Rd./Jeeves, Kristopher ♂ approx. 4-5years old
Co. of Dallas, Texas   SER #81-18036

CRIME SCENE SKETCH (not to scale) Lt. J. G. Cron #66, Physical Evidence, Dallas SO

<u>evidence</u> A-Roxann Jeeves
          B-Kristopher Jeeves
          C-Knife
          D-Vehicle of Roxann Jeeves
          E-Crocheted cap

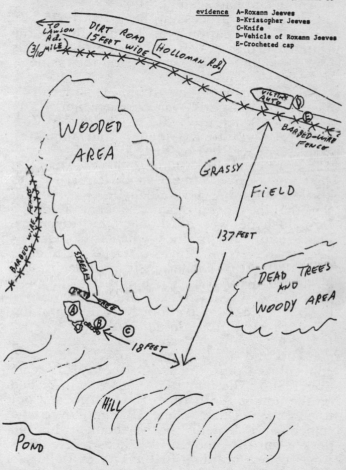

Police sketch of the Jeeves crime scene.

Holloman Rd. for more than 40 minutes; another deputy, J. L. Kilzer, reported that he drove by the scene in his cruiser at 11:07 that morning and had seen nothing.

Crime-scene processing began at 12:25 P.M. No murder weapon was found. Inside the Thunderbird, however, crime lab technicians found good latent fingerprints on the inside of the driver's window.

The blue canvas bag in the Thunderbird's backseat potentially was an even more valuable clue. It definitely did not belong to Roxann Jeeves, or to Kristopher, and almost as certainly it was left by their killer.

In it, investigators found some screwdrivers, duct tape, knives, and a small lemon extract bottle containing formaldehyde. Lt. Forsyth says that the most probable explanation for the formaldehyde was as a marinade for marijuana joints to produce what is sometimes known as Sherman Stick—ultra-powerful dope that is also ultra-dangerous to your health. Explains the detective: "The majority of people I talked to who've tried it said they never wanted to do it again. People at our lab said that quite often it results in brain damage."

Also in the blue bag were a black-knit toboggan cap and a small notebook. There was a gold-colored pin attached to the cap. It read: Super Shit. The name E. Oden was inscribed on the notebook. In time, E. Oden turned out to be Eugene Oden, a local IBM employee who remembered leaving the notebook in his old desk when IBM moved its offices a few miles west from a building in the city of Dallas to the sprawling commercial and residential real estate development known as Los Colinas.

Finding Eugene Oden required an enormous effort. All that it has accomplished to date, however, has been to eliminate Eugene Oden as a suspect in the case.

Finally, the blue bag was found to contain several aged (possibly pre-World War II) brass .38 caliber Remington bullets, and a brown leather holster manufactured by Brauer Brothers of St. Louis, Missouri. It, too, was a comparative antique. A stamped impression on the holster's restraining strap read C O N S T, or perhaps C O 3 1 S T. The impression is very faint.

According to a Brauer Brothers employee contacted by the Dallas County investigators, the company once supplied that type of holster to the military by the thousands, but discontinued the model in 1952.

It seems very likely that the bullets and the holster were stolen, along with the missing murder weapon, undoubtedly a pistol. Larry Forsyth believes that to find their owner and also to solve the mystery of Eugene Oden's notebook—probably would bring him much closer to identifying the killer.

"I've always felt that the holster and pistol had been passed down from somebody's grandfather," he says. "And I think they came out of a burglary. I always hope that somebody will call and say, 'That's my holster!' Then I could go back and start working on that. That holster haunts me—that and the notebook. How the hell did that notebook get from that office building to where that mama and baby were killed, and in that bag?"

Neither sex nor robbery seemed to be motives in the case, and nothing that the sheriff's

The Brauer Brothers holster and Remington bullets.

office learned in the crucial early hours of its investigation brought detectives any closer to understanding why someone would want to murder Roxann Jo Jeeves and little Kristopher.

They discovered that she was a native of Jamestown, New York, in the far western portion of the state, not far from the Pennsylvania border. Roxann Jo Jeeves had married (retaining her maiden name) and moved to Oklahoma City, where she worked for an insurance company for a couple of years. Her ex-husband,

Lt. Larry Forsyth.

Kristopher's father, still resided there. He was not a suspect.

In Dallas, the detectives learned, Roxann led a moderately active social life. She played on a woman's baseball team in the summer, and enjoyed dancing in country-and-western joints with names like "No Whar But Texas" and "The Cockeyed Cowboy."

Her boyfriend of the past 12 months, Jimmy Hoskins, told police he had last spoken to her, by telephone, at about 10:00 on the night before her murder. Jimmy Hoskins was at work the next morning when Roxann and Kristopher were killed. His mother, 53-year-old Louise Hoskins, told investigators that she spoke with Roxann Jeeves, also by telephone, at 10:00

A.M. on the twenty-third, less than two hours before mother and son were found dead. According to her, Roxann and Kristopher were due at Mrs. Hoskins's workplace, Kraft Foods in nearby suburban Garland, Texas, at 11:00. The twenty-third was Kristopher's birthday. As a special treat for him, Mrs. Hoskins was going to take the boy on a tour of the plant.

Still another acquaintance, 37-year-old Danny Binion, recounted to Forsyth that he had visited the Jeeves apartment on the night of the twenty-second. Before leaving at about 10, said Binion, he noticed that Roxann had placed a red box full of car tools near her front door. When Binion asked about the toolbox, she explained that she intended to put it in her Thunderbird's trunk the next morning, "in case I have car trouble."

Danny Binion confirmed Louise Hoskins's account. He recalled Roxann telling him that she and Kristopher planned to meet Mrs. Hoskins at Kraft Foods around 11:00 A.M. the next day. Then, according to Binion, Roxann was going to bring Kristopher to lunch at Binion's club, the King's X, before taking the boy for the last of his birthday treats, a matinee movie.

One of the first witnesses to provide Detective Forsyth with something substantive was 19-year-old Patricia McAvey, Roxann Jeeves's neighbor at The Sussex Place. At about 10:30 on the morning of the twenty-third, Ms. McAvey told Forsyth, she walked out of her apartment to see little Kristopher struggling down the stairs toward his mother's car with a big red toolbox. Patricia McAvey, who was on her way to a doctor's appointment with her

own infant son, asked Kristopher if he needed
any help. The boy declined, explaining that he
thought he was big enough to wrestle the
cumbersome toolbox downstairs all by himself.

She hurried off across the parking lot toward her car. Partway there, Patricia McAvey
turned around to see something she found dis-
quieting, a black male accompanied by a dark-
complected, possibly Native-American, female,
who seemed to be approaching Kristopher
Jeeves in a furtive manner. "They were looking
around to see if anyone was watching," Detective Forsyth remembers hearing from Ms.
McAvey.

The unwholesome-looking duo unnerved Patricia McAvey. "She didn't feel like these people belonged in her apartment complex," says
the detective, even though Ms. McAvey also reported that Kristopher seemed to recognize the
man. "When she got to her car she looked back
one more time and this time she saw the black
male carrying the toolbox in one hand and
holding Kristopher's hand with the other. All
three of them—the Indian woman, too—were
headed in the opposite direction around the
building to the parking lot. That's the last she
saw of them."

Patricia McAvey sat down with a police artist to produce a sketch of the suspect male.
Over the coming days it would be widely re-
produced in the Dallas-area news media. According to her, the man appeared to be about
five feet nine inches tall, and weighed 180
pounds, possibly more. He looked to be in his
early-to-mid thirties. His black hair was cut
short. She remembered him wearing sun-

The Jeeves suspects as Patricia McAvey described them.

glasses, a dirty white T-shirt under a blue jogging top, and light brown pants covered with greasy smears.

The suspect's companion presented an equally derelict aspect. She, said McAvey, was a squat five feet five inches tall, and about 25 years old. The woman's hair was short and brown and frizzy. She wore ill-fitting tan slacks. It appeared that someone recently had smacked her around, giving the woman a black eye.

The next significant witness was Don Crawford, who worked in a gas station near The Sussex Place complex, at the intersection of Abrams Rd. and Interstate 635, the LBJ Freeway, which forms a partial loop around the north, east, and southern sectors of the city of Dallas. Within hours of the murder, Crawford notified the sheriff's investigators that he had pumped gas that morning for Roxann Jeeves; according to her credit card receipt, $31.00 worth.

Crawford remembered that Ms. Jeeves was at the steering wheel of the Thunderbird, and that she said nothing but "Fill it up," at the station. Sitting quietly next to her in the front passenger seat was a black male who looked to be somewhere between 30 and 35 years of age.

The attendant went on to explain to deputy W. L. Mayes that he saw a little boy, maybe 3 or 4 years old, standing up in the backseat. He was wearing a blue coat and blue pants. No one else was in the vehicle. Assuming the black male Don Crawford saw in Roxann Jeeves's Thunderbird is the same individual Patricia McAvey saw with Kristopher that morning, his female companion, whoever she was, seems to have vanished.

Although no one as yet has come forward with evidence of Roxann and Kristopher Jeeves's whereabouts from the time they left the gas station with their passenger until they were found, dead, perhaps less than one hour later, time constraints make it plausible that Ms. Jeeves drove southeast from the station on I-635 past the suburbs of Garland, Mesquite, and Balch Springs, possibly as far as State Route 175, on which she might have continued in a southeasterly direction toward Seagoville. State Route 175 is the major route out into the easterly stretches of Dallas County where mother and son were murdered.

A principal investigator at the scene was deputy R. W. Veatch, and he turned up any number of witnesses. One, 20-year-old Tamera

Burton, reported that she was driving by just as Deputy Baird came upon the Jeeves Thunderbird on Holloman Rd. At that moment, according to Burton, a man she could only describe as "dark" sprinted out of the brush and across a plowed field toward Cartwright St. Tamera Burton was at least 200 yards away when she spotted the fleeing figure. She was unable to describe him, or even to tell his race. But, "He was running as fast as he could," she said in her statement to Veatch, and the subject wore "dark clothing with a greenish look to it."

Another of Veatch's witnesses, 34-year-old Michael Dean Daniel, was an employee at a water treatment plant at the intersection of Cartwright and Lawson, about one-half mile from the murder scene off Holloman Rd. Daniel told Veatch that he left work at noon on the twenty-third, and that his route carried him past Holloman on Cartwright. Just as he approached Holloman, said Daniel (who is white), he saw a black man run out from behind a vacant house and try to wave him down, as if for a ride.

Daniel drove on, but later was able to describe the male he saw as about five feet eleven inches, medium build, and somewhere in his twenties. He told Deputy Veatch the man had facial hair and, despite his frantic attempts to gain Daniel's attention, he kept his left hand hidden inside the pocket of his olive-green military jacket.

Daniel's descriptions were consistent with those of Jim and Marcella Hicks, Seagoville residents who reported to Veatch that they were driving down Cartwright Rd. at about noon, or a little later, the day of the killings. Jack Hicks said he noticed a black man walking and trying to hitch a ride on Cartwright. He remembered the individual as about five feet ten inches, tall, of medium build, and somewhere in his twenties. Hicks said the man was wearing dark clothes and a growth of beard, "mostly stubble."

Marcella Hicks concurred in her recollections, adding that the hitcher's hair was cut in a short Afro and that he wore a "drab green" military-style jacket. Both Hickses and their passenger that day, Marsha Youker, said they noticed the man kept his left hand in his jacket pocket. All three believed they'd recognize the man if they saw him again.

As Detective Forsyth and Deputy Veatch and the rest of the Dallas County sheriff's investigators worked around the clock through the 1981 Christmas weekend, their flow of substantive leads inexorably began to slow, even though the local press continued to show the police composite sketch of the suspect and Schepp's, a local dairy, offered a $10,000 reward for information leading to the arrest of the Jeeves' killer.

One of the last of the useful early witnesses was 35-year-old Katie M. Christian, who contacted the sheriff on Monday, December 28, five days after the murders. Ms. Christian, like Don Crawford, was a gas station attendant. She worked at a Mobil station at the intersection of I-635 (the LBJ Freeway) and Bruton Rd. in Mesquite, about six miles due west of the crime scene.

According to her, at about noon on the twenty-third a black man approximately five feet eight inches tall, medium build, wearing a green army jacket and green cap, walked into the station and asked to use their inside telephone. Ms. Christian refused, directing the man's attention to an outside pay phone. After he placed a call from it, she explained to detectives, the subject loitered around the station for an hour or so, coming inside at one point for a drink of water. The last Ms. Christian saw of the individual he was heading north, on foot, on I-635.

All sensational crimes provoke deluges of anonymous tips to the authorities, and the Jeeves' murders were no different. Although the preponderance of such calls come from pranksters, cranks, and the like, there often are substantive leads to be followed, or information to be gleaned that casts the crime in a certain light. In the Jeeves case, many of the callers suggested that if the detectives dug hard enough they'd find a drug connection in the killings. The discovery of formaldehyde in the killer's blue canvas bag also pointed toward some sort of drug connection, as did the highly suggestive testimony of another of Roxann Jeeves's neighbors at The Sussex Place, Kevin Long.

Several weeks after the murders, Long was involved in a fracas at the apartment complex. It was a matter of routine for the sheriff's investigators to ask him if he knew anything about the Jeeves' slayings. "I wish I could help you guys," Long replied, "but I can't."

The detective started leaning on him. After

three days of their intense attention, Long finally exclaimed, "Look! I'm in a real jam here. But if you give me your word you won't cause me any problems, I'll tell you what I know."

Kevin Long, it turned out, was a parolee. If used against him, what he had to report could have put him back in jail.

According to Detective Forsyth, Long remembered seeing in the complex a black man answering the description of the suspect. In fact, the man had come to Long's door, about three or four days before the murder, asking to borrow a set of battery jumper cables for his car. Kevin Long owned no such device, but as they spoke in his doorway the stranger caught the unmistakable aroma of pot being smoked within the Long apartment.

"Hey man, who's got the reefer?" the visitor asked. Long replied that he did and that some of it might be for sale. As they spoke, the man at the door introduced himself as "G-Man." He said he might be in the market. When Kevin Long shook his hand, he noticed G-Man was wearing a horseshoe-shaped ring, and that there was a long pink scar on his right hand.

The rest of what Kevin Long had to say was even more provocative. He told Forsyth that the selfsame G-Man returned to his door the morning of the murders and purchased a Baggie of marijuana from him. Finally, says Forsyth, "Long told us something about the clothing we've never made public. Something that other witnesses noted. Something unusual."

Kevin Long's information, consistent with a drug-related theory of the murders, still shed no light on another nagging point. Neighbor Patricia McAvey felt that little Kristopher Jeeves recognized the suspect that morning. If she was right, then what, or who, could have been the connection?

One distinct possibility was Roxann Jeeves's brother Kurt, who had come to Dallas from Jamestown the previous summer and lived with Roxann and Kristopher for a few weeks. Some of the telephone tipsters mentioned Kurt by name. Others went so far as to say he had two distinguishing habits: one was to smoke dope regularly, and the other was to associate with blacks routinely. For some reason, whites were nearly excluded from Kurt Jeeves's social circle.

On January 21, 1982, 29 days after the murders, Detective Forsyth traveled about 125 miles southwest of Dallas to the U.S. Army base in Fort Hood, Texas. There he interviewed PFC Kurt Jeeves.

According to Forsyth, he asked Jeeves about suspicious black males at The Sussex Place. Roxann's brother answered that in the summer of 1981 a black male neighbor named Brantley Wood, whose apartment was quite close to Roxann's, had begun dealing drugs. Soon, said Kurt, Brantley Wood had "fronted" him four bags of marijuana to sell. When he didn't move the merchandise quickly enough, Kurt continued, Wood came to the Jeeves apartment and angrily demanded the dope's return.

Another time, he told Detective Forsyth,

Wood answered his apartment door with a knife in his hand. Brantley Wood's explanation for the weapon was that someone had just burgled his place and made off with some of his stash.

Kurt Jeeves would not concede that his lifestyle and such business associates as Mr. Wood might have had something to do with his sister's and nephew's murders. "He readily admitted to associating with nearly all blacks," says Forsyth. "But I got a strange reaction. In the middle of the interview, when I asked him if any of his black friends had anything to do with this, he jumped up and said, "You're not gonna put a guilt trip on me! I didn't have anything to do with my sister's murder, and I'm through talking to you!"

As it turned out, that conversation less than a month after Roxann's and Kristopher's murders was as close as Larry Forsyth would come to unraveling Kurt Jeeves's role in the killings, if any. By the time he got back to Dallas, a call from Jamestown awaited Detective Forsyth. It was from Kurt Jeeves's father, who wanted the Dallas County Sheriff's Office to leave his son alone.

Kurt Jeeves subsequently was shipped by the Army to Germany, where he was found guilty of a drug offense. The Army returned Jeeves to the United States in 1984. He served time in the Louisville, Kentucky, stockade before being dishonorably discharged. "He was kicked out of the Army and given his back pay," says Forsyth. "Almost immediately he went into a black part of Louisville to score some marijuana and was killed because he flashed a big roll of bills. A group of blacks was arrested and convicted, but we could find no connection whatsoever to our case."

Since then, the only significant development in the case came in 1988 with a Crimestoppers television broadcast about the case. After the program, a man called in to say that on December 23, at the corner of I-635 and Bruton Rd. where Katie M. Christian worked at the Mobil station, he saw a black man stop his car to pick up another black—perhaps, but not for sure, the suspect described by Ms. Christian.

So why were the Jeeveses killed? One possibility is that Kevin Long's Mr. G-Man bought his dope, soaked it in formaldehyde, smoked the Sherman Stick, and went off on a psychotic tear. It would be a much closer fetch to imagine the man had a serious beef with Kurt Jeeves and killed Kurt's sister and family as a payback of some sort.

Yet the killer could not have fully considered his crime. It was rash to be seen with his victims in the daytime, and then to murder them with no previously planned means of escape. Sudden anger may have played some part in the crime. Also, why was he hiding his left hand as reported by Mike Daniel, the Hickses, and Ms. Youker? Did Roxann Jeeves bite him or otherwise injure his hand just before he killed her?

None of these questions ever are likely to be answered unless Larry Forsyth someday gets his man. Says the disappointed but determined detective, "Nine and a half years later this case feels like unfinished business to me. It was assigned to me and it was my responsibility to find the person who did this awful deed. I haven't yet and I've gotta solve this before I leave here."

Lt. Forsyth retires in eight years.

Sally and Sal

SALVADOR NÚÑEZ GUARDADO
San Francisco, California

DATE OF BIRTH: July 25, 1951
HEIGHT: Five feet ten inches
WEIGHT: 210 pounds
HAIR: Black
EYES: Brown
DISTINGUISHING MARKS: Heart-shaped tattoo, pierced by an arrow with "RACHEL" written across it on upper right arm. May walk with a limp.
Also known as: Ki-Ki
CONTACT: Inspectors Jeffrey Brosch and/or Edward Erdelatz
San Francisco Police Department
Homicide Division
(415) 553-1145 (Days)
(415) 553-1071 (Nights)

Sally Garrity of San Francisco did not lead an easy life. When she was just 2, says her younger half-sister, Sheri Ysit, their mother abandoned Sally and her brother, Ross, to their aunt Lydia and uncle Colton Henry's care. Five years later, she gave up Sheri, too, leaving the Henrys to raise all three kids. At 18, Sally had a daughter, Yvette, but intra-family strife made it impossible for her to keep the girl, who

Sheri Ysit.

Sally Garrity.

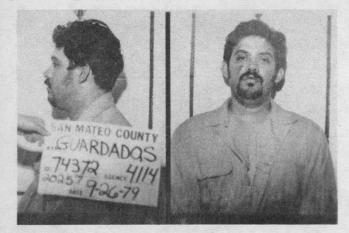

Sal Guardado.

by age 11 was living across the bay in Oakland with Sheri, who was then single.

Another problem was men. Either they were useless, or married, or broke or, too often, all three and worse. Somehow Sally wasn't able to connect with anyone who would, or could, treat her right. Yet for all her hard luck, Sally Garrity's spirits never seemed to falter. "Sally was happy go lucky," says Sheri. "She loved to party, loved to have a good time."

She was 29 in early 1985 and was having a good time one night in a San Francisco bar when Sally, a Native American of Shoshone-Paiute descent, met Salvador Guardado, a Mexican-American not long out of the joint after serving a sentence for attempted murder and arson.

"Auntie" Lydia Henry

Sally Garrity would never know of Salvador
Guardado's prison past; in fact, neither she nor
any member of her family knew his full name
for sure. In the short while that their romance
bloomed it was enough for Sally that he came
with few of the usual glaring deficiencies of
character or class—at least not from her point
of view. "He had a car and a job and he was
really sweet and nice to her," says Sheri, who
was 25 years old at the time. "He was like the
world to her. I said, 'You finally did it! You
finally got a good man!' I was kinda jealous."

So smitten was Garrity that the silliest things

made her happy. She thought it "cute" for example, that her new beau was known as Sal, and that she was called Sally, like a rhyme sorta. The woman was easy to please. In March of 1985, about a month after they met, Guardado moved in with Sally Garrity, who was then living with Lydia Henry—whom everyone called Auntie—in Mrs. Henry's apartment on Shipley near Fifth, south of San Francisco's Mission District.

Sally earned a few dollars here and there making decorative clothing, beadwork. Sal had a job in a pizzeria, or so he said. Within days of moving his gear to Sally and Auntie's place, Guardado sold his car. Then, on a visit to the pizzeria, Sally and Sheri discovered that he only worked part-time, and not much at that. Soon enough, all Sal ever wanted to do was drink beer and go bowling. He was nuts about bowling, and even had his own custom bowling ball that he brought with him to the apartment.

Something odd then occurred. Auntie reported that one day while riding on a city bus she was accosted by a strange woman. "This lady turned around in her seat and said, 'Give this to Sally, God bless her,' " explains Sheri Ysit. "It was a Christian calendar with Jesus stuff on it."

Who was the woman?

"She didn't know her! She just said, 'Give this to Sally. She'll need it.' Strange, huh?"

You bet.

This was in March, about the time that Sally and Sal started quarreling in earnest over his sloth and general slovenliness. Auntie, who didn't have much use for Sal herself, explained to Sheri that "she tried to stay out of it, but it was noticeable. Sally kept telling him he should look for a place to live, that they were bothering Lydia, but it only made him drink another beer and get abusive. He got real bossy, like it was his house."

On Mother's Day, 1985, Sheri and Yvette came over from Oakland for a visit. Yvette gave Sally a card. Sheri brought fresh cut flowers for Auntie—something she'd never done before. The gesture sparked a second strange interlude.

It turned out that Auntie had lost an older sister years before, and ever since she had associated the bouquets of cut flowers at her sister's funeral with death.

"Here, Auntie! These are for Mother's Day!" Sheri announced in good cheer.

"Ooouuuuuhh!" answered the older woman, looking appalled and a bit frightened.

"This ugly chill went through her. She said, 'Get those away from me!'

" 'What?'

" 'They remind me of death. I never have had cut flowers since Paula died, because they remind me of death!'

"It gave me a really creepy feeling. I go, 'Okay, Auntie. I'll give them to Sally.' "

With that she did, reports Sheri, who goes on to relate how the sisterly gift enraged the increasingly loutish and possessive Sal, now like a millstone around Sally's neck. Guardado, says Sheri, pitched her flowers out the window and then stormed out to buy his own flowers, which Guardado then presented to an understandably shaken and perplexed Sally Garrity.

About a week later, Sheri saw Sally and Sal at a so-called Indian Pow Wow on the campus of Stanford University, about 30 minutes south of San Francisco. At the annual affair, which features cultural events, dancing, craft sales, and the like, Sally told Sheri she was "fed up" with Sal. For the first time, Sheri also could sense that her half-sister was physically afraid of her boyfriend. "I can't stand him! I can't stand him! I wish he would leave," Sally kept saying, an edge of panic in her voice.

The only witness to the final episode of the Sal and Sally story was Auntie. As she later told police investigators, at around noon on Thursday, May 23, 1985, Guardado came into her kitchen as she was having a bite to eat. He wanted to know if Auntie would go buy some items at Walgreens. She said she would. "But he came back into the kitchen again," recounts niece Sheri, saying, 'Auntie, aren't you going to Walgreen's?'

"She said, 'What's the rush? I'm trying to eat. I'll go when I go.'

"Finally, she left. Sally was in the living room, beading an eagle pattern. She was so proud of that! He came up behind her and strangled her while she was working on the border outline of that eagle."

Guardado evidently throttled Garrity with a ligature. According to Inspector Jeffrey Brosch of the San Francisco Police Department's Homicide Division, he used either a telephone cord or one of the several cat leashes that Auntie had in the apartment.

"Then," continues Sheri Ysit, "he waited for Auntie to kill her, too. He dragged Sally into their room and put her on the bed. The bedroom was right by the front door. Auntie came home about 20 minutes later and saw the bedroom door was closed. She sat down on the couch and started to watch soap operas.

"She heard a sort of click, the doorlock. He came up beside her with a pillow and pushed her down and grabbed her by the throat to strangle her with his bare hands. She pushed the pillow away and saw him and she said, 'Why, Sal? Why?' At that point he took his bowling ball off the floor and started clubbing her in the head with it."

Seriously injured, Auntie fell unconscious, "Then," says Sheri, "he left her for dead."

Salvador Guardado's behavior with Auntie just prior to murdering her niece Sally strongly suggests premeditation. But he could not have thought the crime through entirely, because Sal fled the moment he thought Auntie was dead, leaving behind all his clothes and business papers (which helped lead police to members of his family) and even his cherished custom-drilled bowling ball.

Since then he has been spotted in Hawaii as well as in Guadalajara, Mexico, where Guardado's father reportedly lives, and in and around San Francisco, which makes Sally Garrity's survivors very nervous. Sheri Ysit, who finished raising her slain sister's daughter, Yvette, moved Auntie out of the city and onto a reservation in Nevada. Sheri subsequently married and moved out of Oakland. Today, she continues to live in the Bay Area with her husband, a mechanic, a stepdaughter, and a recently born son.

Sheri's still scared of what Sal Guardado might try. She thinks she even might have seen him once, standing outside a Popeye's fried chicken outlet in San Francisco. The experience unnerved her. "I kinda got scared," she says. "What do I do? Go looking for a cop? And what do I say, then? 'Oh, this guy over there killed my sister.' And what if it wasn't him? I really don't know what I would do if I actually saw him."

The Toy Texan

Austin, Texas

According to his family and close friends, rare book dealer and historian John ("Johnny") Holmes Jenkins III, 49, of Austin, Texas, was in good spirits on the bright April Sunday in 1989 when Jenkins climbed into his gold Mercedes and drove southeast 30 or so miles from Austin into Bastrop County. He certainly gave no indication of despondency or depression, emotions which in any case seemed utterly alien to him. Jenkins, the author of a well-respected bibliography of Texas historical tracts and treatises entitled *Basic Texas Books*, was at work on the biography of Edward Burleson, a patriot of the Texas revolution, and he believed he had at last pinpointed where Burleson's father was buried. Jenkins was headed down into Bastrop County to see if he was right.

The question of Johnny Jenkins's frame of mind is important because the sheriff of Bastrop County, Con Keirsey, believes that the book dealer himself was responsible for the

Johnny Jenkins.

quite large bullet hole discovered later that same Sunday in the back of Jenkins's head when his body was recovered near a boat ramp on a turbid stretch of the Colorado River in Bastrop County.

If Sheriff Keirsey's right, then Johnny Jenkins certainly selected an unconventional and melodramatic way to kill himself, which *would* have been in character. However, the Bastrop County official who determines official causes of death, Justice of the Peace B. T. Henderson, thinks someone besides Johnny Jenkins pulled the trigger. Many who knew the dead man concur. "If that sheriff had been in a room for one minute with Johnny Jenkins," one of Jenkins's employers told a reporter, "he'd know he's barking up the wrong tree. He'd know about the force of his personality, his confidence, his assurance to himself and to those around him that any problem could be overcome. What it gets down to is that the sheriff didn't know Johnny Jenkins."

Maybe no one did. "The truth is," said one acquaintance in the book trade, "that he was a very complex person, not a simple man."

Johnny Jenkins's business interests were eclectic. He sank considerable sums into a nonremunerative oil-drilling operation. He once backed a feature-length horror movie, *Mongrel*, which was humanely destroyed soon after its release.

Jenkins also had another name, Austin Squatty, his sobriquet when he competed in the company of world-class poker players in Las Vegas and elsewhere. Jenkins wasn't call Austin Squatty because he waddled when he walked, although he did. And according to an article by Calvin Trillin in *The New Yorker* magazine, they didn't call him Austin Squatty because he was short, perhaps no taller than five feet six inches. No, Trillin's sources suggested the nickname derived from Jenkins's poker-table habit of sitting cross-legged, "the way Indians in movies sit around the campfire," as Trillin puts it. In other venues, Jenkins was referred to as the Toy Texan.

It is unclear whether Johnny Jenkins ever won much money playing cards; there has been speculation that he was, in fact, a poor player and deeply in debt to unsavory elements in Nevada and maybe New Jersey. If so, then Johnny Jenkins's real cause of death could have been a welshed chit.

Sheriff Keirsey offers perhaps the soundest rebuttal to that idea. "If you seem to be welshing on a gambling debt," Keirsey told Trillin, "the first thing they want to do is put some hurt on you—break your legs, smash up your face, do some odds and ends. If they do have to kill you, they'd make it obvious, to leave a message."

There is little that's obvious to be concluded from the physical evidence at the boat ramp scene of the crime. Jenkins's gold Mercedes coupe was parked at the river. Its left rear tire was flat and the passenger-side door was open. His wallet lay nearby, empty save for the victim's social security card. His Rolex watch was gone, as were Jenkins's credit cards and an estimated $500 in cash he is thought to have been carrying in his wallet that day. Because of this, many of those who think he was murdered believe the motive was money and that the killer, in all probability, was a stranger.

Their reasoning seems sound, except to Sheriff Keirsey. Yet no theory of Johnny Jenkins's violent death can be considered without reference to certain other curious and poorly-understood features of his business life. These include fires and forgery.

In the first instance, Jenkins-owned establishments were hit by conflagrations three times—in 1969, 1985, and in 1987. He collected a $3.5 million insurance settlement after the 1985 blaze. The 1987 fire was ruled an arson, although no suspect was ever named.

The forgeries were a more complicated matter. According to investigations undertaken in the main by Texas printer and bookseller Tom Taylor, beginning probably in the late 1970s some one or more people produced and sold a variety of forged Texana documents. The bogus documents included at least 20 copies of the 1836 Texas Declaration of Independence. Some sold for $40,000 and more. One of the fake Declarations found its way into the Dallas Public Library's collection. Former Texas governor Bill Clements bought another. Yale University acquired at least two of the forged documents.

Book man Tom Taylor's detective work brought him in time to the state of Mississippi and Pass Christian, a tiny hamlet where he found C. Dorman David, a onetime Houston rare-document dealer, former heroin addict, and ex-con, who quickly owned up to his role in the fakery. David, who also once had been Johnny Jenkins's partner in an Austin western-art gallery, admitted forging several historical documents, including the Texas Declaration of Independence. But he also claimed he had no intention of ever selling the fakes. Instead, insisted David, he meant to sell the documents, marked as reproductions, to institutions that could not afford the real thing. This would be part of an effort to establish himself as an expert on forgeries.

The fact that the forgeries were discovered, he later told reporter Lisa Belkin of *The New York Times*, demonstrated the truth of what he said. "I'm an artist," David said to Belkin. "I believe in my heart that if I wanted to I could make something no one could detect."

There are those who doubt what C. Dorman David claims. And it is not at all clear if David was the only source of the bogus papers. What is known is that several people bought and sold them and profited from the trade. Tom Taylor succeeded in tracing the provenance of 36 forgeries. According to Trillin's account, five of the documents were sold by David. Nine other were traceable to a Houston dealer, William Simpson, who had no knowledge that they were fakes. The remainder, 22 fakes in all, were vended by Johnny Jenkins's company.

No criminal charges ever have been filed in connection with any of the forgeries, and apparently no prosecutions are anticipated. Conspiracy theorists might argue this is because the one person who probably knew most about the case is now dead. On the other hand, no one publicly connected with the forgeries— either as a winner or loser—appears to be a viable suspect in Jenkins's death.

According to Sheriff Keirsey's analysis, the fires and forgeries played a subtle, indirect role in Johnny Jenkins's demise. By early 1989 there was plenty of speculation about his practices circulating within the small, clubby world of rare-book dealers, many of whom disliked Jenkins purely on account of his style. The world at large wasn't acting any friendlier, either. In the spring of 1989, the Federal Deposit Insurance Corporation sued Jenkins for $1.3 million in connection with a loan he secured for his oil-rig operation. An Austin bank had foreclosed on his combination warehouse and bookstore, and he could look forward to the humiliation of having the property sold at public auction.

Hence the Keirsey theory. "His esteem and his prestige and his status had diminished in the last year," the Bastrop sheriff told Trillin, "and he couldn't live with the stigma of defeat. His family says he was always able to pull out, but pretty soon you use your coupons up."

There'd be less dispute over Con Keirsey's conclusions had gunpowder been detected on Johnny Jenkins's hand. It wasn't. And although that doesn't disprove the sheriff's conclusion, it is consistent with another troublesome detail: namely, the death weapon has not been recovered.

How can a person shoot himself in the back of the head and then secrete the weapon? One theory Calvin Trillin uncovered is that Jenkins punched several holes in a large, plastic soft-drink container, and then tied the perforated bottle to his gun. According to this speculation, when he fired the fatal bullet the gun-and-bottle device dropped into the river and floated along until the container filled with water and sank, possibly quite a distance downstream from Jenkins's dead body. It is also distinctly possible that Jenkins simply blew himself away and dropped the gun in the water where, despite an intensive search, it remains. Stranger things have happened.

One thing that almost everyone agrees upon about Johnny Jenkins's death is that it would have tickled Johnny giddy to attract so much attention. The deed, whoever did it, also helped rescue Jenkins's businesses since his lenders all had policies on his life. The warehouse/store that was about to be auctioned is now owned, without attachments, by the Jenkins Company. From this perspective, Johnny Jenkins's death may have been the best deal he ever did.

There is vigorous dissent. "People say, 'Oh, it's Johnny's last scam,' " an admirer and employee, Michael Parrish, told a reporter. Parrish, who thinks his boss was murdered, resents the idea that Jenkins engineered the episode. "They say, 'He pulled the wool over everyone's eyes. He's up there laughing.' But it's hard to laugh when you're dead."

Domestic Violence

THOMAS ROSS WILLIAMS
Mesa, Arizona

DATE OF BIRTH: October 14, 1940
HEIGHT: Five feet nine inches
WEIGHT: 150 pounds (approx.)
HAIR: Black
EYES: Brown
CONTACT: Mesa Police Department
Detective Mark Jones
(602) 644-2002

It was Tuesday evening, November 29, 1983, five days after Thanksgiving, and a late autumn chill had fallen over suburban Mesa, Arizona, directly southeast of Phoenix. Virgil Wike, 64, and his wife Marjorie, 63, were watching television together in their trailer on East Englewood St. at a little past nine that night, when Virgil decided the cool weather warranted another log in the fireplace.

Wike rose and walked outside to his woodpile. He tarried there a moment, enjoying a pipe of tobacco, when suddenly Wike heard a loud commotion next door at the Williams's trailer. He discerned a crashing sound, as if someone was trying to kick in the trailer door. Virgil Wike hurriedly knocked the dottle out of his pipe, ran back inside his trailer, and

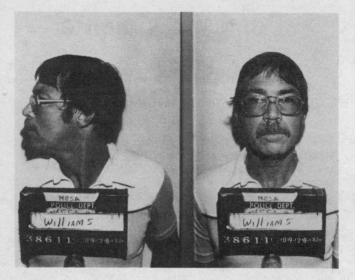

Tommy Williams.

called the Mesa police. Then he grabbed Marjorie and dashed with her into their back bedroom, the better to eavesdrop on yet another of Tommy and Maxine Williams's locally notorious family rows.

"I heard two distinct voices," Marjorie Wike later told police. "I could immediately tell it was Thomas and Maxine. I knew them well. They had lived there for more than seven years, and they had had many fights before."

"Maxie!" Mrs. Wike remembered Mr. Williams shouting at his estranged spouse. "Why did you do it?"

"You know why!" Maxine Williams yelled in reply.

At that moment, Marjorie Wike explained,

she heard the "low level" sound of two gun-shots fired within her neighbors' trailer. That's when the Wikes called the cops again.

A few minutes later, Mesa police department patrolmen Bill Rogers and Adam Bustos, to-gether with Lt. Harry Boden, arrived at the Williamses' residence, 63 East Englewood. They found that the middle window of the west door, by the kitchen, had been smashed in; there were glass shards all over the kitchen floor, as well as on the adjoining utility room floor. The investigating officers also recorded that an empty leather holster, discarded and probably forgotten, lay on the floor.

They walked to their right toward the rear bedroom in the south end of the trailer, the room closest to the Wike residence. On the way, they found Maxine Williams's purse with $153 cash in it. The motive for the break-in was not money. A few steps farther on, the officers noted that the bedroom door had been dam-aged. It was partially unhinged. They contin-ued through it into the bedroom where they discovered Mrs. Williams, 43, quite dead from a gunshot wound in her right temple. Another bullet had ripped through the south bathroom wall. Subsequent investigation would reveal that the second slug exited the trailer through the bathroom, then whizzed through a metal storage shed and slammed into the concrete exterior wall of a neighboring house before it fell harmlessly to the ground, where the spent round was later recovered for ballistic tests. Back in the bedroom, Mrs. Williams's gold-colored metal wristwatch was discovered to have been torn from her wrist in the struggle with her assailant. It lay on the bed near her.

From the outset, the police had no reason to suspect Maxine's murderer was anyone but heavy-machine mechanic Tommy Williams, 43, her husband of 12 years, from whom she was trying to gain a divorce. Based upon what the neighbors and Maxine's son, 18-year-old Richard Carl Gohl, had to report, the only real mystery in the case was that Mrs. Williams hadn't died sooner at the hands of the brutal, unbalanced Tommy Williams.

According to her son's written statement, Maxine was a battered wife throughout most of her marriage, suffering repeated broken noses (at least seven), fractured ribs, black eyes, and bruises. Once, reported Gohl, Tommy Williams kicked his wife several times, and then took his boot off and hit Maxine in the head with it. On another occasion, Williams menaced them both. "He blatantly threatened myself and my mother, saying, 'I'll blow both your fucking heads off.'"

"All of these things led to their separation," Richard Gohl wrote. Gohl explained how he had come home from his college fraternity house one afternoon that autumn to do some laundry. "When I walked inside I could see that Thomas (Tommy as we called him) had struck again. Both of her eyes were black and swollen. Her nose had been broken again. And she could hardly move or breathe comfortably because several of her ribs had been broken. I looked at her feeling disgusted and questioned, 'Tommy?'

"She said, 'Yes.'

"I asked, 'Why?'

"She answered, 'Because he was pissed.'"

Ordinarily, it required no evident provoca-

STATEMENT OF FACTS
MESA POLICE DEPARTMENT

CASE NO. _____

STATEMENT OF _____

PART _____ P.M. / A.M.

FINISH _____ P.M. / A.M.

PLACE _____

STATEMENT OF _____

ADDRESS _____   AGE ___ SEX ___

PHONE _____

②

and my mother's lives saying "I'll blow both of your fucking heads off" in anger.
    He also used her and took cash from her. She would take money from my mom, and give her none. She would cook for him and do errands and _____ chores for him; but he showed no gratitude, and gave her no freedom. Yes he took material objects from her and then on Tuesday, November 29 he took the last thing he could ever take from her, her life. Pretty shitty, huh?
    Well all of these things lead to their separation, and a pending divorce. Despite the separation he continued to bother her, harass her, and physically abuse her. On Thursday, just several weeks ago I went to her home at 83 E. Inglewood, to do my laundry. I'm living in a fraternity house in Tempe, and we have no washers or dryers there. When I walked inside I could see that Thomas (Tommy as we called him) had

WITNESS: _____

SIGNATURE _____

Part of Peter Gohl's handwritten statement detailing Tommy Williams' abuse of his mother: ". . . on Tuesday, November 29 he took the last thing he could ever take from her, her life. Pretty shitty, huh?"

tion for Tommy Williams to become "pissed," and then to express his manly wrath by knocking around his wife. After their separation, he still came by the trailer to maul and harass Maxine, but then Tommy would withdraw to his new address, 746-C South Alma School Rd. in Chandler, just south of Mesa, which he shared with Cynthia ("Cindy") Ann Hoke, 26, and her brother, 17-year-old Jeffrey. Williams had met Ms. Hoke at Empire Machinery, an auto parts supply house where she worked.

Meantime, Maxine found herself a lover, too. At the time, this seemed understandable enough in light of the horrors she endured at home. In retrospect, it probably cost Maxine her life.

The other man, Ned Rosen,* was married. Rosen told police that his wife had discovered the affair in late October of 1983, and that he broke off with Mrs. Williams the week before Thanksgiving.

On November 15, Rosen related, he took a call at home from Tommy Williams. With his wife listening in on an extension, Rosen heard Williams accuse him of sleeping with Maxine. Williams threatened to come over with some friends to beat him up. "You're lucky to still have your life," Williams allegedly said, "and Maxie is, too. I told Maxie that if she ever took anybody else inside that trailer I would blow them both away."

Virgil and Marjorie Wike told police they saw Tommy Williams's tan-colored Ford Ranger pickup truck parked in front of 63 East Englewood from approximately six o'clock until seven the night of Maxine Williams's murder.

*pseudonym

Then Tommy departed, apparently, and Maxine placed a call to the Rosen household, looking for Mrs. Rosen. According to Mrs. Rosen's later sworn statement, Maxine Williams insisted over the telephone for 45 minutes—until nine o'clock—that she come out that night and meet her at a nearby bowling alley to talk. If she would not, Maxine threatened, then she'd come to the Rosen residence herself.

It was just a quarter-hour or so after Mrs. Williams hung up that her husband returned to East Englewood St. In an odd and so-far-unexplained twist in the story, at about this time a male telephone caller (Tommy Williams?) dialed a complete stranger, Dee Ann Marsh of Mesa, and demanded to talk to someone named Cindy. In the background, as Dee Ann Marsh later recounted to the police, she heard a woman talking in a loud voice, saying, "Tommy, you've done it now! You are going to go to jail!"

Some weeks before, Maxine Williams had sworn out a complaint against her husband, and had obtained a court order legally forbidding him from calling the trailer or coming near it. Perhaps Maxine was the mystery woman whom Dee Ann Marsh overheard warning "Tommy" that he'd violated the order and was going to be arrested as a result.

Ms. Marsh had no idea who was calling for Cindy, or what the conversation on the other end of the line was about. "ut up and be quiet," she heard the unidentified man say, "and sit down or I'll shoot you in the head." Something like that.

The "Cindy" Tommy Williams might have been trying to telephone as he stood in the trailer, menacing Maxine Williams with his gun, presumably was Cindy Hoke, but the number he dialed by mistake, the Marshes' home telephone, was much closer to the Rosen family number than it was to Cindy Hoke's. All that can be reasonably surmised is that, in his rage, Tommy Williams wanted to speak with his girlfriend, whose number he confused with the Rosens'. Whatever the truth, Dee Ann Marsh always refused to repeat her experience in court. She told the police she was afraid because of Tommy Williams's reputation for violence, and she remains so today. "I told the police and I told you," she says, "I just don't want to get involved."

After weeks of threatening to shoot someone in the head, and then doing it to his wife, Tommy Williams decided to leave town—immediately—with Cindy Hoke. Her younger brother Jeff later told police that Williams telephoned him at home at approximately 10:30 that night, a little more than an hour after the murder. Williams said he was at a North Phoenix motel with Jeff's sister, and that Jeff was not to wait up for them that night. "Something has happened to Maxie," Williams told Hoke, "and I'll be blamed for it." He also asked Hoke to work Cindy's 8:00 A.M. to 4:00 P.M. shift at the Empire Machinery Co. (where Jeff also was employed, as a janitor) the next day, so that she wouldn't lose her job. His sister couldn't make it herself, said Williams, because she was going to accompany him on an appointment at his divorce lawyer's office.

The next afternoon, Wednesday, November 30, the police found Williams's tan Ford Ranger parked on West Main St. in Mesa, in front of the Enterprise Leasing and Car Rental Agency. A check revealed that the vehicle was registered in Ms. Hoke's name, possibly to mask its ownership in the pending divorce settlement. The Mesa police staked out the Ranger for two days before seizing it.

On Thursday, December 1, the police were contacted by Terry Pachelo Bilducca, who identified herself as one of Cindy Hoke's coworkers at Empire Machinery. Ms. Bilducca told Detective Jim Mason that Cindy had telephoned. "I guess you heard what happened," she quoted Hoke. "It was an accident." Cindy Hoke also informed Ms. Bilducca that she intended to be back at work at Empire Machinery by Monday, December 5. She added that Monday was the day that Tommy Williams expected to turn himself in.

Then Jeff Hoke received a letter from his sister. It was postmarked November 30, in Tucson, Arizona, about 115 miles southeast of Mesa. In the note, Cindy Hoke asked Jeff to retrieve the Ford pickup, and provided him directions to the Enterprise Leasing office on West Main as well as a set of keys. Hoke immediately turned the letter over to the Mesa police.

Within hours, Mesa detectives Mike Johnson and Mark Jones were en route by car to Tucson. When they arrived there, however, a check back with police headquarters in Mesa disclosed the news that Williams and Hoke had contacted the FBI in Flagstaff, Arizona, which is about 140 miles *north* of Phoenix. The couple told Special Agent Stephen H. Enfield that they were in New Mexico, that they wanted to give themselves up, and that they would be driving west from New Mexico on Route I-40 in a brown-and-white 1973 Chevy sedan.

Four and a half hours later, Detectives Johnson and Jones pulled into Flagstaff where the fugitives already had been placed in custody,

read their Miranda rights, and had undergone
a preliminary interrogation. Sgt. Byron Allen
of the Flagstaff police department debriefed
Johnson and Jones on the questioning.

According to Sgt. Allen, Tommy Williams admitted going to the trailer that night. He further
conceded engaging in "a verbal argument" with
his estranged wife. In Williams's version of the
fight, it was Maxine who pulled the gun and
squeezed off the shot that blew through the bathroom wall. Then they struggled for the handgun,
said Tommy, and as they did the weapon discharged again, accidentally. He said Maxine collapsed at that moment, but he thought she only
had fainted from fright. "I didn't know she was
even hit," he reportedly told Officer Allen. Tommy
Williams then recounted how he fled from the
trailer and tossed away the gun as he headed for
a Denny's restaurant to call Cindy Hoke.

When Detective Mark Jones tried to interview
Williams and Hoke, they revealed that they had
been married on December 1 in El Paso, Texas,
and that neither of them had anything further
to say until they had legal counsel. Williams did
insist that his companion—and wife—knew
nothing of the events in the trailer until they
had returned from Texas as far as Albuquer-
que, New Mexico, where he had telephoned the
FBI in Flagstaff.

The next day, both fugitives were returned
to Mesa where Tommy Williams was formally
accused of first-degree murder and Cynthia
Hoke, despite her new husband's assurances
of her ignorance and innocence, was charged
with one count of hindering prosecution.

Cynthia Hoke-Williams ultimately served five
years in prison. Upon her release, she left the

area. Tommy Williams's attorney plea-bargained his client down to a manslaughter charge. As a result of the plea deal, Williams would have spent no more than 15 years in prison. While out on $35,000 bond as he awaited sentencing, however, Tommy Williams vanished. He so far has evaded recapture.

In death, his wife Maxine had become a statistic; one of the roughly 4,000 American women who die each year from domestic abuse. "He used her and took from her," Maxine's son Richard wrote in his statement. "He would take money from my mom, and give her none. She would cook for him and do errands and chores for him, but he showed no gratitude and gave her no freedom. Then, on Tuesday, November 29, he took the last thing he could ever take from her, her life. Pretty shitty, huh?"

All-American

STANLEY BEATTY
Sacramento, California

DATE OF BIRTH: November 6, 1969
HEIGHT: Five feet eight inches
WEIGHT: 160 pounds
HAIR: Black
EYES: Brown
DISTINGUISHING MARKS: Small scar on left forearm
ALSO KNOWN AS: Reggie Smith and "Supreme"
CONTACT: Sgt. Joe Dean
         Sacramento County Sheriff's Office
         (916) 440-5057

The results of a recent study by the National Center for Health Statistics, released in March of 1991, are stunning. According to the report, homicide has become the leading cause of death among young black males in America. Unsurprisingly, the vast majority of these murders are committed with guns. "As a black man and a father of three, this really shakes me to the core of my being," Dr. Louis W. Sullivan, U.S. Secretary of Health and Human Services, told an audience at the time. "Do you realize that the leading killer of young black males is young black males?"

Here's a case indicative of this appalling trend.

Stanley Beatty.

Kyron L. Vandell, 22, was a star football player at Sacramento City College. In one season, the five-foot ten-inch 190-pound halfback had rushed for 1,106 yards in 240 carries. Three hundred of those yards came in his last game, a 30–20 conference championship victory over American River College. During two years on the team, Vandell had scored 208 points; only two other players in the history of California junior college football ever rang up more points. He was voted a junior college all-conference, all-state, and all-American offensive back. He also won a football scholarship to Washington State University, where Vandell was scheduled to enroll as a junior in the au-

tumn of 1990. "He was an all-American player
and an all-American person," WSU head football coach Mike Price would later say. "He
worked all his life to get where he was."

On a night in late June 1990, Vandell was so-
cializing at Brannan's, a bar in Sacramento's
K Street Mall. Also at Brannan's that night was
Thaddeus ("Tee") Williams, known to the Sacramento police as a drug dealer and street
punk from New York, who with an unnamed
cousin was hassling a young woman of Vandell's acquaintance.

According to witnesses, the girl asked Vandell to help her. He and Williams squared off
in the bar, and then walked outside at Vandell's suggestion. There, Tee Williams received
a thorough thrashing. Kyron Vandell "kicked
his butt," as one source puts it. As Williams
picked himself off the pavement, said witnesses, he vowed vengeance against Vandell.

Fifteen days later, at 2 A.M. on Thursday, July 12,
Vandell was seated in his car in the parking
lot of a Black Angus restaurant at 6601 Florin
Rd. in south Sacramento when, as Sacramento
County Sheriff's spokesman, Ed Close, relates,
Williams and three other young black men approached. Williams was carrying a length of
pipe, for which Vandell chided him. "If you
want to fight me," witnesses recalled Vandell
saying, "fight me one on one."

Onlookers reported that Thaddeus Williams
did put down the pipe, but at the same time
one of his associates, a New York dice player
and hustler named Stanley Beatty, opened up
with his .380 semiautomatic pistol. David and
Dinah Ray, a married couple who'd just exited
the Black Angus and were crossing the parking

lot toward their car, both were hit in the leg. Both later recovered. A friend of Kyron Vandell, Corey Baugh, also took a Beatty bullet in the leg, and was rushed by ambulance to the UC-Davis Medical Center for treatment. Kyron Vandell, Beatty's target, was hit once in the head. He, too, was taken to the UC-Davis hospital, where Vandell was pronounced dead about four hours later.

Because Tee Williams was a reputed member of the dreaded "Crips" drug gang, the Sacramento Sheriff's Office wasn't surprised to hear from a source they trusted that the shooting was gang-related; that Kyron Vandell was in fact a member of the rival "Bloods" and that is why he was killed. The sheriff, in turn, identified Vandell as a Bloods gang member to the local news media.

Corey Baugh's father responded with instant indignation. "My son," Mr. Baugh wrote in a letter to the press, "was shot down on the streets of Sacramento and his friend was killed. Instead of dealing with a friend and the injury to my son, I'm dealing with the accusation ... that this tragedy was a gang-related killing and shooting. I feel that my son was victimized by these statements." Mr. Baugh went on to characterize the gang references as "irresponsible, reckless and false."

Three days after the murder, the sheriff retracted the gang allegations. "We're wrong," said Ed Close, "and we're apologizing. It wasn't something that we put out in a cavalier manner. We received that information later in the day after the shooting occurred and felt that we took it in good faith, and felt it was good information."

After her son's funeral at St. Paul's Baptist Church, Kyron Vandell's mother, Barbara Vandell, spoke to the press, too. She was hardly mollified by the official apology. "They caused a lot of turmoil in my family and a lot of unnecessary hurt, a lot of mental anger because it was not true," Mrs. Vandell said bitterly of the sheriff's office. "They will never be able to retract these things. But I'm thankful he was buried with honor and this rumor was buried with him."

She no doubt would be even more grateful if her son's killer could be brought to justice. Following the shooting, Tee Williams vanished, only to be captured in Sacramento in September of 1990 and extradited to New York on pending drug charges. Stanley Beatty, the shooter, also is named in outstanding New York warrants for car theft, drug possession, and attempted murder in connection with his alleged shooting of Andre Williams of Staten Island on November 12, 1988. Beatty, says Sgt. Joe Dean of the Sacramento Sheriff's Office, has not been seen in Sacramento, or New York, since the Vandell murder. There has been one unverified tip that the fugitive is in Puerto Rico.

Crimes of Opportunity

Skagit and Snohomish Counties, Washington

On Wednesday, November 18, 1987, Jay Roland Cook, 20, and his girlfriend, 18-year-old Tanya Van Cuylenborg, both of Oak Bay, British Columbia, a little town on Vancouver Island, boarded an auto ferry at Victoria, on the southern tip of the island, for the scenic trip across the Straits of Juan De Fuca to Port Angeles, Washington. The couple was headed down to the United States with $570 in cash and travelers' checks that Jay's father, Gordon Cook, had given them to pay for some furnace parts they were to pick up for him the next day in Seattle.

In Port Angeles, Jay and Tanya debarked the ferry in their bronze, '77 Ford van and steered south for some sightseeing along Route 101, about a hundred miles down to the town of Shelton. There they turned northeast on Route 3 toward Bremerton, where they planned to catch a second ferry across the Puget Sound to Seattle.

Subsequent police inquiries would reveal

Tanya Van Cuylenborg.

Jay Cook.

that Cook and Van Cuylenborg stopped to make a purchase in the town of Allyn on Route 3, between Shelton and Bremerton, and that they bought their Bremerton ferry tickets later that day. It is presumed that Cook and Van Cuylenborg drove the Ford van onto the boat, and that they accompanied the vehicle on the short voyage to Seattle. To date, however, no one has reliably reported seeing the young people on the ferry that evening.

Nor were they ever seen alive again.

Western Washington seems to experience far more than its share of aberrant, serial, and sex-related homicides. Ted Bundy hunted there in the 1970s, and perhaps earlier. Bundy's successor, the so-called Green River Killer—or Killers—ranged around Seattle and down to Portland, Oregon, murdering at least 49 females, mainly prostitutes, in a brief, mid-1980s binge. Lately, Washington paraphile and child killer, Westley Dodd, has wormed his way into the crime spotlight. Dodd currently awaits (impatiently, he says) execution at the state prison in Walla Walla.

Because of this recent history, Washingtonians are perhaps quicker than most to assume that any disappearance or murder in their state is the work of another marauding maniac. In the Cook and Van Cuylenborg case, the dread was heightened by the fact that three other couples had vanished in western Washington over the past two years. Those who had been found had all been found dead. This time, however, Washington's experienced corps of newspaper crime reporters barely had the opportunity to begin sampling speculation as to the Canadian couple's fates before they were known.

- On Tuesday, November 24, a man out for a walk near the town of Alger in Skagit County, well north of Seattle, came across a partially-clad body in a ditch. It was Tanya Van Cuylenborg. She had been raped and shot once in the back of her head.
- On Wednesday, police recovered the '77 Ford van parked near the Greyhound Bus Depot in Bellingham, perhaps 30 miles north of where Tanya's body was found.
- On Thursday, Thanksgiving Day, 1987, a pair of hunters found Jay Cook dead under a bridge near the town of Monroe, in Snohomish County, 20 miles or so northwest of Seattle, and roughly 45 miles south of Alger in Skagit County. Cook had been strangled to death with a ligature.

According to articles by reporter Mike Boroughs and others on the staff of the *Skagit Valley Herald* newspaper, as well as interviews with sources close to the investigations, the physical evidence recovered from the crime scenes and the van suggests that both Tanya Van Cuylenborg and Jay Cook were killed on the night of the eighteenth. Jay most likely was murdered first, and dumped as the couple's abductor, or abductors, traveled north with the Ford van.

Then Tanya was sexually assaulted, shot dead, and disposed of in Skagit County before the van was abandoned in Bellingham. A clear inference—and perhaps one that the police were *supposed* to make—is that their quarry continued north into Canada from Bellingham, possibly aboard a coach from the depot.

How did the crimes occur?

This appears to be a matter of opportunity seized. Cook and Van Cuylenborg were open and trusting in the manner of small-town natives; it would not have been difficult for a friendly stranger to strike up a conversation with them on the ferry. Either one might have discussed why they were coming to Seattle, and let slip that they were carrying cash. If their killer was a single individual—almost certainly a male—he might have asked for a ride once they landed in Seattle. Judging from the wire-plastic restraints later recovered from the van—these were similar to the restraints used in Bobbie Oberholtzer's murder (Section One, Chapter 1)—he had thought ahead about committing this crime, and probably had committed one or more like it before.

Another possibility is that there were two killers. The strongest evidence for this is the different means of murder, the more "intimate" strangulation of Cook (who was not otherwise assaulted) as opposed to the relatively impersonal execution-style slaying of Van Cuylenborg after her rape. There seem to be two distinctly different personalities dispatching two different victims.

Very little more can now be said of the case, except that so far detectives in Snohomish and Skagit counties have not been able to conclusively link the Cook-Van Cuylenborg murders to any of the other, also still-unsolved, couple murders committed in the region. A reward of

$100,000 has been established, principally from corporate contributions and from the British Columbia Bar Association.

Readers with information are asked to call either the Skagit County Sheriff's Office at (206) 336-9450, or the Snohomish County Sheriff's Office at (206) 388-3393.

Death in the Big D

Dallas, Texas

Dallas, Texas, is famed for its beauties; "the prettiest girls in the world," according to a local boast, which may not be an exaggeration. Yet the Big D also is one of the more violent major metropolises in the United States—perversely so for a city blessed with so many gorgeous women.

Some Dallas neighborhoods, especially those with many singles' apartment complexes, are plagued by sex offenders. In 1990, 1,344 women reported to the police that they had been raped in the city, a huge number of victims considering that they represent but a fraction of the total. Experts say that nine in ten rape victims still chose to bear their pain and outrage in silence rather than report the crime to authorities.

Dallas, the eighth largest city in the United States with a 1990 population of 1,058,000, also suffers along with the rest of America's urban centers from a rising epidemic of murder—even though its citizens fairly bristle with fire-

Ashley Reed in high school.

Reed in photo
taken just
before her
disappearance.

arms purchased for their personal protection. In 1989, there were 351 homicides reported to the Dallas Police Department. In 1990, the number of murders in Dallas jumped to 447, a new record. By comparison, San Diego, population 1,156,000, had 135 reported murders. And in Phoenix, with 1,014,000 residents, the police received 128 homicide reports in 1990.

Out of the carnage in Dallas come two illustrative cases, both still unsolved, that recently have scared the daylights out of many of the prettiest girls in the world. Each story is a graphic example of just how perilous life in Dallas can be, especially for women.

Ashley Reed of St. Cloud, Minnesota, came to Dallas with her mother, Karen Reed, in October 1989, a month before her nineteenth birthday. According to published accounts, the pert and innocent-looking brunette with the thick Minnesota accent had been a cheerleader, homecoming queen, and president of the student council back at Harding High School in St. Cloud. She also had been offered a scholarship to the University of Minnesota campus in St. Cloud.

Ashley had some problems, though. "She was not nearly as straight as I was led to believe when I first got the case," says Dallas Police Department homicide detective John Westphalen. "She and some other kids were accused of stealing from their employer, quite a substantial amount of money. There never were any charges filed, but restitution was made. She just got caught up in a deal with what other kids were doing, I think."

Dallas was a logical spot for Ashley Reed to start over. Her maternal grandmother, Eileen

Hogstad, lived there, as did her uncle, Robert Hogstad. Her mother, Karen, 42, found a North Dallas apartment for herself and Ashley, and Karen's 2-year-old son, Josh, and went to work as a business form designer at Standard Register, Mrs. Reed's employer when she lived in St. Cloud. Ashley took a job waiting tables at a restaurant called JoJo's, and began making new preparations for college.

"Ashley had everything planned," her mother later told the Edgar Award-winning crime writer, Carlton Stowers, for a *Dallas Observer* article. "She would work for a few months, helping me get settled, then she would enroll at the University of North Texas for the spring semester."

"Thus," wrote Stowers, "Ashley's life [became] a routine of work, occasional trips to a nearby mall for shopping or a movie, and solitary visits to a neighborhood Denny's restaurant where she would sit in a back booth and write long letters to friends back in Minnesota. It was there she smoked cigarettes, a secret, newfound habit of which she was certain her mother would disapprove."

A waitress at Denny's later informed police of a young man she'd frequently seen flirting with Ashley in her back booth. According to prevailing theories of the case, this probably was the man that Ashley told her mother about, by telephone, on Saturday, January 13, just before six o'clock in the evening.

Excitedly, as Karen Reed remembers, Ashley described how she'd been invited to a rock concert in Corsicana, about 48 miles south-southeast of Dallas on Interstate 45. Because Ashley always was cautious around men she didn't know well, she was going to drive her own car, a brown 1984 Citation, and planned to meet "Dave," her date, at an International House of Pancakes (IHOP) in Mesquite, directly east of Dallas.

She discussed with her mother what she intended to wear; a Guess brand denim skirt, black pullover shirt, black flats, and the brown bomber jacket Karen had given her for Christmas. Ashley also promised that once she and her date arrived in Corsicana she would call to tell Karen what time to expect her home that night.

The Mesquite IHOP was near an exit off I-635, the LBJ Freeway. Employees there were able to provide a good description of the man the police believe is "Dave." He was polite and friendly, appeared to be about 25 years of age, or a bit older, and dressed in neo-cowboy: tan boots, tan cowboy hat, and a tan corduroy jacket with brown patches at the elbow. He was sitting alone at the counter that evening, drinking coffee, when the IHOP phone rang. A woman was calling. She explained that she was to meet her date there and described the cowboy at the counter, with whom she wished to talk.

"Dave" took the call, spoke for a bit, and then hung up. He told one of the waitresses that it had been his date calling and that she had gone to the wrong IHOP looking for him. The waitress specifically recalled the cowboy explaining that his girl was "from up North and doesn't know her way around very well."

A few moments later, "Dave" placed two calls from the bank of pay phones near the IHOP's entrance. He then returned to his cof-

The police sketches of "Dave."

fee until shortly past seven, when a brown Citation with a female at the wheel pulled up to the restaurant. "That's her," he said as he walked out and climbed into the Citation's passenger seat.

If all had gone according to plan, Ashley and "Dave" easily would have made it to Corsicana by 8:00 p.m. When 9:30 came and went without Ashley's promised phone call home, Karen Reed in her apartment back in Dallas began to worry. She called her mother to see if perhaps Ashley had telephoned Mrs. Hogstad instead. No, she had not, but Eileen counseled her nervous daughter to relax. Ashley was a completely reliable young lady, she reminded Karen, and probably had a reason for not calling. Maybe she couldn't find a working pay phone. Maybe she just forgot, said her grandmother. Stranger things had happened.

Karen Reed fell asleep in a while, but awoke at 2 A.M. with a gnawing premonition. By four o'clock on Sunday morning, January 14, she was calling the police in Dallas, Mesquite, and Corsicana. Meantime, Eileen Hogstad started a telephone canvass of local hospitals, suspecting that Ashley might have been in a car wreck.

Nothing.

The next day, Monday the fifteenth, Karen's brother Bob drove out to Mesquite where he found his niece's brown Citation, its hazard lights flashing, parked alongside a freeway access ramp near the IHOP where Ashley is presumed to have picked up "Dave" the night before. The Citation was pointed north, the opposite direction from Corsicana. Its driver's seat was pushed far forward, the way that five-foot two-inch 115-pound Ashley usually positioned it. There was no evidence of a struggle inside the automobile. Her car keys were not in the ignition, and the battery was dead.

Interviews with attendants at the Mobil gas station nearby established that the Citation had been parked where it was found, hazard lights flashing, since eleven o'clock, or earlier, the previous night. That explained the dead battery. It also suggested that wherever Ashley was, she and "Dave" had not gone very far together in the Citation. There also was no evidence, and no witnesses, to establish that they ever made it to Corsicana.

Volunteer searchers scoured the open fields and a creek bed near where the car was recovered. They found nothing. On the Tuesday and

Wednesday following Ashley's disappearance, her mother, uncle, and grandmother stood on the freeway shoulder with signs asking motorists to report anything they might have seen at the cloverleaf intersection that weekend.

The only reports of Ashley's whereabouts that the family, or the police, ever received were of the mistaken, or crank, variety. As Stowers noted in his article, "Ashley was seen at a truckstop near Fort Worth, hitchhiking . . . she was working as a topless dancer in a Dallas nightclub . . . she was in a bar near Oklahoma City with two men and a woman, high on drugs, her hair teased, and wearing a revealing mini-skirt . . . she had forsaken her family and friends and moved into a lesbian lifestyle in Dallas's gay community."

Such implausible tales only intensified the nightmare of worry and fear that engulfed Karen Reed, and complicated a police investigation that was going nowhere, fast. "Every time I get a call like that, I say to myself, 'That isn't the girl I'm looking for,' " Dallas Police Department Youth Division detective John Easton told Stowers several months after Ashley's disappearance. "Still, I have to check it out."

Christina ("Chris") Gill turned 20 the Monday that Bob Hogstad found his niece Ashley's brown Citation on the freeway ramp near the Mesquite IHOP. A Dallas native, Chris lived at home with her parents, John and Bess, in a northeast neighborhood of the city. She stood five feet six inches and weighed a slim 95 pounds. Her eyes were brown and her hair was black. She wore it long, with bangs. According

Christina Gill.

to what Chris's father, a consultant/technician in the printing industry, told writer Floyd Whaley for a *Dallas Observer* piece, his daughter had graduated from a local high school and was taking a few liberal arts courses at a Dallas-area junior college. She said she might take up some sort of career in the media. Chris Gill, reported Whaley, "was a young woman who her father described as an intelligent late-bloomer, hyperactive and easily bored. Like many young people, she had a chameleonlike quality that allowed her to move from the hard-

rock set to the debutante crowd with a change
of clothes. . . . She 'acted independent among
her friends, but she was actually insecure and
looked to her parents for support and defense
from the world,' " says Gill.

In all, Chris Gill seems to have been entirely
normal, just like Ashley Reed. "She wasn't out
on the street every night howling at the moon,
by any means," says Dallas Police Department
homicide detective Jim Gallagher. "She wasn't
down in the front row of the church every Sunday, either."

On Thursday night, May 3, 1990, Chris and a
friend planned to go night-clubbing in Deep Ellum, an old industrial and warehouse district
of Dallas lately reborn as a popular restaurant, art gallery, and nightlife area. For some
reason, Chris's friend decided at the last moment to stay home. So Chris Gill pulled on a
white T-shirt, black tights, a long black skirt,
and a wide black belt, then took off for Deep
Ellum in her black 1989 Mustang.

According to Detective Gallagher, Gill's first
stop was a club called On The Rocks where a
hard-rock band was playing that night. She
knew members of the band, and met up with
several friends at the club. Later, says Gallagher, the group drove up to North Dallas to
another club, The Basement, and then everyone drove back down to Deep Ellum again.
Chris Gill was at On The Rocks as the 2 A.M.
closing time approached.

Thenceforth, the record of her actions is
murky and a bit confused. Everyone in her
group seems at least to have had something to
drink, perhaps a lot, and perhaps a little dope,
too. "I don't have any signed affidavits saying

narcotics were used that night," explains Gallagher, "but drugs were used regularly in this circle of friends, everything from marijuana to LSD."

Gallagher's witnesses told him that Chris Gill was plenty stoned by the shank of the evening. Patrick Brignon, a doorman at On The Rocks, confirmed this to Floyd Whaley. "I've never seen her in that state before," Brignon told Whaley. "She was never, ever like that."

Earlier that night, as Jim Gallagher recalls, it was agreed among Gill and her group that they'd all meet for some after-hours partying at one of their number, Steve Townsend's, apartment. Then there was a missed connection. Not only did her friends allow the dangerously drugged Ms. Gill to climb behind the wheel of her Mustang, no one told her that the planned party at Steve Townsend's place had been called off.

"She takes off into the night," as Jim Gallagher puts it, tersely. "And she doesn't come home."

Chris's destination, the Town Plaza apartments on Park Lane near the North Central Expressway, was one of those Dallas neighborhoods popular with the city's sex offenders. "Years ago when I was working rapes," explains Gallagher, "I worked *many* in that area. There are lots of young single women around."

The next morning, May 4, at about sunup, Steve Townsend came home and noticed Chris Gill's black Mustang parked about a hundred feet from his apartment door. "He didn't think much about it," says Gallagher.

Later in the morning, a Town Plaza maintenance man and a cleaning woman found a cosmetic bag and some scattered articles near the car. "This stuff changed hands two or three times," according to Gallagher, "finally ending up in the manager's office. Come to find out, this property belonged to Christina."

At first, Bess and John Gill weren't overly concerned that their daughter hadn't come home yet. "Mrs. Gill," says Gallagher, "said it happened before when she'd been out partying somewhere and felt like she shouldn't drive home, or whatever the circumstances. Early the next morning, she'd call and say, 'Mom, I'm over at Suzie's house. I didn't want to call you last night and wake you. I'll be home by noon.' "

By Friday afternoon, however, the Gills did begin to worry. Bess started calling around, trying to locate Chris through her friends. That night, John Gill reported his daughter missing to the Dallas police and a "wish to locate" directive was issued to all patrol officers.

As was true of the Reed case, Chris Gill's disappearance initially was handled by the Dallas PD's Youth Division. Although John Gill later would be strongly critical of the Youth Division detectives' work (indeed, Gill has been critical of the whole department), Jim Gallagher insists that the early investigation was thorough and competent. He points out that there was no reason, at first, to assume Chris Gill had met with foul play. It would be fully two months before her case and Ashley Reed's were taken from the Youth Division and made the responsibility of homicide detectives.

"We have a different perspective to offer," Detective Westphalen, who took over the Reed case from John Easton, told reporter Nancy St. Pierre of *The Dallas Morning News.* "We'll look at these cases as potential homicides, not just missing people. We have certain ways and methods that are more detailed . . . and we have more time to work on these cases than other detectives."

The homicide detectives were deeply grateful for the positive, tireless help both families offered in the search for their daughters. If every suspected murder received the public attention these two cases did, the abysmal cleared-by-arrest rate in the United States would improve dramatically.

Posters of both girls were displayed all over the Dallas area. Ashley's father, remarried and living in Boston, came to town to assist in the search. So did her older brother from Michigan. Chris Gill's brother Scott came north from Houston to be of help. John Gill quit his job to devote his full-time efforts to finding Chris. Gill had posters printed and hired a local private investigator. By the end of 1990, he would spend an estimated $100,000 investigating his daughter's disappearance.

Yet for all the effort, cooperation, and determination to solve the two mysteries, there were precious few good leads to follow. Detective Westphalen says he reinvestigated the Ashley Reed case from the start, going so far as to find an old boyfriend in Minnesota who, in the past, had knocked Ashley around from time to time. The young man was nowhere near Dallas on January 13.

Besides the waitresses' descriptions of "Dave"—which were used to produce a composite sketch that was circulated with Ashley's photo—and some so-far unidentified latent fingerprints lifted from her Citation's interior,

the only other unequivocal evidence in the case
was developed the week after Ashley disappeared.

Two men telephoned 911 to report they'd
seen a purse along a southeast Dallas County
roadside near a gravel pit where they'd been
fishing. Coincidentally, the site was not too far
from where Roxann and Kristopher Jeeves
(Section One, chapter 4) had been murdered
eight years earlier.

The fishermen left the handbag where they
discovered it, they said, although neither it, nor
any of its contents, were to be found in a later
search. When questioned in person, however,
the men were able to describe the purse, and
articles they'd seen within it, in detail. These
included a temporary Texas driver's license,
some family photos, and some credit cards from
Minnesota. "We're about 99 percent sure it was
Ashley's purse," says Westphalen.

But what significance was there to the discovery? There are two speculative scenarios.
One is that both Ashley and "Dave" were victims, possibly of a hitchhiker, who robbed and
killed them both somewhere near where her
purse was seen. If Ashley or "Dave" is ever
found, the other one won't be far away.

Detective Westphalen favors another possibility. In it, Ashley and "Dave" headed south on
I-635, following the highway approximately 13
miles to the intersection with I-45, where they
turned south toward Corsicana. "I'm not saying
it happened this way," he cautions, "but the
theory is they got down there off of I-45 and, for
whatever reason, they exited on Belt Line Rd.
[about 8 miles south of the intersection of I-635

and I-45] and headed east to where her purse was eventually seen by the fishermen.

"I think she was killed down there; probably put in a field or in one of those gravel pits. Then he got back in the car and drove back up northbound on I-635 until he got back to the IHOP. Then he parked her car, turned the flashers on, and walked over to the IHOP where he had his own car and drove away."

Chris Gill's fate is more certain. On the afternoon of Wednesday, December 5, 1990, a squirrel hunter reported to the Dallas police that he'd discovered what appeared to be a human body, 8 feet up in a tree along the Trinity River floodplain in south Dallas, an area known as the Trinity River bottoms.

It was a human, a nude female, but there was very little left of her. John Gill recognized some pieces of jewelry found with the remains as quite similar to Christina's. Also, the three physicians who compared the dead woman's teeth to Christina's dental records all agreed there was a match. It was impossible to tell if she had been sexually assaulted. A forensic anthropologist examined a fracture in her skull and concluded that Christina had died from blunt trauma to the head.

But how did she get up into that tree, and how long had she been there?

"We kicked around the theory that the girl was kidnapped, brought into that area, sexually assaulted," says Gallagher. "She flees her attacker. She climbs up into the tree, naked, and dies. Nobody finds her. I don't know. What do you think?"

What Gallagher thinks is that Chris Gill drove straight to the Town Plaza apartments that night and that someone accosted her there; someone with a car who either abducted Chris by force or subterfuge or, in Ted Bundy fashion, cracked her over the head from behind, possibly as Chris was exiting her Mustang, which would account for her cosmetic bag being found next to the car the following morning.

Christina's father, John Gill, 45, has received reports that his daughter was sold into white slavery and also that she was murdered during the filming of a snuff movie. Gill indicated to Floyd Whaley that he tends toward a theory that his daughter deliberately was drugged that night at On The Rocks, and then was kidnapped in Deep Ellum. Gill told Whaley that Chris's Mustang was driven to where it was found as a red herring. "This was supposed to look like someone got grabbed in the parking lot," Gill told Whaley. Further, Chris's father suspects she was kept alive for several months before her murder. He thinks the authorities, both local and federal, know more about the case than they are willing to say, possibly to cover up their own complicity, or incompetence.

Detective Gallagher politely denies the charges of incompetence. He accords John Gill courteous respect. "Mr. Gill," the detective said to Whaley, "has never interfered with our investigation. When I've asked him for things, he's given them to me. . . . His only intent from day one has been to help us in any way."

Gallagher believes that Chris Gill was killed within hours—no more than a few days—of her abduction. "We had heavy rains in the springtime," says Gallagher. "And the river crested the day after Christina was missing. After that, it started to recede. Based on that, this young lady went into the river the day she was grabbed, or within a day or two. There is no other explanation why this young lady is eight feet high in a tree in a river bottom that was not accessible to anyone, except by boat, for months. She went into the river pretty quick."

As far as is known, Chris Gill and Ashley Reed were unacquainted, nor did they have mutual acquaintances. However, there were enough superficial similarities between their cases to raise one other question: Could the same killer have struck twice? Neither Detective Westphalen, nor Gallagher, believe so. "But never say never," Gallagher adds.

That, in essence, is how the girls' families try to look at the cases, too. Although the reality of what probably happened to her daughter sometimes confronts Karen Reed with shattering finality, she still clings to her hopes. In January of 1991, on the anniversary of Ashley's disappearance, Karen told Bechetta Jackson of the Dallas *Times Herald* that the family had celebrated Ashley's twentieth birthday two months before. "In her heart," wrote Jackson of Karen Reed, "she knows Ashley is still alive. She just has to find her. 'I'll never give up. Ten years from now, I'll still believe that I'll find my daughter.' "

In another part of town, John Gill continues on with his own obsessed search for the truth. He has given readers of the *Dallas Observer* a number to call if they have any information about Chris (214) 348-5076. "I won't quit," he told Floyd Whaley, "I won't quit until I get an answer."

Like Little Richard

JAMES FRANCIS EDWARDS
San Francisco, California

DATE OF BIRTH: August 19, 1950
HEIGHT: Five feet eleven inches
WEIGHT: 220 pounds
HAIR: Blond-Gray, balding
EYES: Gray
ALSO KNOWN AS: Peter Paul Provost, Robert Charles Edwards
OTHER: Wears thick eyeglasses
CONTACT: Inspector Edwin Kenney
       or
    Inspector Michael Mullane
    San Francisco Police Department
    Homicide Division
    (415) 553-1145 (days)
        553-1071 (nights and weekends)
       or
    Any FBI office

Pudgy, soft-spoken James Edwards seems to have been lost in turmoil throughout most of his adult life. Once a respected Mormon in his native Utah, Edwards developed severe problems with his sexual identity, began expressing his desires inappropriately, and wound up sentenced to a 15-year stretch for child molestation at the state prison in Draper.

James Francis Edwards.

He was released after 10 years, then was arrested in Arizona for carrying a gun. His wife divorced him. His parole was revoked. As a result, Edwards headed west for San Francisco, where he submerged himself among the city's homeless, leading the vagrant life with a succession of gay companions.

"He'd stay with them awhile, and then he'd turn on them," says Homicide Inspector Edwin Kenney of the San Francisco Police Department. "I guess he was a suppressed homosexual. I don't think he knew what he was. I guess that was one of his problems."

Edwards held the occasional job as a security guard, clerk-typist, or janitor. In fact, ac-

Lamar Vaughn.

cording to his friends, by early 1989, he seemed to be pulling himself back together. He had risen in the working world to become the assistant manager of an apartment building in San Francisco's Tenderloin district. And although James Edwards had very little money, he was able to feed himself and to afford decent clothing.

Then the criminal side of his nature resurfaced. In May of 1989 on a San Francisco street, a very expensive Ampex video camera-recorder was boosted from an auto belonging to a producer for the CBS television program, *48 Hours*. Not long after the equipment was stolen, Edwards appeared with the gear asking

$400 for its return. The CBS crew called the cops instead, and James Edwards found himself back behind bars.

He was set free again after pleading guilty to a reduced charge of possession of stolen property. But Edwards—fearful that his prison record would mitigate against leniency from his judge—declined to appear for sentencing in late 1989, and became a fugitive.

As Inspector Kenney has retraced Edwards's life on the lam, it appears that he drifted into a hobo tent encampment in San Francisco's Mission district, and began taking his meals at the privately financed Martin de Porres charity soup kitchen at 225 Potrero Ave., about a five-minute walk away. This may have been where he met 47-year-old Lamar Vaughn, who soon became Edwards's new companion. "Lamar," says Morcy Burkett, a regular at the soup kitchen, "had been with everybody who would let him close, or who didn't care what they did with their body."

James and Lamar supported themselves on the street by panhandling and, perhaps, a little petty thievery now and again. Their union was not a happy one for long. Vaughn was made uncomfortable by the large-caliber handgun Edwards carried, and he frequently complained that his friend often disappeared for days without explanation.

"I didn't blame him," says another Martin de Porres habitué, a man who wishes to be known only as "Dutch." "Jim was paranoid, always thinking someone was after him, always saying he was going to rob a bank and live in southern California."

It was just such a plan, says Inspector Kenney, that may explain the trip Edwards and Vaughn made to Reno, Nevada, on Saturday, November 3, 1990. Or they might have gone there simply to do a little gambling. No one knows for sure.

What is certain is that they returned together to San Francisco late on Sunday, the fourth, and showed up Monday morning for breakfast at the soup kitchen on Potrero. Witnesses have told Inspector Kenney that Jim and Lamar were bickering, and that Edwards seemed more perturbed than usual. "You wouldn't let me alone all weekend," he reportedly complained to Vaughn. "It was the worst weekend of my life!"

The squabbling continued. At one point, Edwards rose and went to the men's room. When he returned, say onlookers, Vaughn had produced a one-by-one stick and began jabbing at Edwards with it, trying to force him away from the table. With an estimated 60 to 100 people watching them, Vaughn prodded Edwards toward the door, repeating "Get on out! Get on out!" as they moved across the room.

At the door, Edwards suddenly reached inside his belt, produced his handgun, and squeezed a single, point-blank round into Vaughn's head. Then he replaced the weapon and stepped outside, calmly strolling away.

"I wasn't here," says Morey Burkett, "but a couple guys told me he never blinked. Lamar gave a hoot like you might expect from Little Richard, and dropped straight to the floor. Most of the fellows kept eating. Wasn't nothing they could do."

Edwards has not been seen since. Some friends reported to Inspector Kenney that he'd talked of going to Mexico. There's also a possibility he's relocated to New York State, where he has family. Kenney believes Edwards probably has continued living as he did in San Francisco, and does not underestimate the odds against recapturing him. Not only is Edwards at home with people who try to avoid contact with police, but he neither drinks nor uses drugs. If he can avoid physical confrontations, he'll be difficult to catch.

Is Ed Baker Dead?

Houston, Texas

Edward Gerald Baker, 52, was by reputation as intelligent as he was rich. But the Houston oilman also had certain weaknesses—notably women and gambling—that reportedly created major financial strains for him. How major? Baker misappropriated as much as $10 million of other people's money, according to lawsuits filed by his business associates. Some of these people sent Baker menacing letters, says his lawyer. Were they the persons responsible for his murder? Or did Miami mob bosses, from whom Baker allegedly borrowed large sums, order a hit when he didn't pay off?

Could be, says his widow, Sandra, who herself lives under a shadow of suspicion in the case. Other people believe strongly that a financially ruined and emotionally-distraught Edward Baker killed himself. Finally, cognoscenti of the case (as well as some self-interested life insurers) maintain that the 30-odd pounds of burned bones and other human debris found in the front passenger-side seat of Baker's charred Jaguar could be the murdered remains of someone else entirely. Under this theory, Ed Baker possibly faked his own death and then disappeared with all or some of the missing loot, probably to his favorite place on earth, the Caribbean.

"He was a very intelligent man," says Bob Gale, a Houston private detective who frequently worked for Baker. "He's living it up somewhere far from Houston. I've never felt anything else."

"It's either one of the most clever suicides or one of the most clever murders ever," said Harris County sheriff's captain Mike Smith at the time of the crime.

"Edward Baker was an entrepreneur living the American Dream, and then he screwed the family pooch," an unnamed business associate told journalist Kathryn Casey for a *Houston City Magazine* story. "If he didn't die in a ball of flame in his '84 Jaguar, he died in the flame of his own greed."

The blackened hulk of Baker's Jaguar was discovered about 9:30 A.M. on Friday, November 8, 1985, by farmers in a rice field 2 miles north of Katy, Texas, in extreme western Harris County, about 25 miles due west of downtown Houston. Inside the vehicle, police found Baker's .32 Smith & Wesson: One round had been fired. They also discovered a shotgun in the car, plus three fire-damaged gasoline cans. These apparently had contained the fuel used to torch the Jaguar.

In touches that film director David Lynch might admire, Baker's wedding ring was found fused by the fire's heat to the metal of the Jag's interior, whereas another of Baker's rings was recovered with nearly no damage to it. More bizarre by far was the discovery of a dead man, about 25 years old, lying in the grass about a quarter mile from the car. He was handcuffed and had been beaten to death. The body was clad only in a shirt with a camouflage pattern on it. Neither this victim nor his killer ever have been identified, nor—except for physical proximity—can detectives connect the dead man with the burned-out Jag or its gruesome contents.

Joe Jachimczsk, the county medical examiner, determined that a person definitely had been cremated inside the car, but he could not be certain that fire was the direct cause of death. Jachimczsk found a gunshot wound in the victim's head. He also noted that Ed Baker suffered from marked coronary arterial sclerosis. If that was Ed in the car, then he might have succumbed to an infarct.

Jachimczsk thinks it was. He at first identified the remains as Edward Baker based on a few teeth dentures. Investigating officers were dubious of this finding, because Baker was known to possess a second pair of caps and could well have planted them as evidence. Later, Jachimczsk strengthened his identification by establishing a match between two jawbone fragments, as well as the victim's palate, with Baker's dental X-rays.

"The big handicap," the medical examiner explained at the time, "is that we don't have enough of him left. We know there was a gunshot wound to the head. But we don't know whether it was self-inflicted." In the end, he would conclude that the death most likely was a suicide, but Jachimczsk added that he guessed the victim might have been afforded some assistance.

"We can't rule out a homicide," says Ronnie Phillips, a detective with the Harris County sheriff's department, one of the six law enforcement agencies to have investigated Baker's death.

Also familiar with the case is Terry Wilson, an assistant Harris County district attorney. Wilson conditionally accepts that the remains in the Jaguar really were those of Edward Baker, "but I never ruled out the possibility that it was somebody else in that car," he says. Wilson is dubious of Jachimczsk's suicide theory. The assistant DA notes that extensive experimentation has shown fairly conclusively that Baker couldn't have both shot himself and ignited the gasoline. But beyond the few facts established to date, Wilson sees little hope of proving anything to everyone's satisfaction until, or unless, a snitch surfaces. "I would guess that until some crook runs his mouth off, we won't solve the case," he says.

Edward Baker was of average height and weight, and above average good looks—about which he was vain. According to private investigator Bob Gale, Baker had at least two facelifts. He wore expensive clothing and enjoyed being driven around Houston in a stretch limo. By contrast, Baker's four-bedroom, Concord Colony subdivision residence in western Harris County was comfortable but nothing special, says Gale. The beige house was worth perhaps $100,000, not much more than his Jaguar and clothes, and was thoroughly unremarkable except for its extensive rose gardens, another of Baker's passions.

There were quirks and dark places in Baker's world, as well. Bob Gale reports that at one time his client was an extortionist's target, and that much of the work Gale did for Baker was involved in stopping the blackmail. Gale won't, or can't, reveal who was bleeding his client, or what the extortionist had on Baker.

The private investigator is more open about the females in Baker's life. While an earnest womanizer, Ed Baker nevertheless was "uncomfortable" with his women, says Gale, and he often instructed the investigator to follow them. Bob Gale recalls shadowing various wives and girlfriends "to Florida, New York, California—all over."

The oilman also routinely asked that his employees at Vanguard be surveiled.

Baker married four times. His first wife Sally, whom he married in 1953, died in a 1973 car accident. His second marriage, to Mary Ella Walker, ended in divorce. His third wife's name was Karen Wallbridge. He met her at a meeting of est guru Werner Erhard's often-lampooned human potential training program. Baker married Wallbridge in Las Vegas in September of 1984. Less than two weeks later, Baker filed for an annulment, claiming he was drunk when the wedding ceremony took place. On April Fool's Day, 1985, Baker and Wallbridge were divorced. A month later, he married Mrs. Baker Number Four, Sandy, age 41, who had been his secretary.

Ed Baker started out as a traveling shoe salesman, then moved to insurance and real estate sales before discovering his forte, the oil-drilling business—or, more exactly, the oil-drilling promotion business. Through his Van-

Edward Baker with Sandy, Mrs. Baker #4.

guard Groups International, Inc. (the Jaguar's personalized license plate read V-OIL-1) he put together tax-advantaged partnerships for well-heeled, would-be oilmen eager to turn a buck, or at least to save one from the IRS. Typically, 12 to 24 partners joined his ventures, and for a while many of these investors apparently got rich right along with Ed Baker. "For the investor with tax problems this was a honey of a deal," one of the partners later told reporter Casey. "Baker was getting the reputation of a man who delivered."

Sometime before his death, however, Edward Baker altered his practice; he continued accepting syndicate investments, but he stopped using the money to drill for oil. No businessman, even one astute as Edward

Baker, can manage such thimble-rigging for-
ever. Eventually, his partners began compar-
ing notes, and then they sued Vanguard. A state
district judge, William Powell, was appointed
a special master to investigate Vanguard's finances. It was about this time that Baker began spending significantly more time in
Nevada where, at his death, he owed three ca-
sinos $50,000.

"A lot of men who get into financial trouble
try anything to make the big hit," says Bob
Gale. "That's the reason he gave me for his
gambling. He had a lot of faith he would hit it
big."

Baker's attorney, Ward Busey, thinks the
stories of his deceased client's gaming are
overplayed. Busey also seriously doubts that
Edward Baker killed himself. "Ed never gave
me any indication he even contemplated suicide," says the lawyer.

To the contrary, Busey maintains that Baker
wrote him that he was being threatened and
that he feared for his life. Possibly believing
that his days were numbered, Baker redrew his
will, by hand, and sent a copy to Busey. In the
document, his new wife Sandra was left
$500,000. Baker's two natural daughters by
previous marriages were given $225,000 each.
His son, Blair, was left $150,000.

Baker at the same time sent letters to two of
his life insurers. These notes directed the companies to cancel Vanguard Co. as his beneficiary and to replace it with members of his
family. "I received a copy of the letters in the
mail from him the day after he died," says
Busey. "Apparently he realized his estate
would be tied up for quite some time and

wanted assurance that his family would be taken care of."

The only person to publicly claim knowledge that Ed Baker contemplated suicide is his widow, Sandy. She told the police Baker had discussed suicide at length with her in the days prior to his death. She went on to report her husband even had checked out which life insurance companies paid in case of suicide.

A second possibility, said Mrs. Baker, was a hit man. She told investigators that Ed owed the mob half a million dollars, and that these creditors wanted their money, or Ed's life. Investigators were unable to substantiate either the amount of this alleged debt, or the identities of the alleged gangsters to whom Mrs. Baker said it was owed.

In Mrs. Baker's version of events, her husband took the death threats against him seriously enough to advise her she'd be safer to leave Houston for a time. According to the famous Houston private investigator, Clyde Wilson, whom Mrs. Baker hired soon after Ed's death, she did leave as her husband suggested. When Wilson asked Mrs. Baker why she didn't go to the police, he says, she answered: "I didn't want to get involved."

Sandy Baker hired an attorney, Mike Hinton, at the same time she engaged investigator Clyde Wilson. At Wilson's suggestion, she submitted to an independent lie detector test, administered by polygraph operator Bob Musser in Wilson's office on November 13, five days after her husband's Jaguar, with perhaps her husband in it, was found in the rice field.

Musser asked Mrs. Baker if she knew who arranged her husband's death, and "did you ever participate in any plan to allow Edward Baker to be injured?" He made several similar inquiries, and then asked, "Are you withholding any information today concerning the death of Edward Baker?"

Sandy Baker answered no to all the questions. Musser's machine detected stress. "We felt she was trying to hide something," he told a reporter. "It looked deceptive in nature." In his full report, Musser wrote, "Her physiological responses are in such a pattern to cause the examiner to believe that she is in fact withholding information concerning the death of Ed Baker."

What examiner Musser detected possibly was affected by the widow's emotional state and by the prescription tranquilizers Mrs. Baker was taking. But when she first agreed to a second lie detector test, and then didn't show up for it, both attorney Hinton and investigator Wilson quit the case. Clyde Wilson claims that he threw Mrs. Baker out of his office.

Wilson, who thinks Ed Baker was murdered and that Sandy Baker hired the hit, recalls one odd episode from his brief involvement with the case. He says a gas station attendant called him to report that while recently servicing Mrs. Baker's automobile he saw a paper sack full of cash on the floorboard. It looked like all $100 bills, said the attendant. When Wilson put sheriff's investigators onto this witness, "he suddenly forgot what he had told me."

No arrests ever were made in the Baker case, and as time passes the prospects of finally solving the bizarre episode continue to dim. So far, three life insurers have paid on Baker's policies; his widow, who still lives in Houston, reportedly has collected $300,000 from them.

Two others balked. First Colony Life Insurance Co., which insured Baker's life for $500,000 payable to his second wife Mary, says the policyholder killed himself and therefore First Colony won't pay. Old Line Life Insurance Co. also contested a claim for $1 million. In the end, Old Line paid the money to trustees in charge of liquidating Vanguard. The insurance company said it couldn't determine who the proper beneficiary should be. Nor is Old Line any more certain of what actually befell Edward Gerald Baker than anyone else. Says Richard Colquitt, an attorney for Old Line: "All I can say is, we are not prepared to take the position that Mr. Baker is dead."

A Serpentine Saga

STEPHEN LESLIE WILSON
Olancha, California

DATE OF BIRTH: March 23, 1945
HEIGHT: Five feet, nine inches
WEIGHT: 190 pounds
HAIR: Blond or light brown
EYES: Blue
DISTINGUISHING MARKS: Scar on right shoulder from tattoo removal; appendectomy scar
ALSO KNOWN AS: Michael Eisenberg, John S. Harden, John Harding, John Hardy, David Billups, Glen Charles Moyer
CONTACT: William Barcklay
FBI
Sacramento, California
(916) 481-9110

Olancha (Pop: 100) is a high-desert farming hamlet near the sinuous, southward-flowing Los Angeles Aqueduct at the intersection of California State Routes 395 and 190. The little town is situated just below the massive eastern escarpment of the Sierra Nevadas in Inyo County, about 25 miles southeast of 14,495-ft Mt. Whitney, the tallest mountain in the 48 contiguous states.

In 1978, Stephen Leslie Wilson, 33, moved north from San Diego to Olancha, where Wil-

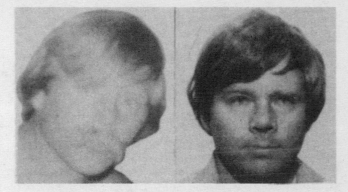

Stephen Wilson.

son, handy at any number of crafts and trades, found work in a clay mill. Divorced and an Air Force vet, he was proud of his powerful physique, but occasionally embarrassed by a surprisingly high-pitched voice Wilson cannot prevent from piping and squeaking. He was friendly and likable to folks in Olancha when it suited him, and is remembered there as a self-styled ladies' man, albeit the sort with a violent temper, known to physically abuse his female companions.

Olancha is small enough for everyone to know everyone else, as well as everyone else's business. So it was that not long after he came to town Wilson discovered, and soon began to woo, Callie Thornburgh, daughter of farmer Bill Thornburgh, one of the more respected and successful citizens of sprawling Inyo County. Bill Thornburgh didn't think much of Stephen Wilson, and the feeling was mutual. Nevertheless—and strongly against her father's wishes—Callie agreed to marry Wilson.

After a few months, he started beating her, which is when Bill Thornburgh started pleading with his daughter to come home for her own protection. After a few months more of Stephen Wilson's abuse, Callie did so. A divorce ensued. According to investigators, when the divorce was final Stephen Wilson went looking for his ex-father-in-law. He already had told several people of his intent to get even with the old man for meddling in his marriage.

Early on the morning of May 30, 1979, Thornburgh was out on his land, repairing irrigation equipment. It was the last anyone ever saw of him alive. At first all that the folks in Olancha and their local authorities knew was that both Bill Thornburgh and Stephen Wilson were missing. They *assumed* that foul play was at the bottom of the disappearances, which is why a murder warrant was sworn out against Wilson. His bail, if he was caught, was set at $50,000. About a month later, after Wilson's pickup was found abandoned in the San Diego area, bail went up to $250,000.

Still, Bill Thornburgh's exact fate wasn't known until several months later. On Christmas Eve, 1979, a 15-year-old dirt biker discovered Thornburgh's remains in a ditch near the Los Angeles Aqueduct where it crosses southward from Inyo into Kern County, some 30 miles directly south of Olancha. Thornburgh, who was in an advanced state of decomposition, was identified through dental charts and X-rays. Cause of death, said the medical examiner, was a single bullet in the back of his head.

After the forensic experts were through, Bill Thornburgh was cremated according to his wishes, and his ashes strewn over the Sierras.

An annual Inyo County snow ski tournament later was established in his honor.

Stephen Leslie Wilson, meantime, relocated to Florida, where he assumed an alias, John S. Harden, and went to work as a construction laborer in the Miami area. It took a real fluke to flush him out.

In July of 1981, an Alaska state Fish and Wildlife Protection Agency officer cited a visiting Floridian for fishing in Alaska without a proper license. The tourist, John S. Harden, produced his Florida driver's license for identification. The game warden noted Harden's appearance and that it matched the photo on the license. Then he jotted down Harden's Florida address.

Several months later, while perusing a stack of FBI "Wanted" fliers, the Alaskan official came across one with Stephen Leslie Wilson's mug shot on it. He recognized Wilson at once as John Harden. The warden then called the FBI in Anchorage and gave the Feds Harden's Florida address.

According to FBI Special Agent William Barcklay in Sacramento, when the Bureau sent an arrest team to Harden's house, the fugitive killer's female companion told them, "I just put him on a plane to visit some people in Las Vegas." The FBI was waiting for Stephen Wilson when he landed in Nevada. "He was arrested without incident," says Barcklay.

In March of 1982, 33 months after murdering Bill Thornburgh, Wilson was returned to Inyo County and placed in jail at Independence, the county seat, a few miles north of Olancha. Wilson admitted the slaying, telling interrogators how he accosted Thornburgh that morning in his fields with a .357 Magnum, then kidnapped the farmer and executed him. But Wilson also pleaded innocent to responsibility for the crime by reason of insanity.

A June trial date was set, and then postponed until autumn. Superior court judge Don Chapman rejected a change of venue motion filed by Wilson's court-appointed lawyer, Inyo County public defender Dean Stout. According to Stout, his client then developed concerns that a trial to determine his sanity (Wilson's guilt was established) might prove too heavy an emotional burden on his family, who lived in neighboring San Bernardino County. Furthermore, if a jury accepted Wilson's insanity plea, the defendant was looking at the possibility—if not the probability—of spending the rest of his life in a mental institution.

In October, just as jury selection began, Wilson entered a new plea to second-degree murder. Judge Chapman accepted it, gave Wilson 25 years to life, and sent the confessed killer south to begin his prison term at the California Institute for Men in Chino, just east of Los Angeles. In December, Wilson was relocated to Folsom Prison, northeast of Sacramento.

Stephen Leslie Wilson's serpentine saga seemed finally to have come to its end. But there were several more surprises in store.

On the morning of Thursday, August 2, 1984, Wilson was one of about 200 inmates working under the supervision of 20 guards in the prison warehouse, about a half mile inside Folsom's perimeter fences. According to Lt. Ted Zink of the prison staff, a commercial truck, sent to pick up some metal beds, arrived from outside the prison at 9:10 that morning. Just then, two inmate forklift operators in the warehouse collided their machines, affording Stephen Wilson a moment's confusion in which to dive and secrete himself inside the truck. The warehouse guards then routinely resealed the vehicle, which consequently was waved out through Folsom's gates without ado.

As reporter George Rentschler of the Inyo *Register* reconstructed the escape, inmate Wilson's disappearance wasn't noted until 10:45. Prison officials immediately telephoned the trucking company in Bright, about 25 miles away, where the truck, seal still unbroken, was parked. Wilson, however, wasn't still inside; he'd taken with him a pair of metal cutters from the prison tool room and had cut his way to freedom through the truck's roof. Lt. Joseph Gonzalez, Folsom's Escape Detail commander, told Rentschler that Wilson, who was clad in prison-issue T-shirt and blue jeans, either jumped from the truck when the driver stopped for coffee in the town of Folsom, about 2 miles from the prison, or in Bright, just before the prison notified the company of his escape.

Either way, he was long gone; the first successful escape from Folsom in 15 years. During the following days several sightings of Wilson were reported, but despite the best efforts of thirty searchers using dogs and helicopters to comb the northern California countryside, Wilson could not be found. "It was obviously something he had planned for a while," said Lt. Zink.

This time, Wilson stayed gone, too. Four months after his escape, on December 17, 1984, he telephoned one of Folsom's guards at home to wish the man a happy holiday; he also asked to be remembered to others on the prison staff

who'd treated him "kindly." According to a
story by reporter Rebecca Cheuvront, one of
George Rentschler's colleagues at the Inyo *Register*, the guard (who declined to be identified)
said he spoke with Wilson for about 25 minutes. Once he overcame his surprise, the guard
explained, he tried to elicit some clue as to
where his former prisoner had settled. But Wilson wasn't about to be snookered. All he would
say before ringing off was that he was "somewhere north of Sacramento."

"He could be anywhere," Lt. T. J. Smith of
the Folsom staff told Cheuvront. "There's not
enough information to change anything."

The mystery of Stephen Wilson's whereabouts persisted for more than five years. During that time, according to FBI agent Barcklay
in Sacramento, the fugitive acquired a new
name, Glenn Charles Moyer, and gradually migrated southeast once more to Florida. Wilson-
Moyer stopped for a while in Oklahoma, and
then in Texas, where he met a new companion,
a young woman who recently had been severely injured in an auto accident that killed
her husband. In time, she moved on with the
man she knew as Glenn Moyer, settling at last
in St. Cloud, Florida, not far from Orlando.

"He was self-employed as a home construction
worker," explains Agent Barcklay, "doing all
sorts of work. He was building houses. He could
do electrical work. He could do plumbing work.
He built the house he lived in, built it from the
ground up." Barcklay adds that while in St.
Cloud, "Wilson avoided any criminal activity." He
also installed an elaborate weight-training room
in his house, bought himself a boat, and took up
scuba diving and fishing as hobbies.

Then came another unwelcome bolt out of the blue for Stephen Wilson, a threat to his freedom almost as unexpected and annoying as his identification eight years earlier by the alert game warden in Alaska. On Friday, February 16, 1990, Wilson learned that on Sunday the eighteenth, he was to be profiled on the weekly fugitive-hunting television program *America's Most Wanted.*

"Believe it or not," says Bill Barcklay in Sacramento, "someone from his family found out and told him. We're not sure on this, but after he got wind of it he told his girlfriend with whom he was living that his father was seriously ill and he would have to leave immediately."

Wilson-Moyer blew out of St. Cloud just ahead of his would-be captors. That Sunday night, the first call placed after his segment aired on *America's Most Wanted* was from a neighbor in St. Cloud who recognized Wilson's unique squeaking voice on an audiotape made while he was in Folsom.

Stephen Wilson continues to elude recapture, although he has made his presence felt. A year after fleeing from St. Cloud, he sent a videotape to the program *Inside Edition,* in which Wilson said he wanted to "air my side of the story." This side includes an unspecified "reason" for murdering his former father-in-law, and a plea that he, Wilson, wasn't such a bad sort after all. He did insist that he'd never surrender. Subsequently, Wilson has contacted another national show, *Unsolved Mysteries,* trying to advance his version of events, as well as several local television stations in the Sacramento vicinity.

Wilson hasn't forgot old acquaintances, either. As he repeatedly pleaded for understanding from the media, says Agent Barcklay, the killer also contacted and threatened both his ex-wives, and has warned people in the Olancha area that they are on his "hit list."

The FBI has learned that Wilson's habit is to repeatedly grow and remove facial hair while on the run, and he sometimes darkens his hair with dye. He is sufficiently dedicated to maintaining his muscles that he is likely to live near, and frequently use, gym facilities. He also seems to have acquired a passport. With it, the Bureau believes, Wilson has traveled to Mexico and possibly other countries. One source in St. Cloud reported the fugitive had visited Australia as Glenn Charles Moyer, but this has not been established for a certainty.

SECTION TWO

CENTRAL

"A Special Case"

DENNIS MELVYN HOWE
Toronto

DATE OF BIRTH: September 26, 1940
HEIGHT: Five feet nine inches
WEIGHT: 165 pounds
HAIR: Dark brown to gray
EYES: Brown
DISTINGUISHING MARKS: Severely diseased teeth; scar under chin; little fingers are crooked
ALSO KNOWN AS: Michael Burns, Wayne King, Ralph Ferguson, Jim Myers
OTHER: Wears mustache and smokes unfiltered Players cigarettes
REWARD: $100,000 (Canadian)
CONTACT: Inspector Wayne Oldham
Metropolitan Toronto Police
(416) 324-3312
Fax: 324-3302

Police detectives, as a rule, are wary of the press. "A lot of the young detectives are down on the media," says Inspector Wayne Oldham, 45, of the Metropolitan Toronto Police. "You know, 'Nosy bastards. They get in your way. They won't help ya.' I say to them, 'You just listen to me for a minute.' And I give ten illustrations of how the media have helped solve crimes." One of Oldham's favorite examples is the 1983 murder of 9-year-old Sharin Morningstar Keenan, as traumatic and frustrating a case as the veteran Canadian detective ever has handled.

Sharin, about four feet nine inches tall and approximately 80 pounds, was the eldest of three children in the family of Brendan Caron, 35, and Lynda Keenan, also 35, a common-law couple whose principal source of income in early 1983 seems to have been the occasional sale of food-dehydrating devices that Caron, an unemployed printer, vended from the family's rented house at 493 Dupont St. in the northside, blue-collar Toronto neighborhood of Casa Loma. According to Wayne Oldham, Caron and Keenan were "sort of hippie residue from the sixties." Besides Sharin Morningstar—so named, her father would explain to newspeople, because to him and Lynda Keenan a morning star symbolized love—the couple had a second daughter, 6-year-old Celeste, and a son, then 4, named Summer Sky.

Their oldest child was a free spirit, with long dark hair and brown eyes. When Sharin smiled, which was often, a dimple formed on her right cheek. Just a fourth-grader at Jesse Ketchum Public School, she'd already written plays and had produced neighborhood puppet shows with her friends. "I love everything," Sharin wrote on a poster she made at school. She also feared nothing, because Sharin had never been exposed to, or frightened by, any evil in the world. "She didn't know about irregular behavior," explains Inspector Oldham. "Sharin was very trusting."

On Sunday afternoon, January 23, 1983, at about three o'clock, Lynda Keenan and her

Sharin Morningstar Keenan.

daughter were out walking together when they happened to pass Jean Sibelius Park, a small playground about a quarter mile from their Dupont St. house. Sharin, who was dressed in a white blouse and blue-green kilt under her knee-length, brown, quilted coat, asked if she could stay and play awhile. Her mother said yes, but told her to be home within an hour.

Around 4:15, Brendan Caron walked the few blocks from 493 Dupont to Sibelius Park, expecting to find his daughter on the slide, or swingset. He meant to accompany her home. Instead, Caron discovered the playground deserted; there was no sign of Sharin anywhere. Since Sharin Morningstar Keenan *never* went anywhere without first informing her parents,

Brendan Caron and Lynda Keenan instantly
were fearful. At 6:15 that evening, the Toronto
Metropolitan Police were notified that Sharin
Keenan was missing.

In many U.S. police jurisdictions, the cops often wait a day or more before acting on the report of a missing person, even when the lost
individual is a child. Not so in Toronto. That
night, according to *The Toronto Star*, fully 50
Metro cops canvassed the neighborhood looking for Sharin. They found nothing, no evidence
and no witnesses.

The next day, Monday, 100 uniformed officers from five precincts undertook a house-to-
house search of the Casa Loma area, and
beyond. On succeeding days, bloodhounds were
brought in. A rooftop reconnaissance by heli-
copter was conducted. Photos of Sharin were
released to the Toronto press and thousands
of fliers bearing her likeness were distributed
throughout the city.

The hunt for Sharin Keenan was intense, but
as early as midday Monday the police began
losing reasonable hope they'd find her alive.
Monday noon, a pair of homicide detectives,
David Boothby and Wayne Oldham, were assigned to the case.

Their logical first suspect was Sharin's father.
Early on the Sunday of her disappearance, she
had quarreled with her siblings, Celeste and
Summer Sky, and been punished for her behavior by Brendan Caron. "We had to look
closely at that," says Oldham.

It didn't take the homicide investigators
long, however, to satisfy themselves of Caron's
innocence. That left them with two distinct
possibilities to explore. One was that a pedo-

phile had struck, and two was that Sharin, alive or dead, was not far from where she'd last been seen. "History is a great teacher," Oldham explains. "Statistically, you don't look beyond your nose until you make sure that you have to. Also, there's a certain type of character that commits an offense like this. They're a very rare breed, thank goodness."

While a list was compiled of the nine or ten pedophiles (as these offenders were then known) in the Toronto area, a Casa Loma resident came forward with a report that about 4:00 on Sunday afternoon he'd seen a girl answering Sharin Keenan's description at Jean Sibelius Park. She was talking to an adult male, according to the witness, and this man seemed to be coaxing the little girl to accompany him somewhere.

The information reinforced the detectives' suspicions, yet they still had little to go on. In the seven days following her disappearance, the police had launched several exhaustive searches of Sharin's neighborhood and had turned up nothing of value. In the midst of this impasse, according to what David Boothby later told Larry Collins, a *Reader's Digest* writer, he and Wayne Oldham were sitting together in their car, parked alongside Sibelius Park. Boothby sensed strongly that Sharin was not far away. "We've got to go back," he remembered saying to his junior partner. "We've got to get into every house in this neighborhood."

Two days later, on Tuesday evening, February 1, the police search team of Sgt. Michael Pedley and Constable Brian Lawrie came to the door of 482 Brunswick St., a seedy, three-story

Inspector Wayne Oldham.

rooming house about a hundred yards from Sibelius Park. Although the address had been
checked before, it and all the other residential
structures in the area were being reinvestigated. This time, those within were politely
pressed to permit basement and attic searches,
as well as a quick glance into every spare or
little-used room.

At 482 Brunswick, the tenants reported to
Pedley and Lawrie that one of their number, a
man calling himself Michael Burns who lived

on the second floor, hadn't been seen since Monday, the twenty-fourth. Pedley and Lawrie went upstairs and opened Burns's door. They discovered a dingy, 9-by-12 room that opened on to a balcony, which wrapped around the front of the house. According to Burns's neighbors, in the few weeks he'd lived at the rooming house, Burns spent considerable time standing on the balcony, gazing to his right and across Brunswick St. toward the children playing in Jean Sibelius Park.

His vacated room was mostly bare. Pedley and Lawrie moved around in it, noting a bed, a table, a closet, a couple chairs and an ordinary-looking refrigerator. They also discovered articles of clothing Burns had left behind, together with an audio cassette player and some scraps of paper bearing his handwriting. Apparently, their suspect had left in a hurry that Monday. But if he was their man, what had Mike Burns done with Sharin?

The grisly answer was in his refrigerator. When the officers opened it that evening, they discovered Sharin Morningstar Keenan stuffed inside the appliance. She was partially clad. Later investigation would show Burns probably brought Sharin to his room alive, and then raped and manually strangled her to death shortly thereafter. Then he stuffed her into the refrigerator and was gone by early the next morning.

It had been Brendan Caron's ghastly premonition that his daughter would be found dead in a refrigerator; he shared this dread with Patricia Orwen of *The Toronto Star* just hours before Sharin's body was discovered on Tuesday. Later that evening, he identified Sharin at the city morgue. "There was no use kidding myself," he told reporter Orwen. "When I saw her lying there on her side with her hair flowing down her back, I knew it was her. I know my daughter."

Caron offered a poignant account of how he and Lynda Keenan broke their heart-wrenching news to Sharin's little brother and sister. "We told the children that they would see Sharin only once or twice again," he recounted. "We said she'd be lying down and that she wouldn't be able to speak. We said she was going away. I think they knew what happened."

Toronto, a clean, peaceful city where violent and aberrant crime is significantly rarer than in U.S. urban centers, reacted with shuddering revulsion at the Caron-Keenan family tragedy. "This was a special case," remembers Wayne Oldham, "because of the impact on the community, and the indelible impression that's left on so many people's minds.

"Not that all life isn't precious. It is. And all murder is tragic. But the rape and murder of a 9-year-old is particularly troubling. And you get caught up in this. You have to."

Interviews with the tenants at 482 Brunswick yielded a surprisingly comprehensive portrait of the suspect. The roomers gave detectives Boothby and Oldham a full physical description of the man they knew as Mike Burns, down to important details such as his painful dentition. They remembered that Burns was continually applying a topical analgesic in order to deaden his mouth pain.

He was friendly, they said, and of average size; about five feet eight inches tall, 160 pounds, and somewhere in his late thirties.

Burns talked of being from western Canada, Saskatchewan, and mentioned that he was working for an unnamed hosiery manufacturer located on Spadina Rd. in Toronto's garment district.

That information alone was enough to narrow the search to a particular hosiery house whose owner immediately recognized Mike Burns, a stock clerk, from his neighbors' description. The employer confirmed much of what the roomers said, and was able to add a birthdate, September 26, 1940, from Burns's job application.

According to this man, Burns had come to work early on Monday, January 24—the morning after Sharin's disappearance—and asked to borrow $200 to pay for emergency dental work. "His employer believed this story," says Wayne Oldham. "He gave him the money and bingo, he's gone. That was the last time the suspect was seen by someone who knew him."

Working from the recollections of the rooming house tenants and the hosiery maker, police artist James Majury drew a composite sketch of Burns. The drawing, together with a written profile of the suspect (including particulars such as his habit of calling people turkeys and his quick, militarylike stride) was released to the Toronto media two weeks after Sharin Keenan's body was found.

What ensued, Wayne Oldham explains, was a major stroke of serendipity, luck entirely attributable to the positive power of the press. Bob McCafferty, 33, a transient then living at the Single Men's Hostel in downtown Toronto, saw the Burns sketch at a newsstand, or kiosk, and felt he recognized the figure. When Mc-

Cafferty read the written description, he was even more certain. The only problem was, the man called Mike Burns in the papers was actually named Wayne King, as far as Bob McCafferty knew. Curious, and apparently willing to be of help to the investigation, McCafferty called the cops.

"The media help you recruit the community, deputize them," says Wayne Oldham. "McCafferty put this together for us. If we hadn't associated Wayne King with Michael Burns, how would we ever have gotten that?"

Indeed, but there remained much dogged sleuthing to be done.

Bob McCafferty told Oldham and Boothby of meeting Wayne King in a Toronto men's hostel, and of traveling with King west by bus in search of work in Regina, the provincial capital of Saskatchewan. Officials at the hostel in Toronto confirmed that a Wayne Edward King had stayed there. They had a bit more information, too. According to the rules of the place, all residents had to produce valid Canadian birth certificates. King, who didn't have one, filled out a birth certificate application in the spring of 1982. A copy of the application remained on the hostel's records. Among the many interesting items on the application was King's date of birth, September 26, 1940, precisely the same date of birth Michael Burns listed on his employment application at the Spadina Rd. hosiery company. King listed his place of birth as Regina.

The Toronto detectives sent the birth certificate application to Regina, where it was checked against Saskatchewan's complete register of vital statistics. The information didn't match that of any known person, Wayne Edward King or otherwise.

It looked like a dead end until Boothby and Oldham sat and pondered a bit longer over the compelling coincidences of birthdates for King and Burns. What if, they surmised, this unknown suspect—Mr. X—lied *some* of the time, but not always. Why not ask the Regina police to go back to the records, cross-checking all males born on September 26, 1940, for additional coincidences with the Wayne Edward King application information?

The Saskatchewan provincial vital statistics were not computerized; the records search and cross-referencing all had to be done by hand. In the end, however, the hundreds of hours of arduous research paid off. On his Wayne King application, Mr. X had listed his parents as Clifford King and the former Helen Leskiew. In Regina, a sharp-eyed cop pulled out the birth certificate for a Dennis Melvyn Howe, born September 26, 1940, and remarked that Mr. Howe's parents were Wilfrid Clifford Howe and Helen Vivian Leskiew.

Inspector Oldham in Toronto quickly pouched a set of Michael Burns's fingerprints to Regina. On the afternoon of March 4, 1983, 40 days after Sharin Keenan's murder, Oldham took a call from Detective Sgt. Norm Marchinko of the Regina police. "Confirmed," Marchinko told Oldham. "That's your guy."

So Mr. X, the unknown suspect, was neither Mike Burns nor Wayne King but, in fact, Dennis Melvyn Howe.

"Who is this Dennis Howe?" Oldham asked.

"He's one bad sonofabitch, I'll tell ya," was

Dennis Howe in a photo from the 1970s.

An artist's interpretation of how he might appear today.

Marchinko's reply. "He's got a horrific record."

Michael Burns turned out to be a Regina resident whose identification had ben lost or stolen in 1982. Further investigation revealed that Wayne Edward King was a real person, too. He was a convicted robber who had done time with Dennis Howe in a Saskatchewan prison. And Dennis Howe was every bit the horrific outlaw that Marchinko described.

According to *The Toronto Sun*, Howe's father was a sex offender himself; Wilfrid Clifford Howe had done hard time for having intercourse with Dennis's half-sister. As a youth, the newspaper reported, Dennis was an antisocial loner who'd amassed 15 criminal convictions by his twenty-second birthday. One was for stealing his mother's paychecks. Others were for breaking into neighbors' houses. Still others were for robbery. In 1965 he was convicted of raping a 13-year-old girl. In 1977, after breaking parole, he attempted to abduct a 29-year old Regina woman.

In all, Dennis Howe had spent more than half his adult life behind bars when he was released again in Saskatchewan, on February 19, 1982, under so-called mandatory supervision parole. Howe disappeared almost immediately, and his whereabouts were totally unknown to the authorities until they identified him, just over 12 months later, as Sharin Keenan's killer.

Unfortunately, he has been at large ever since.

"We've had literally hundreds and hundreds and hundreds of sightings," says Inspector Oldham, who today remains in charge of the case even though he has left the homicide squad and now is in charge of a police station in north-central Toronto. "But I haven't been able to confirm one of them. Not one *single* sighting. Not a single person has been able to say to me, 'I know Dennis Howe, and I've seen him.' "

The inability to bring the killer to justice has not been for want of effort. The case received saturation coverage in the Canadian press. All appropriate American as well as Canadian police authorities were alerted, Oldham and Boothby even went so far as to publish Howe's likeness and dental records in the official Canadian Dental Association magazine.

Wayne King has speculated that his old prison buddy is in Texas; Howe allegedly discussed moving to Texas while still in prison. Wayne Oldham thinks not. "Why Texas and why not Alaska?" he asks.

Another possibility is that Howe is dead. "Of course," says Oldham, "that would explain everything. I don't think he's the type of guy who would take a chance on a border crossing. He could not go to a hospital or a dental clinic. He'd be fried like an egg. But he had abscessed teeth. So maybe he died shortly after the offense. He's the type of guy that's more likely to hide in the bush than in the city. Possibly he's perished somewhere."

To date, no one knows for sure.

Setup

Cook County, Illinois

Murdered sheriff's officer Ralph Probst, 30, was the stiff-necked, by-the-book kind of cop who made enemies as a matter of principle. For example, in his three-plus years with the Cook County, Illinois, sheriff's department, Probst deliberately provoked the enmity of a reputed local mob *capo*, Sam Di Stefano. He also may have imperiled his physical safety among rogue elements inside his own department.

Whoever is responsible for the deputy's death—mobsters, fellow officers, or possibly a coalition of the two—the killing almost certainly was a setup requiring the victim's unwitting cooperation. Probst had to be in the right place—the kitchen of his ranch-style duplex at 8802 Corcoran Rd. in Suburban Hometown, Illinois—at the right time—10:00 P.M. on Monday, April 10, 1967—for a lone shooter to direct a single .41 Magnum round into Ralph's skull.

A onetime chemical engineer and father of

Ralph Probst.

Robert Borowski.

three, Probst had in his brief career as a cop handled the usual assortment of law enforcement duties from writing traffic tickets to working undercover as part of an anti-gambling task force in Cook County's notorious Cicero district. At the time of his murder, he was taking canine patrol classes at a special Chicago Police Department training school.

According to his fellow deputy and patrol partner, Robert Borowski, however, Probst had confided that he was pursuing some sort of independent, top-secret investigation on the side. "I'm working on something," Borowski remembers his pal Ralph telling him. "When I solve it they're gonna make me sergeant." Borowski thought his friend was joking, but so certain was Probst of his coming promotion and raise, reports another acquaintance, that he ordered a new car in anticipation of it.

The night of his murder was intended to be a quiet evening at home in front of the television for Ralph and his wife, Marlene, a dispatcher with the Hometown police department. Their children, Ronald, 11, Maureen, 7, and Sherry, a 2-year-old infant, were put to bed early. After the news, Ralph and Marlene watched a popular 1960s TV series, *Felony Squad*. Then the Probsts, with their German shepherd Paddy snoozing contentedly nearby, tuned in the annual Academy Awards show from Hollywood.

Together, they watched Estelle Parsons accept the best supporting actress Oscar for her role as Warren Beatty's sister-in-law in *Bonnie and Clyde*. Rod Steiger won the Oscar for best actor for *In the Heat of the Night*. Time passed. The typically tedious telecast dragged on. Well before Mike Nichols took the best director Oscar for *The Graduate*, Marlene Probst had dozed off on the couch.

"The next thing I heard was a loud explosion," she recollected years later to newspaper columnist Phil Kadner. "As I got up I saw smoke coming from behind the TV set, which was just off the kitchen. When I went into the kitchen I found Ralph lying on the floor in a pool of blood."

It was a little past ten o'clock.

The bullet had entered the back of Probst's head, exited his chin, then came to rest atop the kitchen stove. The mortally wounded deputy was rushed by ambulance to a nearby hospital and pronounced dead shortly thereafter.

Four days later, at Ralph Probst's funeral, Deputy Bob Borowski stood over his slain partner's casket and made a vow. "Buddy," he said, "I'm not going to give up until I catch the person who did this."

At first, there were plenty of potential suspects, including Mrs. Probst. A neat, round bullet hole was discovered in the Probsts' kitchen window, and it appeared to have been made by a bullet leaving, not entering, the kitchen. If so, more than one shot had been fired that night, and the crime had not occurred as Marlene Probst recounted it.

However, subsequent ballistic tests demonstrated conclusively that just a single bullet had been fired, and probably no more than a couple inches from *outside* the house. The .41 slug carried muzzle gases with it inside the Probsts' kitchen, which explained the puff of smoke reported by Ralph's widow. But the discharge also caused an implosion, not an explosion, at the point of impact with the window-pane, creating a crater normally diagnostic of a shot fired from within.

This evidence also raised other probabilities. Ralph Probst's murder clearly was not a random bit of violence. The killer was waiting for his or her target, and unless this person placed undue faith in luck, he or she would not have simply stood outside the kitchen window, hoping to get a clear shot. Someone lured Ralph Probst into his kitchen at just that hour.

One way to do so would have been to telephone Probst; the receiver he was likely to use was the kitchen wall unit. However, Marlene Probst believes that such a call would have awakened her. Therefore, absent other pieces of the puzzle, it seems plausible that Officer Probst arose from the couch at about ten o'clock and went into the kitchen to make a preplanned call, perhaps connected to his secret investigation. Under this theory, as he turned his back on the window and reached for the receiver, his killer gunned Probst down.

The Sam Di Stefano connection was explored. A couple months before the murder, Di Stefano was confined to the Cook County Jail Hospital. Deputy Ralph Probst, part of the hood's guard detail, one night discovered Di Stefano holding court from his bed. There were several people in the room enjoying a take-out Chinese meal. Someone had sent Di Stefano a big fruit basket. Probst, strictly hewing to the letter of the law, banished the visitors, confiscated the fruit and handcuffed the prisoner to his bed. "You'll be sorry you treated me this way," Di Stefano is reliably reported to have croaked in anger at the deputy.

During the later Probst murder investigation, Di Stefano was repeatedly questioned about the threat. The old man denied ever making it, and denied any knowledge of the killing. In April of 1973, Sam Di Stefano himself was murdered.

Another candidate for suspicion was a local thug and thief, Frank Calvese. According to Bob Borowski, Ralph Probst visited Calvese's house on several occasions directly prior to Probst's murder; since cop and criminal hardly were pals, these trips likely were made in connection with Probst's independent investigation.

Also, the Probsts' neighbor across Corcoran Rd. told investigators that a man he recognized as Frank Calvese inquired about renting his house some weeks before the shooting. As the neighbor showed him around the residence, Calvese supposedly asked if the house had the same layout as the Probst place across the street.

This witness later developed a memory lapse. "Gee, they killed Ralph," he said to Borowski. "What could they do to me?"

Frank Calvese also is since deceased.

The most troubling—and intriguing—possibility is that Ralph Probst was executed by one of his own. There is no direct evidence of this, just some inconsistencies and coincidences that have led Bob Borowski to wonder about his brother officers.

What, for instance, happened to Ralph Probst's notebook? Marlene Probst remembered that Ralph carried it with him everywhere, and Bob Borowski says that such a notebook is clearly evident in some of the crime-scene photographs. Yet it never was listed as a piece of evidence, and has never shown up. Possibly Ralph Probst's notebook contained the secret of his murder.

Then there is Ralph's old friend and police academy classmate, Lt. James Keating, the onetime head of the Cook County sheriff's intelligence unit, who is now doing time for taking bribes and for his role in a conspiracy to murder Dianne Masters, a Cook County educator. Columnist Kadner reports that Keating was the first officer to arrive at the Probst house that night, and also was among the first to appear at Dianne Masters's residence the night she was killed.

"That is strange, isn't it?" Bob Borowski asks. He hopes someday to visit James Keating in prison to discuss the Probst murder.

Before then, perhaps, the snitch that Borowski hopes is out there somewhere will come forward with some useful information. It'll be worth $2,000 if such news leads to an arrest and conviction in the Probst case.

In the meantime, Borowski does what he can to keep the case alive. Four years ago, on the twentieth anniversary of Ralph Probst's slaying, Borowski used his own money to place ads in both the *Chicago Tribune* and the *Sun-Times*. "Unsolved homicide," the ads read. "Anyone having information on the murder of Cook County Sheriff's Police Office[r] Ralph Probst please write." A post office box number was provided.

"I got several responses from the ads," says Borowski, "and spent my own time and money following them up, but nothing came out of it." Four years later, there's still nothing, yet Bob

Borowski will not forget his graveside pledge to his fallen partner. "I think about Ralph every day," he says. "And I mean every day since April 10, 1967."

The Cook County Sheriff's Police Department has assigned responsibility for the Probst investigation to Sgt. Larry Evans and Investigator Jim Bredecan. They are reachable at (708) 865-4700.

Plotkin's Demise

FRANK JOSEPH PERFETTI
Bloomfield Township, Michigan

DATE OF BIRTH: August 27, 1958
HEIGHT: Five feet eleven inches
WEIGHT: 165 pounds
HAIR: Brown
EYES: Blue
REWARD: $2,000 from the Oakland County, Michigan, Chamber of Commerce
CONTACT: Lt. Jeffrey D. Werner
Bloomfield (Mich.) Township Police
(313)644-6161

As far as his family or neighbors knew, Jack Plotkin was exactly what he seemed, a quiet, 37-year-old guitar and stereo equipment dealer who lived alone at 785 Hickory Grove Rd., a nondescript residential structure in an older neighborhood of Bloomfield Hills, Michigan, a generally affluent suburb of Detroit. There was no air of intrigue or criminality about Plotkin, no hint of violence in his manner or lifestyle. In short, there appeared to be nothing extraordinary about Jack Plotkin until his house burned down.

On the morning of January 15, 1988, a new white Yugo was seen being driven away from Plotkin's house. Shortly thereafter—at 11:42 A.M.—

the Bloomfield Township fire department received a radio call that the house at 785 Hickory Grove was ablaze. Firefighters arrived at the scene to find Plotkin's place completely engulfed in flames; there was no hope of saving the structure, or of rescuing anyone trapped inside.

Once the fire was extinguished and the gutted hulk had cooled, investigators began to sift through the ashes. They found a number of gas cans; the first of several pieces of evidence that would establish arson as the cause of the fire. They found the blackened remains of Plotkin's dog in what was once his kitchen. And they discovered 60 or 70 pounds of marijuana, some of it charred, divided into large plastic packets.

But where was Jack Plotkin himself? The only trace of him at the house was his two cars, a 1984 Chevrolet sedan and an '86 Ford Mustang, both parked in his driveway.

A check with Plotkin's relatives, who also lived in Bloomfield Hills, disclosed that Jack hadn't been seen or heard from for a few days, which was unusual. Ordinarily, the police were told, he kept in close touch with the other Plotkins, who also seemed genuinely surprised to learn of Jack's marijuana stash.

Additional inquiries revealed that the reserved Mr. Plotkin, responsible family member or no, was an active drug dealer who operated from behind a carefully maintained veneer of suburban respectability. Furthermore, says Lt. Jeffrey D. Werner, commander of the Bloomfield Township Police Investigations Division, the deeper his investigators probed Jack Plotkin's hidden life, the more frequently they turned up the name Frank Joseph

Frank Perfetti.

Pcrfctti, whom Werner today describes as "very close" to Plotkin in thc drug business.

Frank Perfetti, then 29, lived in Mt. Clemens, about 20 miles northeast of Bloomfield Hills. As was true of Jack Plotkin, he had no police record. Similarly, Perfetti was described by friends and family as quiet and a bit of a loner. He collected guns, enjoyed snow skiing, and was an avid amateur airplane pilot (a useful skill in his line of work.)

Other facts, however, interested the police more. One was that Frank sometimes drove a new white Yugo, owned by his mother, and this car precisely fit the description of the vehicle seen leaving Plotkin's house the morning of the

Jack Plotkin.

fire. Second, said Mrs. Perfetti, the Yugo was gone—and so was her son.

Perfetti and Plotkin were presumed to have left the Bloomfield area, probably in the Yugo. Missing persons reports were prepared and distributed nationally for both men. There was no response. Weeks passed. Winter turned to spring and still there was no progress in the case, and no good leads. Then came the sixth of April 1988, when Deputy Dwayne Engler of the Cowlitz County Sheriff's Office in southwestern Washington State telephoned the Bloomfield Township police with a partial answer to their riddle. Engler reported that local loggers, working in the woods about a quarter mile east of north-south Interstate 5 in Cowlitz

County, had come upon wild creatures pawing and sniffing at the bones and flesh of a human hand sticking up from a shallow grave on the forest floor.

The loggers chased off the animals and called the cops, who came out and processed the gravesite. Working from fingerprint cards provided earlier in the missing person reports, as well as descriptions of the missing men's belongings, the Cowlitz County authorities identified the remains as those of Jack Plotkin. Deputy Engler also reported that the Cowlitz County medical examiner had determined Plotkin's cause of death was multiple gunshot wounds.

Later investigation showed that Frank Perfetti, or someone closely matching his description, checked into a motel in Kelso, Washington, near where Jack Plotkin was found, after their disappearance from Michigan and prior to the discovery of the shallow grave. Altogether, there was sufficient evidence to charge Perfetti with Plotkin's murder, and with the arson at 785 Hickory Grove.

Lt. Werner explains, without elaboration, that the police now know Perfetti murdered Plotkin in his house the morning of January 15, then torched the place. Somehow, he was able to transport the dead man undetected approximately 2,000 miles—no mean feat—to the woodland site where, if Perfetti had any luck at all, Jack Plotkin's remains would never be found.

The problem for the police then became to hunt down Frank Joseph Perfetti, an obviously resourceful fugitive who would be doubly difficult to catch because he's never been fingerprinted. "He's really a tough case," acknowledges Lt. Werner.

In truth, law enforcement officers in California have had one good chance to recapture Perfetti, and they blew it. In the spring of 1988, Frank Perfetti was working in South Lake Tahoe as a night clerk at the Montgomery Inn. According to a female acquaintance there, Perfetti was living under his own name. Ever the sport, he also had recently taken up mountain-bike riding.

A couple weeks after Jack Plotkin's body was found, the police in South Lake Tahoe raided a private residence in the vicinity. The cops were in search of a number of suspected drug dealers, and had a list of those they intended to detain. In the house at the time of the raid was Perfetti. He gave officers a false name, but produced no corroborating identification. This discrepancy notwithstanding, because Perfetti was not on the police raiders' hit list, they turned him loose.

After he left the premises, his leather jacket with Perfetti's actual ID in one pocket was discovered. One suspect in the house told officers that "the guy who just left" owned the jacket.

When the police later ran a routine check on Perfetti and discovered who had slipped through their grasp, they went to his room at the Montgomery Inn where they found his belongings and some drugs. Three years later, in the spring of 1991, his mother's white Yugo showed up in Boulder, Colorado, bearing stolen Colorado plates. The Yugo's driver was questioned and released; he knew nothing about the case. Otherwise, there has been no trace of Frank Joseph Perfetti, and the authorities have no idea where he might be.

"God only knows where he is now," says FBI Special Agent Jack McDonough of the Bureau's Troy, Michigan, office. "Until he's arrested and fingerprinted, we'll be hard-pressed to find him." Perfetti's family, says Lt. Werner, reports that they have heard nothing from him and they now think that Frank is dead. Werner won't discount that possibility. "I think he's found himself a new life," explains Werner, "or he could be dead from some drug deal gone bad."

Family Man

Lincoln County, Oklahoma

The call came to the Lincoln County, Oklahoma, sheriff's office on Saturday evening, November 12, 1988. An anonymous motorist wished to report that he'd seen a motionless figure—possibly a drunk or a druggie—slumped to the ground near an outdoor pay phone at a small rest area on the westbound side of I-44, the Turner Turnpike, near Chandler, Oklahoma, about 35 miles northeast of Oklahoma City.

The Lincoln County sheriff relayed the motorist's information to the Oklahoma Highway Patrol, which dispatched Trooper Steve Newby to investigate the report. At about 8:00 that night, Newby pulled his cruiser off I-44 and into the small rest stop. The trooper noted a black Kenworth tractor hitched to a Contract Freighters, Inc. (CFI) trailer in the parking lot. The truck's running lights were on, and its engine was idling. Close by stood the open-air phone booth. The receiver was dangling on its cord from the hook and, yes, splayed out on the gravel in the dark was a very drunk- (or stoned) looking fellow—undoubtedly the Kenworth's operator.

Steve Newby looked again at the prone figure, a young male about five feet ten inches tall and weighing maybe 170 pounds, and noticed that he seemed a little *too* motionless. He wasn't breathing. Newby approached the inert body and then discovered why. There was a gaping crimson gunshot wound in the man's back.

Someone had pumped a 12-gauge round of double-aught buckshot into the trucker. It was clearly an ambush murder, and the victim probably had been slain from behind as he tried to place a call from the phone booth. Indeed, it appeared that the first warning the trucker had of his mortal peril was when his slayer squeezed off the fatal blast.

The only simple part of the ensuing homicide investigation was to establish the victim's identity. He was 27-year-old Dwayne McCorkendale of Kansas City, Kansas, a husband and father of two who'd been driving for CFI, a Missouri freight hauler, since August of the preceding year. The day of his murder, McCorkendale had been en route from Joplin, Missouri, to Oklahoma City with a load of auto parts.

Detectives soon discovered that Dwayne McCorkendale did not fit the hard-living truck driver stereotype. He was devoted to his wife (and longtime sweetheart), the former Joanie Hammer, whom McCorkendale married in her hometown of Tacoma, Washington, on Valentine's Day, 1985. He was, as well, a proud papa, always eager to show off pictures of his twin

Dwayne McCorkendale and his rig.

daughters, Brianna Melissa and Brena Holly, born on January 30, 1987.

McCorkendale neither smoked nor drank—not even coffee, according to his father, Milford McCorkendale, a Kansas City chemical worker. Nor did Dwayne take unnecessary risks in an often hazardous business. He did not, for example, pick up hitchhikers. The space next to him in his Kenworth cab was always occupied by a small refrigerator.

"You know what you find in truckers' trucks?" Milford McCorkendale asks rhetorically. "Booze. Drugs. Tobacco. Girlie magazines. And what did they find in his truck? None of that! His Bible. And in the refrigera-

McCorkendale with his twin daughters.

tor, some chocolate milk and white milk he'd bought in Champaign, Illinois."

Losing his son to a highway homicide devastated Milford McCorkendale. "Everybody's got problems," he reflects. "And everybody's going to react differently to something like this. But until you've gone through it, you don't know what it's like. He was a son that *anybody* would have been proud to have."

The McCorkendale murder profoundly affected Dwayne's employer and fellow truckers, too. Four days after the killing, CFI posted a $10,000 reward. Readers of *Truckers News*, a trade publication, set up an educational trust fund for McCorkendale's infant daughters. Altogether, these contributions exceeded $2,200. "We were really overwhelmed," Joanie McCorkendale told the paper. "The moral support and the caring has meant so much to all of us."

The murder's motive, apparently, was robbery. "You could never picture Dwayne McCorkendale being in any kind of trouble at all," says Paul Renfrow, a spokesman for the Oklahoma State Bureau of Investigation (OSBI). "And from the scene you could tell there was no confrontation. It's very apparent that he stepped up there to use the phone, and was probably counting the change in his hand when he was shot. They shot and killed him and then checked to see if he had any money on him."

McCorkendale's wallet was missing, and is presumed stolen.

"What makes this case particularly brutal," Renfrow continues, "and why we have placed so much emphasis on it, is that most robberies that end in violence begin with a confrontation and then escalate into violence. This *began* with violence. They killed him to see what kind of money he had on him. We speculate they got away with probably less than $25."

Renfrow uses "they" advisedly. Following the murder, truckers throughout Oklahoma and surrounding states reported strange incidents in which they were harassed by a group of two or three people marauding the interstate highways in a brown (or perhaps red) Ford Pinto. In some instances, truck drivers recollected the Pinto dodging in and out of traffic, swerving in front of them and taunting them on CB radio.

Other truckers reported seeing the Pinto at truck stops. "The circumstances weren't always the same," says Renfrow. "But they were similar enough to make us wonder. A brown Pinto would pull up to a truck driver. A woman would get out and approach him, needing either money or drugs. Then maybe another car would pull into the stop. The people in the Pinto [often described as two males, a white and a black] would become very nervous. All three'd jump in and speed away. It was as though they were getting ready to set somebody up and it never quite happened."

The brown Pinto was seen on I-44 at about the time of Dwayne McCorkendale's murder. It is known that Dwayne had been on his CB several times that afternoon—his handle was "Double Whammy"—telling other truckers he intended to stop where he eventually did in order to telephone ahead to Oklahoma City and back home to Joanie in Kansas City. Those in the Pinto might easily have heard these conversations and were laying in wait for McCorkendale when he stopped to make his calls.

Such informed speculation has served to shape the McCorkendale murder investigation, but there is as yet no physical or eyewitness evidence to link the brown Pinto, or its occupants, to Dwayne McCorkendale's death. To date, the OSBI has no known suspects in the case, nor has the agency released any sketches of suspects.

Late in 1990, the case was portrayed on the television program, *Unsolved Mysteries*. According to Renfrow of the OSBI, the TV reenactment of McCorkendale's killing netted 400 telephone tips. Many were from Alabama, and came in response to one trucker's on-air recollection that the woman who approached him said she needed money to get home to Alabama. Of all the calls, says Paul Renfrow, about two dozen have required careful attention.

"I have to say," he adds, "that the people in the Pinto may not have anything to do with this. They're just our strongest lead. But we definitely must locate them to either confirm or eliminate them."

Readers with relevant information about the McCorkendale case should contact the Oklahoma State Bureau of Investigation at the OSBI 24-hour dispatch center: (405) 848-6724.

Two Mistakes

ROLAND PARQUETTE
Chicago, Illinois

DATE OF BIRTH: December 25, 1948
HEIGHT: Five feet eleven inches
WEIGHT: 175 pounds
HAIR: Blond
EYES: Green
CONTACT: Chicago Police Department
Area Five Violent Crimes
(312) 744-8903 or 8364

James Ward's first error was to answer his telephone.

It was the evening of October 7, 1981, in a mostly white, working-class neighborhood of northwest Chicago. Ward and a friend, David Beach, were sitting together in the living room of his rented apartment on West George St., a residence Ward shared with his girlfriend, Debra Ohlson-Parquette, and another woman, Sharon Stanholz. Neither woman was at home.

At eight o'clock the telephone rang. The caller was Debra Ohlson-Parquette's hot-tempered husband Roland—self-employed carpenter by profession and gun enthusiast by avocation—from whom she'd been separated for about a year. Parquette, a Marine veteran, asked to speak to Debra. Ward inquired as to the caller's name. When Parquette identified himself as Debra's estranged spouse, Ward irately called him a "jack-off," and demanded that Parquette never call the apartment again. He slammed down the telephone.

Roland Parquette had never been arrested for assaultive behavior; his brief rap sheet indicates arrests for auto theft, marijuana possession, and unlawful use of a firearm. But despite the relative inconsequence of his recorded offenses, Parquette's violent nature and low tolerance for abuse apparently were well appreciated by James Ward. During the next hour, David Beach would recall, Ward sat peering out the first-floor apartment's window, searching the gloom of twilight on West George St. for signs of his rival, and nervously second-guessing himself for calling Parquette a jack-off.

It wasn't until after nine that night that James Ward finally felt the danger had passed. Reasonably certain that Parquette would leave him alone, Ward relaxed, took off his shirt, and sat down to watch television with David Beach while he waited for Debra to come home from a dental appointment.

He was about to make his second, fatal, mistake.

Instead of brushing off Ward's insult, Roland Parquette in his apartment on West Summerdale St. "decided to do something about it," as the subsequent police report states. He donned his shoulder holster and inserted a .45 automatic in it. Then Parquette took out a .22 Derringer and placed it in his pocket. Lastly, he stuffed a .44 Magnum in his belt. Then Roland Parquette headed for West George St.

Roland Parquette.

David Beach told police that the apartment doorbell rang at 9:20. He explained that Ward arose and walked to the front door to answer the bell. Beach then heard a whispered exchange in the doorway, followed by what sounded like an explosion. Beach jumped to his feet and ran toward the noise. He encountered James Ward stumbling backward into the dining room.

"Roland shot me," Ward said as he crumpled to the floor. "Help me."

James Ward died on the dining-room floor from a single .44 Magnum round through his chest. Debra Ohlson-Parquette returned home shortly thereafter. Though stunned by the murder of her boyfriend by her husband, she was able to compose herself sufficiently to tell police where Roland was living. Two hours later, Parquette was arrested at his West Summerdale residence. He offered no resistance and, after having been read his rights, promptly confessed to the murder. "He would give no reason for the shooting other than he was angry at the victim," reads the police report. The arresting officers confiscated 17 firearms at Parquette's apartment, including the .44 Magnum murder weapon.

On November 12, 1981, Roland Parquette was indicted for murder, "home invasion," and armed violence. He came to trial and was convicted about one year later. In January of 1983, Parquette was sentenced to 20 years in the Illinois State Penitentiary.

Two years after that the Illinois Appellate Court agreed with Parquette's lawyer that his client's prosecutor may have made certain improper remarks during his summation before the jury. The appeals judges ordered Parquette's case returned to the original court for further action.

In the interim, Parquette was eligible for release under an appeal bond. A judge set the amount within Parquette's budget, and the convicted killer was set free pending adjudication of the improper remark issue. That July, as the course of hearings progressed and his chances for winning a retrial seemed to disappear, Roland Parquette decided to do likewise. He has not been seen since, and Illinois authorities say they have no clue as to where the fugitive Parquette may be.

Her Pet

RICHARD GERARD BOCKLAGE
Kansas City, Missouri

DATE OF BIRTH: July 12, 1957
HEIGHT: Six feet two inches
WEIGHT: 190 pounds
HAIR: Brown
EYES: Brown
DISTINGUISHING MARKS: Long surgical scar running vertically under each armpit
ALSO KNOWN AS: Dick Bock, Robert G. Cass
OTHER: Avid and experienced outdoorsman
CONTACT: Any FBI office
         (I.O. #5078)

The year 1980 began with a bang for Richard Gerard Bocklage. True, the handsome and customarily amiable 22-year-old from St. Louis was beginning to sweat his grades at the University of Missouri School of Pharmacy in Kansas City, but that problem seemed inconsequential when compared to his blossoming romance with 35-year-old Tatiana ("Tanya") Kopric, a gynecologist at Kansas City's Truman Medical Center. The Yugoslavian Kopric met Bocklage at a party in January, and soon thereafter bedded him, aggressively. Tanya knew what she wanted, and Richard was glad that he was it.

Richard Bocklage.

At least for a while.

Dr. Kopric was nothing if not focused. According to reporter Philip L. Burgart of the *Kansas City Star*, she took her early medical education at Belgrade University in her native Yugoslavia, from which Tanya Kopric graduated in 1970. She then studied in West Germany for three or four years before accepting a 1975 internship appointment at the Montgomery, Alabama, Medical Foundation. From there, she moved to Vanderbilt University to begin her specialty, ob-gyn, which she would complete in June of 1980, after a two-year residency at Truman in Kansas City.

All the while, according to her good friend Zlata Gregoric, Tanya shared all that she could with her family. "She helped them all," Ms. Gregoric told the *Star*, "her brother, her sister, her parents. She would send them money, clothes, suitcases, radios, and other things, all the time."

When Dr. Kopric decided to help herself to

Richard Bocklage, she believed she was acquiring a gentle, playful young lover. Bocklage was not particularly intelligent or disciplined—two reasons he was washing out of pharmacy school—but he at first seemed a fine companion for the older woman. He was low-key and casual, dressing for the most part in comfortable western clothes. He didn't smoke and he didn't drink and he didn't do serious drugs, at least not routinely.

Not long after the affair got underway, however, Tanya Kopric began to see that her beau had an unsteady hold on his emotions. Sometimes, Bocklage exploded into irrational rages against Tanya. Other times, he was her obedient pet.

Speaking of pets, he had one of those, too, an adult giant python that Richard kept in the bathtub or basement of the house he sometimes shared with his cousin, a doctor. The snake unsettled Tanya. "If I marry Richard," she once asked her good friend Zlata Gregoric, "what do you think? He's going to have this ugly snake in the basement? If I have children it's going to come into my room and eat my baby!"

Tanya further confided to her friend that she had experienced some strange behavior on visits to Richard at his doctor cousin's house. Once, says Ms. Gregoric, Bocklage "was acting crazy. He wasn't drunk, but something else. He was laughing and acting very odd." On another occasion, Tanya found her boyfriend perched on the roof. Bocklage explained that he thought someone was trying to break into the residence. Says Ms. Gregoric: "This time she said she was thinking, 'Something's wrong with this man.' "

Indeed.

To be fair, however, Dr. Kopric seems to have harbored a few goblins of her own. "She was not always easy to get along with," says a former colleague. "I did caution Richard."

He recalls one time that she visited the house, expecting Richard to be at home. Informed that her lover instead was at a Kansas City Royals baseball game, Dr. Kopric broke out several windows in anger.

Zlata Gregoric demurs at this image of Tanya as overbearing and too tightly wound. "She was a nice, easygoing person, and very sharp. She was so fond of him at the start, but then everything turned into a lemon."

One problem was money: Tanya was earning a good salary and Richard wanted to help her spend it. He ran up enormous charges on her credit cards, and lobbied hard that summer for her to buy them an expensive house in an up-scale Kansas City neighborhood. According to Kansas City police detective Warren Miller, sources told him that when Dr. Kopric rejected this insistent suggestion, Bocklage "tossed a fit."

Richard Bocklage's native good humor was further strained, and then shattered, by his failure in pharmacy school. Although Bocklage had been on notice since the start of the year that his low grades jeopardized readmission in September 1980, he apparently was able to wish away this unhappy fact.

On August 13 the pharmacy school officially notified him that he had flunked out, and Bocklage's appeal of this ruling was denied on September 12. He refused to accept the news. "Becoming a pharmacist was like a pipe dream to him," says Detective Miller. "You couldn't convince him that he wasn't going to become a pharmacist. After he got kicked out he would continue to go to class, even though he wasn't a student. He'd sit in the back. He'd go to labs and work on his own. This was a kid who couldn't face reality."

Bocklage had sufficient grasp of his predicament to beg Tanya Kopric to intercede on his behalf with the dean. She declined to do so and, at the same time, finally told Richard it was over between them. "She realized that he was a loser," opines Detective Miller.

On September 18, Bocklage removed a .45 pistol from its box at his cousin's house, placed the weapon in a manila folder, and then headed for campus. Witnesses reported Richard searching for the dean who'd dismissed him. After two hours, he gave up and drove over to Tanya Kopric's apartment in the 2900 block of Baltimore Avenue.

At 7:53 P.M., Tanya Kopric pulled into the parking area of the apartment house. Some children's toys had been left in her assigned stall, so she paused for a moment with her engine idling as a neighbor removed them. Once her space was cleared, she pulled in the rest of the way, shut off her engine, and turned to gather some papers next to her on the front seat. She suspected nothing.

Just then, according to witnesses, Richard Gerard Bocklage eased out of a nearby vehicle and walked over to Kopric's car. There, he coolly pumped three shots from his .45 into her face, instantly killing the lover who'd spurned him. Then Bocklage returned to his vehicle and drove away.

Several days later, Dr. Kopric's family in the town of Rijecka on Yugoslavia's northern Adriatic coast received an unsigned letter, postmarked September 15. The writer informed the Koprics that their Tanya was a "Communist bitch" who had been assassinated because of her political views. Later analysis showed that Richard Bocklage was the author of the note, which clearly established his premeditation on the September 18 shooting. "The fact that he planned to do it allowed us to get a capital murder charge," says Detective Miller. "This could mean the death penalty."

Of course, the authorities will have to capture Richard Bocklage first. On his way out of town, he left his orphaned giant python near the Kansas City Zoo, intending for the zoo to adopt the snake. A few weeks later, his abandoned 1975 Oldsmobile was recovered in Canada, where the police believe Bocklage may still be. According to one of his uncles, says Detective Miller, Bocklage occasionally talked of trying gold or silver mining someday, dreams he held almost as closely as his desire to be a pharmacist. "We think that's why he went to Canada," says the detective.

First Date

JUAN GONZÁLEZ
Brookfield, Illinois

DATE OF BIRTH: June 24, 1956
HEIGHT: Five feet seven inches
WEIGHT: 170 pounds
HAIR: Black
EYES: Brown
CONTACT: John C. Hymel
         Chief of Police
         Brookfield, Illinois
         Tele: (708) 485-8131
         Fax: (708) 485-9508

Pretty Yolanda Martínez de la Torre awoke with a happy giggle on Saturday morning, March 15, 1986. The 17-year-old high school junior hardly could wait for the evening and her big date with Manuel Calvillo. All day would be spent in nervous preparation of her dress, makeup, hair, and nails, all to be lovely as possible for Manuel.

Yolanda lived with her mother, Maria Martínez de la Torre, and three younger siblings in Logan Square, a neighborhood of North Chicago. She was an intelligent girl with a sunny disposition, a straight-A student who worked hard in school and hoped for a scholarship so that she could study computer science in col-

Yolanda Martínez de la Torre.

lege. On that Saturday, however, Yolanda's
mind was faraway from books and study.

Her mother, a single parent since the children's father had deserted his family three
years earlier in Mexico, was a strict discipli-
narian. Although her oldest child had attracted
many would-be beaux since her early teens,
Maria Martínez de la Torre never had allowed
Yolanda to go on a date, nor anywhere but to
school on her own.

That's what made the night of March 16 so
special. After a week or more of pleading, her
mother finally had agreed that Yolanda could
attend a birthday party with the 22-year-old
Calvillo—permission contingent upon his
promise to bring her home early and his accep-
tance of Verónica Martínez de la Torre, 15, as

a chaperone, or *dueña*, for her older sister. "She had gone out with a group of kids, boys and girls, before," Yolanda's best friend, Melida Henríquez, later commented to the Chicago *Sun-Times*, "but this was the first time she'd gone out with just one guy."

Misfortune arose at once. The party that evening was a dud, about as tedious as such evenings can be. It appeared to a disappointed Yolanda Martínez de la Torre that her first date was going to compare unfavorably with a night at home in front of the television.

Then Manuel Calvillo had an idea. He remembered that one of his friends, 18-year-old Rubén Herrera, was being married that day, and that Herrera and his new bride, Della, had invited Calvillo to their wedding party in Brookfield, a blue-collar bedroom community of about 20,000, located approximately 15 miles west-southwest of downtown Chicago. There was scant debate after Calvillo described the planned celebration to Yolanda and her little sister, especially after he told them there'd be a live band on hand.

The Herreras, who expected more than 300 guests that night, had rented Brookfield's capacious Sokol Hall on the corner of Prairie Ave., a main commercial thoroughfare in the east end of town, and Southview St. When Calvillo and the two girls arrived, they parked in the cramped lot directly adjacent to the three-story brick structure, then walked to their left around the building to its front steps on Prairie. They ignored the party-goers at the bar and tables on the first floor, and instead threaded their way up past several groups of children playing on the staircase to the third-floor gymnasium where a band, as promised, was playing. Yolanda Martínez de la Torre, who loved to dance, soon lost all sense of time.

Hours later, at just before midnight, 28-year-old Martín Collazo was standing at the first-floor bar with a couple friends when Collazo was accosted by a fourth man he'd seen around town but knew only as a macho lowlife named "Juan"—Juan González, a 29-year-old janitor who had come to the party, uninvited, with his pregnant wife. Apparently, Mrs. González had noticed Collazo and remarked to her moody and jealous-natured husband that she once dated him. It is not known if González was drinking or under the influence of drugs that night.

Still according to Collazo, González swaggered up and began annoying him with gratuitous impertinences, the substance of which was that Juan didn't like Martín's face. Collazo replied in kind and then agreed to the inevitable next suggestion from González that the two step outside to more fully air their differences. Collazo, however, also was mindful of Juan González' habit of hiding weapons on his person—Gonzalez had been busted in 1981 for carrying a concealed handgun—and therefore asked along his two buddies just in case.

The four men stepped out the front door of the Sokol Hall just after midnight and walked to their right, toward the parking lot. But as they rounded the corner of the building, González spotted a pair of Brookfield police officers, Richard Sebek and Fred Marek, about 120 feet away at the rear of the jammed parking lot, assisting a couple with their automobile. According to Officer Marek, who was moon-

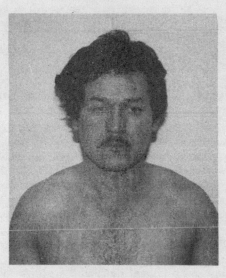

Juan González.

lighting as a security man that evening, he and Sebek were seeking, in vain, to move a heavy cement bumper guard so that the man and his wife could drive directly over the sidewalk and onto Southview St.

Juan González stopped when he spied the cops, and tried to pull Martín Collazo back the other way. Collazo responded by punching González in the eye, knocking him onto his back against the side panel of a parked van. No sooner did González hit the ground, however, than he pulled from his shirt a .45 automatic and started shooting at Collazo.

At the rear of the parking lot, Officers Sebek and Marek heard the gunshots, as well as the screams of frightened bystanders. Sebek

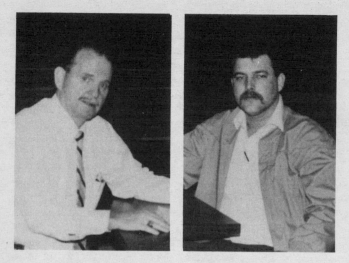

Chief John Hymel (left) and Fred Marek.

sprinted to his cruiser to call for assistance.
Marek unholstered his Smith & Wesson model
29 service revolver and ran to the front of the
hall to investigate. At the corner of the building he encountered Martín Collazo, shot in
both legs, stumbling toward him. Then Officer
Marek saw Juan González, about 10 feet away,
pulling himself up along the side of the van
while shoving a fresh clip into his .45 automatic.

"Police officer!" Marek shouted, pointing his
revolver at González. "Put the gun down!"
González ignored the command and took off
running. However, instead of circling around
the building to an alleyway on the other side—
his only logical possible escape route—González
darted for the front door, pausing briefly to

look at Marek before going inside the Sokol Hall.

Marek, shouting "Stop!" as he pursued González through the door, chased his suspect up the staircase still crowded with youngsters. The officer didn't dare shoot for fear of hitting one of the children. At the top of the stairs, González stopped once again to look back at Marek, then ducked through the doorway into the dimly-lit gym.

The situation now called for extreme caution. Marek, who did not want to provoke a shoot-out on the crowded dance floor, says he quietly followed González into the gym, hoping his suspect was headed for the bandstand on the opposite side where a second set of stairs led down to the street. Instead, to Marek's dismay, González made his way around the throng's periphery and then turned straight into their midst, mingling with those who were standing to admire the better dancers, including Martín Calvillo and Yolanda Martínez de la Torre.

By this time, Officer Sebek had entered the gym, and Officer Marek had closed to within a couple feet of González. "We're in the middle of the dance floor," says Marek, re-creating the scene, "when he turns and points his gun at my chest. I reached out with my left hand and pushed his arm down so that the gun was pointing at the floor. Then I hit him with my right hand, which was holding my service revolver. I caught him just below the collarbone, and we went down."

González, on his back, grappled with Marek for control of his handgun. Then the weapon fired, discharging a .45 round straight up into the ceiling. Yolanda Martínez de la Torre, standing near the light, flinched at the pistol's sharp report and then pivoted toward González just as he squeezed off a second wild shot. This bullet buried itself in Yolanda's skull, precisely between her expressive dark eyes. She was dead in an instant, crumpling against Manuel Calvillo who slowly lowered her lifeless form to the gymnasium floor. Then Calvillo stood and screamed for help.

Meanwhile, Marek continued wrestling and punching with González. He once again managed to push the .45's muzzle toward the floor, only to have the suspect pull his weapon free to fire another round. The slug caught the approaching officer Richard Sebek in his legs.

At last, Marek yanked the handgun free of González' grasp. It skidded away. González then scrambled to his feet and began to flee in the opposite direction, plunging through a by-now utterly terrified crowd of wedding guests. The policeman, whose first concern was to avert further bloodshed, wavered for a moment over whether he should secure González' .45 from a guest who'd picked it up, or to chase the fleeing killer himself. He chose the latter.

González made it as far as the gymnasium door before he was intercepted by burly Austin Rheiner, the Sokol Hall manager. Rheiner stunned the comparatively slight suspect with a shuddering forearm smash, then shoved González back toward Officer Marek, who quickly handcuffed him and took him down to an awaiting squad car. It was about 12:20 A.M. The night of mayhem in Brookfield, at last, was over.

The following afternoon, according to Chicago *Sun-Times* columnist Tom Fitzpatrick, Yolanda's desperate, heartsick mother visited a North Chicago funeral home. "They killed my daughter," she told the director, Eulalio de la Torre (no relation). "What can I do? I have no money."

She was assured by de la Torre that Yolanda would receive a proper funeral, whether or not her mother could afford to bury the girl. Later, a lawsuit was filed against the village of Brookfield. The case was settled out of court for an undisclosed sum, which Mrs. Martínez de la Torre used to take her surviving children back to Mexico.

Juan González was formally charged with Yolanda's murder on Monday, March 17. Also filed against him were three counts of attempted murder and three counts of aggravated battery. Assistant state attorney Colin Simpson asked that no bail be set because this was a possible death penalty case, and because González was a resident alien Mexican national and therefore was more likely to flee U.S. jurisdiction. (Mexico has no extradition treaty with the United States.) Associate Cook County Circuit Judge Rene Goie, in apparent sympathy with Simpson's reasoning, declined his motion but set bail at a prohibitively high $5 million.

"Then in June," relates a bitter Brookfield police chief, John C. Hymel, "González' attorney convinced one of our illustrious judges that this guy wasn't going to skip; that he was a good family man; that if they let him out on bail he'd be sure to show up [for his court dates]. So this judge, in his wisdom, decides he can let González out on $200,000 bond, which means $20,000 in cash in our state."

Mrs. González soon appeared in court with the necessary $20,000. The Brookfield police have no idea where a poor janitor's wife found such a sum. Over the next several months, until December of 1986, her husband did make all his court appearances. The one on December 16, however, was the last court date Juan kept. He has been missing ever since and is assumed to have fled to Mexico.

"It Has to Be Family"

St. Louis, Missouri

The old, three-story apartment house at 5635 Clemens in the Cabanne (pronounced *Cabiny*) neighborhood of St. Louis, Missouri, was at one time a proud structure and a very respectable address. By the early 1980s, however, Cabanne was in steep decline and the sturdy residence on Clemens had become an abandoned, derelict shell. The upstairs floors were forlorn and drafty. Below ground, the aged building's capacious basement storage alcoves—one for each apartment—stood silent and dank as tombs.

On February 28, 1983, a cold and clear Monday, James Brooks, a 29-year-old self-employed auto mechanic, and Gregory Edwards, 23, who was then unemployed, were out scavenging in the vicinity of the dilapidated apartment house; Brooks's car had broken down about a block away and the two men were looking for a piece of scrap metal to serve as a bar, or lever, to help fix the vehicle's drive train. When they got to the alley behind 5635 Clemens,

Brooks and Edwards saw a row of concrete steps leading to the building's basement door. They decided to follow them.

Detective Sgt. Joseph Burgoon of the St. Louis metropolitan police department describes the underground rooms the two men began to explore as pitch black and eerie. "It was like catacombs down there," says Burgoon. The only source of light was Brooks's disposable cigarette lighter, which he flicked on and off as he and Edwards gingerly felt their way through the storage rooms.

The friends inspected two alcoves and found nothing of use. Then they moved on to a third area, which turned out to be the boiler room. In the dark, James Brooks again flicked his lighter, then froze in horror. There on the floor in front of him, partially illuminated by the lighter's feeble glow, was a headless human form, clothed only in a yellow sweater.

"They came flying out of there *real* fast and called the police," reports Detective Burgoon.

Burgoon and the four other homicide detectives on his shift were notified of Brooks's discovery at 3:45 P.M. When the detectives arrived at the scene, the house already had been sealed off by uniformed officers. Fire department personnel were stringing electric lights in the basement.

In the boiler room, the detectives saw that the prone, headless victim was a black female whose hands were tied behind her with a length of red-and-white nylon rope. Jane Doe was very slender and in life stood about five feet three inches tall. "We didn't know what we had at the time," explains Detective Bur-

The abandoned house on Clemens St.

goon. "We thought she might be a prostitute or something."

Not until an autopsy was performed did the police learn that Jane Doe was no hooker but a healthy, adequately nourished, prepubescent female somewhere between the ages of 8 and 11. The medical examiner said the little girl had been raped; there was a "laceration with recent hemorrhage of right lateral wall of vagina." Cause of death was manual strangulation. By the look of her neck wound, and the striations on her exposed vertebrae, the girl's head then had been sawed off with a large blade, perhaps a butcher knife. The medical examiner reported no other signs of injury or physical abuse.

There was almost no blood in her body. It was impossible to tell if she had been bled ritualistically, but the finding did suggest that the victim had been killed elsewhere and then brought to the basement. Consistent with this conclusion was the discovery of blood traces on the basement walls. Apparently, the girl's bloody neck had brushed the walls as her killer carried her down into the boiler room.

A fungus growth discovered on her neck wound provided a means for determining how long she'd been in the boiler room. A specimen of the fungus was taken to the Missouri Botanical Gardens in St. Louis and then was cultivated under the same temperature, humidity, and light conditions as that of the boiler room. It required four to five days for the fungus to grow, indicating that was how long Jane Doe had lain undiscovered.

"It was just a freak thing that Brooks and Edwards stumbled in there and found her,"

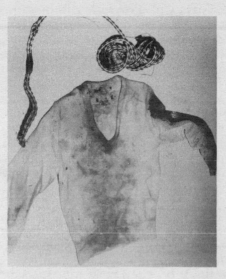

Jane Doe's yellow Orlon sweater
and the nylon ligature.

observes Detective Burgoon. "Otherwise, she
probably would have been in there a long time
and all that would be found was her skeleton."

There wasn't much to be learned from the
girl's yellow sweater. The Orlon garment was
fairly new, well made, and it fit her. The label
had been cut out, pointing to the possibility
that the sweater had been purchased at the
type of discount store where the names of well-
known manufacturers or designers are removed from sale items. No leads ever evolved
from this supposition.

The police at first thought it would be a relatively simple matter to identify the victim.
"We assumed she was from somewhere

nearby," says Col. Leroy J. Adkins, chief of detectives for the St. Louis police, who was a captain in command of the homicide squad in 1983. "We also assumed she had relatives, neighbors, friends, or schoolmates who would report her missing." Instead, as Col. Adkins puts it, "This has been one of the most perplexing cases I have ever seen."

It seemed evident that the killer was a local man, or at least he was familiar with the neighborhood; no stranger would have known about the abandoned basement, much less would he have taken the dead girl back three rooms to dispose of her. Similarly, he must have brought Jane Doe to the house on Clemens St. at night. No one careful enough to hide her as he did would risk being seen and perhaps recognized in the daytime.

Unfortunately, such reasonable assumptions brought detectives no closer to apprehending Jane Doe's killer, nor did they help to establish her identity. So, absent any witnesses to the crime, or any report of a missing child who fit Jane Doe's description, the police began their investigation at local schools.

"We figured this child had to be in school somewhere," says Detective Burgoon. "Right away we checked the schools in the neighborhood there real close, thinking she might have been from the neighborhood or a housing project two blocks north of the house. Nothing. No one fitting her description."

Next, the police went to the St. Louis Board of Education where they secured a complete record of transfers and withdrawals among St. Louis city schoolchildren. Unfortunately, recent school budget cuts had eliminated follow-up record

Detective Joe Burgoon.

keeping. Once a student was withdrawn or transferred, no one double-checked to see that the pupil actually reenrolled somewhere else. Within the previous 12 months, more than 600 young black schoolgirls in St. Louis had been withdrawn from their schools, or were listed as transfers. Detective Burgoon and Detective Wayne Bender personally tracked down each and every one of them.

Still no leads.

The search then was expanded into surrounding St. Louis County. Approximately 150 names emerged and, once again, Detectives Burgoon and Bender tracked down all of them. "That was a lot of tedious work," says Bur-

Col. Leroy J. Adkins.

goon. Some of the girls, from military families, had moved as far away as Europe. When the list was pared down to a handful for whom there was no trace whatsoever, the police arranged for their names and descriptions to be aired on local television. Viewers then accounted for every one of them.

By contrast, the detectives' search for missing black girls in East St. Louis, Illinois, just across the Mississippi River from St. Louis, Missouri, went nowhere. East St. Louis is an urban ruin, "a charred skeleton of a town," as *New York Times* reporter Isabel Wilkerson recently described it, "with its acre upon acre of burned out hulks that were once houses, its sad tales of backed-up sewers and of police cars that run out of gas, of garbage piled so deep that entire streets are rendered impassable and of books so poorly kept that no one can calculate its debt. . . ."

"Some East St. Louis schools sent us their records," says Burgoon. "Others didn't. We talked to social workers and explained to them what our problem was. They said it was just too monumental for them. Parents come in and apply for aid, but they never see these kids, unfortunately."

Nationally, the case was sent by Teletype to police agencies in all 50 states, and the information was re-sent every year on the anniversary of Jane Doe's discovery. Her story was distributed, as well, to every appropriate missing-child registry. In the spring of 1991, Burgoon even told Jane Doe's story to a national television audience on *The Oprah Winfrey Show*.

The case has been placed in the FBI's computer data base of unsolved murders, VICAP. The Bureau would have provided a psychological profile of Jane Doe's killer, says Detective Burgoon, but too little is known about the victim and the crime for the FBI's experts to offer their behavioral insights as to the murderer's possible identity.

In yet another measure designed to make the Jane Doe murder as well known as possible, Leroy Adkins personally contacted every U.S. periodical with a significant black audience, asking each paper and magazine to publish a description of the case. "I've never seen an investigation as intense, as exhaustive, as this one," says Adkins. "We've done everything we can think of."

For a while, Joe Burgoon believed Jane Doe could be a Chicago girl who disappeared in 1980. This lead evaporated when the girl's father reported she once had broken her wrist. Jane Doe's X-rays showed no signs of broken bones.

At one time, the detectives also had a good suspect, possibly Doe's biological father. His name was provided to them by a female acquaintance who reported that she had seen the man with a little girl in a yellow sweater about a week before James Brooks and Gregory Edwards discovered Jane Doe's remains. Subsequent investigation showed that the individual once had been arrested for menacing people with a large knife in a St. Louis city park. The suspect told arresting officers that he was an undercover Secret Service agent. Unfortunately, a DNA test eliminated the man as a possible suspect in the Jane Doe murder.

Today, there is hope that a child killer currently on Death Row in Missouri, might know something about the case. This man, a onetime St. Louis street person, is known to have abused both boys and girls, and may have had both motive and opportunity to kill Jane Doe.

The strongest possibility of all, however, is that the little girl was killed by a close relative and that members of her family have guilty knowledge of the crime. Perhaps she is from an East St. Louis household. And perhaps neighbors and acquaintances were given some story to explain Jane Doe's disappearance in 1983.

"It has to be family," says Col. Leroy Adkins.

"It has to be. And I would say they live right here. When we identify her, we'll probably know who killed her."

Readers with information are encouraged to contact Detective Joseph Burgoon at (314) 444-5371.

SECTION THREE

EAST AND SOUTHEAST

Murder on Wheels

WILLIAM CLAYBOURNE TAYLOR
Marion County, Florida

DATE OF BIRTH: July 2, 1949
HEIGHT: Six feet five inches
WEIGHT: 200 pounds
HAIR: Blond, sometimes dyed red
EYES: Blue
DISTINGUISHING MARKS: Scar at base of right index finger and right middle finger; burn scar on right forearm; half-moon scar on knee
ALSO KNOWN AS: Michael Cauley, or Cawley
REWARD: Unspecified amount from FBI
CONTACT: Any local FBI office
(I.O. #4886)
or
Special Agent Don Dowd
FBI
PO Box 731
Oscala, Florida 32678
(904) 732-7563

QUESTION: *How do you tell the difference between an attorney and a snake in the road?*
ANSWER: *The snake has skid marks in front of it.*

Walter Scott, 64, of Williston in north-central Florida was a retired Immigration and Natu-

ralization Service official who enjoyed certain
genteel pleasures as befit his age and estate.
One such pastime, a weekly favorite, was a leisurely drive with Mrs. Scott and their friends
down through the scenic Florida horse farm
and citrus grove country to Ocala, where Scott
and the rest would enjoy a restaurant supper.

On Saturday night, January 8, 1977, the dinner group was comprised of eight people: Mr.
and Mrs. Scott, Eugene Bailey—the well-to-do
former mayor of Williston, who was 77—
Bailey's wife, and two other couples. They ren-
dezvoused at the Baileys' that evening, then
consolidated themselves into two cars for the
19-mile drive southeast to Ocala. The men rode
in Walter Scott's new four-door Buick. Their
wives followed in another vehicle.

It was a chilly, moonless winter night. After
dinner at the Holiday House restaurant, Walter Scott discovered that one of his tires was
flat. Seeing no purpose in standing around in
the cold, deserted parking lot watching their
men change the flat, the women drove on home.
Twenty minutes later, the tire changed, Scott
and the others climbed into his Buick and
headed home toward Williston, too. It was now
about 9:00.

Approximately midway up rural State Route
27, just south of the Marion County-Levy
County line, a second car drew alongside Scott.
Eugene Bailey, sitting in the backseat of the
Buick, would remember hearing a loud bang;
he thought they had been sideswiped, or maybe
it was another problem with the Buick's tires.
Perhaps one had blown. Then Bailey realized
that the Buick was slowing and veering off into
some scrub growth along the right shoulder of

the road. He also saw that his friend Walter Scott behind the wheel was slumped forward and covered in blood. Scott looked very dead, which he was.

As the Buick slewed erratically to a stop, Bailey and the two other men jumped out of the car, fearful and wondering what was going on. Up ahead, as he later reported, Bailey heard the second car stop. Then, in the dark, a tall, angular male, his face disguised in a ski mask, loomed in front of Eugene Bailey, waving a pistol. After shouting at the others to get out of his way, the stranger opened fire, squeezing four shots at Bailey and hitting him three times before running back to the car. Bailey, who miraculously survived the point-blank barrage, lay on the ground and listened as his attackers raced away. Eugene Bailey had no idea why the assault had taken place.

Neither did the cops. The Marion County Sheriff's Office had no workable theory as to who had set upon the carload of old men, nor could detectives divine any earthly reason why the killers wanted any of them dead. Nothing was stolen, and none of the four men in the Buick was involved in any known personal or business affairs that would help explain the ambush.

Similarly—or at least as far as the police could figure out—the available physical evidence did not point to a suspect, or to a motive. Walter Scott, his autopsy showed, died instantly from a single shotgun blast to his head. Among the usual roadside debris found at the scene of the crime, investigators recovered a discarded McDonald's plastic cup bearing fingerprints of unknown origin, and a pair of pantyhose. Neither item would figure in the ultimate solution of the case. Shell casings found near the Buick indicated the assailant used a Walther PPK. Also, a small, pasteboard address book was discovered along the roadside. None of the names or addresses inside yielded any leads, nor did detectives attach any significance to the single name written on the back of the book: Clay Taylor.

The case lay in limbo for three years, and might have remained there indefinitely had it not been for one Paul Allen and his penchant for beating up his girlfriend, Maxine Peterson. Allen, 47 at the time of the murder, was a nickel-and-dime hood, con artist, and former bingo hall operator who lived with Maxine, then 51, on the outskirts of Gainesville, about 12 miles east of Williston.

After the Scott killing, Paul and Maxine, a registered nurse, moved to Opelika, Alabama, where Allen ran his various scams and, from time to time, smacked around Maxine—a habit, together with drunkenness, that he'd recently developed. One day, according to Gerard King, the Marion County sheriff's detective who led the Scott murder investigation, Maxine Peterson tired of Paul Allen's abuse and presented herself to authorities with the news that she wanted to tell them a few things about her bruiser.

First, Ms. Peterson said, she had overheard Allen and an Ocala attorney, Raymond Ellis Taylor, Jr., plotting the 1977 ambush homicide. "If I can just get rid of that old bastard," she quoted Taylor as telling Allen, "I'll be set for life." Next, Peterson continued, Paul Allen left their Gainesville residence before 8:00 on

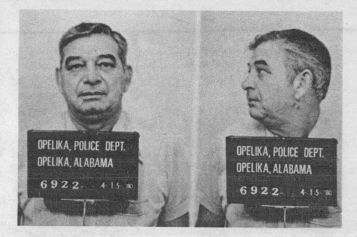

Paul Allen.

the Saturday night that Walter Scott was killed, and didn't come back until 11:00. Allen seemed nervous to Maxine that night, and he was drinking to excess.

Still according to Peterson, Ray Taylor came around two days later, and started berating Paul Allen for "getting the wrong guy." Taylor had with him four firearms: two shotguns, a Winchester 30.30 rifle, and a Walther PPK. "We've got to get rid of these guns," Peterson heard Taylor tell Allen. "Next time you go fishing, throw these in your favorite fishing spot."

Unbeknownst to Allen, Taylor, who had purchased the guns in Ocala the previous month, already had called the Levy County sheriff to report them stolen. This relationship was not founded on frankness, or mutual faith.

Allen, said Peterson, wrapped Taylor's four guns in a pink blanket and stowed them under

Maxine Peterson.

their bed for a couple days. Then Paul and Maxine drove west to the Withlacoochee River near Yankeetown on the Florida peninsula's Gulf coast, where Allen pitched the weapons into the water.

Paul Allen evidently recognized that Maxine Peterson's testimony would place his own future in substantial jeopardy. So, following his eventual arrest—and in exchange for 12 years of probation—Allen also agreed to share what he knew. It was a lot, and it was very strange.

According to Allen, Ray Taylor was referring to the wealthy Eugene Bailey when he talked about the "old bastard" he wished to get rid of. Walter Scott was not the target. Taylor, who

Ray Taylor.

practiced law in Ocala but who lived in Williston and also rented a small office there from Eugene Bailey, was acquainted with the ex-mayor's son and daughter, and reasoned that he somehow might be able to insinuate himself into their financial affairs if the old man died.

Taylor, says Gerard King, was going broke. His third wife, Jane Ann, had just left him, returning with the couple's two children to her hometown of Dayton, in mountainous southeast Tennessee, about 40 miles north of Chattanooga. King goes on to say that the attorney was tenderly consoled during this difficult period by his Williston legal secretary, Nancy Perez. But his permanent *answer* to his finan-

Eugene Bailey.

cial woes, as Taylor saw it, was to gain admin-
istrative control of Eugene Bailey's estimated
$2.5 million estate. Taylor, observes Gerard
King, "was a scumbag lawyer with a pretty
rotten reputation. He thought that getting rid
of Bailey would be the quickest way to make
money. It was just a gamble on his part that
he'd get the estate."

When, at trial, prosecutors presented evidence of this motive in the killing, Eugene
Bailey's son was incredulous. "We never would
have given the estate to Ray to handle!" he told
the police and federal agents. (His father, Eugene, was nonplussed, period. "I thought he
was my friend!" Bailey reportedly exclaimed

when told that Ray Taylor had plotted his murder.)

But the case's strangeness by no means ended with motive. Paul Allen informed the police, and later the court, that Ray Taylor, with whom he'd associated in several shady deals over the years, including an abortive casino operation, had been planning Eugene Bailey's murder for quite some time, and that there was a third member of the conspiracy, the actual triggerman, Ray's younger brother, William Claybourne Taylor, known as Clay.

Clay Taylor, at the time of the murder, was married and the father of two children who lived with their mother in Jacksonville, Florida. Tall and lank, a sometime disc jockey, bartender, musician, and dance instructor, Taylor had a strong taste for liquor and pornography and, according to his girlfriend, Patti Randall, possibly a bisexual orientation. Randall, a student at the University of Florida in Gainesville, where she first met Clay Taylor, would relate to police that Taylor once told her that if for any reason he ever had to run or hide from the cops, he might "go find a fag and live off of him." He was residing in Chattanooga in December of 1976 when big brother Ray called Clay down to Florida to help with the proposed hit on Eugene Bailey.

Clay, like Ray, was a Marine Corps veteran with a disposition toward violence. In Vietnam, Clay was cited for striking his sergeant. While stationed in California, he came under suspicion for robbery and was charged by the military police for possession of an unauthorized firearm, a .25 automatic.

As Paul Allen told the story, Ray Taylor in

Clay Taylor.

December 1976, had planned for him and
brother Clay to follow Mr. and Mrs. Bailey
home from the Williston Elks Club one night,
and to murder them somewhere on the highway. Allen and Clay Taylor went out as directed, but couldn't find the Baileys. When the
two returned to Taylor's house to report their
lack of success, "Ray was mad as hell at them,"
says Gerard King. "Then Clay got mad at him,
stormed out, and flew back to Chattanooga."
The conspirators regrouped on January 8.

Gerard King.

That afternoon, Ray Taylor gave the other two their orders, and their weapons, at his house in Williston.

Allen recalled how he and Clay, using a car borrowed from a friend of Patti Randall, staked out the Bailey house that evening; they wanted to be sure this time that they knew where the Baileys were headed. They followed the group down to the Holiday House. While the Baileys, the Scotts, and the others dined inside, Allen and Taylor let the air out of one of the Buick's tires.

Then they tailed Scott back north on State Route 27 until the preappointed stretch of road near the county line where Allen, at the wheel, pulled even with the Buick as Taylor, on the passenger side, put on his ski mask, rolled down his window, pointed the shotgun at Walter Scott, and pulled the trigger.

Watching the Buick swing rightward into the trees, Paul Allen pulled over in front of it. Clay Taylor tried to jack another shell into the shotgun. It jammed. He threw the weapon to the car floor and grabbed the Walther PPK. Once they stopped, Taylor ran to Eugene Bailey, blasted at the victim four times, and then ran back to the car, accidentally dropping Patti Randall's address book (the one with his name written on the back cover) as he did so. The address book became a valuable piece of corroborative evidence, tying Clay Taylor directly to the crime, and helping to confirm Paul Allen's testimony.

After the crime, Allen testified, they returned the guns to Ray Taylor at his Williston house, where the killers enjoyed a couple drinks before Allen drove home to the place he shared with Maxine Peterson.

The most important physical evidence was the handguns. Maxine Peterson led Detective Gerard King to the exact spot on the Withlacoochee River where, she said, Paul Allen threw the guns into the water. For two days, Marion County divers—including King himself—searched the river bottom for the weapons. No luck.

The detective then considered that maybe he needed to consult with an expert on the Withlacoochee's idiosyncrasies of flow and swirl, someone who might have a better guess where the guns had come to rest. South of Yankeetown, in Crystal City, he found Carl Adams, an officer with the Florida Marine Patrol. When the cop explained about the guns and his need for help, Adams remembered that a Seminole Indian artifact hunter named David McCramie had, in fact, found a couple guns in the Withlacoochee some time back. The exact date of discovery was just three weeks after the Scott murder.

McCramie turned the weapons—including a Walther PPK—over to the local Citrus County sheriff, who consulted the National Crime Information Center. NCIC informed him that the handguns had been reported stolen a month before by a Ray Taylor of Williston in Levy County. A few days later, however, when the Levy County sheriff tried to return the guns to Taylor, he learned that the attorney had suddenly relocated to Tennessee—Dayton, Tennessee, to be exact—where Taylor quickly put his marriage back together and found work at a fast food joint while he began studying to pass the Tennessee bar.

The sheriff kept custody of the Walther PPK which, because it had been in the water only a short time, was more than suitable for the tests Detective King of Marion County ordered to determine whether or not it had been used in the attempt on Eugene Bailey's life. According to the state crime lab in Orlando, it was. Based on this final piece of evidence, in May of 1980, King obtained murder warrants and extradition papers signed by then governor, Ruben Askew.

Paul Allen was arrested in Opelika. Ray Taylor was taken into custody in Dayton where, in the 40 months since the murder, he had passed the state bar and metamorphosed from a murderous, womanizing shyster into a popular Tennessee state prosecutor with a happy marriage (Jane Ann taught school) and a reputation for being tough on crime. Taylor's local friends and colleagues were highly surprised by the charges.

His much less circumspect younger brother Clay, by now estranged from both his wife and Patti Randall, was collared at his Chattanooga workplace, an Arthur Murray dance studio.

Of the three, so far only Ray Taylor has been tried in the case. In December of 1980, an Ocala jury found him guilty for his role in the murder and assault; the judge sentenced Ray to 25 years in prison. He soon will be eligible for parole, but may face additional, unrelated criminal proceedings. In the course of investigating Taylor's background, says Gerard King, he uncovered some very suspicious circumstances surrounding the 1967 drowning death of Taylor's second wife, Merrilee, at Parris Island, South Carolina. Originally ruled an accidental death, Merrilee's case was reopened by the Beaufort County police after consulting with Detective King. A murder warrant against Taylor was sworn out, and it remains active. A detainer also has been filed, and will be activated whenever Ray Taylor is released from prison in Florida.

Gerard King says the motive in the alleged murder might have been money—again. There was a $1,000 policy on Merrilee's life, which paid double indemnity in case of accidental death. Taylor reportedly used the insurance settlement money to get started toward his college degree.

Clay jumped his $20,000 bond in Chattanooga in May of 1980. He was reported seen with his father, Ray Taylor Ellis, Sr., in Panama City, Florida, a few days later. In October, he visited an old friend in Red Bank, Tennessee, presumably looking for some help.

Paul Allen testified against Ray at the trial, then moved to West Virginia where Allen took up a new line of work, fencing hot antiques. A year later, in 1981, he died suddenly of a heart attack. The FBI closely investigated Allen's death, making sure it was from natural causes, because triggerman Clay Taylor was on the loose and had several good reasons for wanting his erstwhile coconspirator dead.

Since then, Eugene Bailey has expired, peacefully, of natural causes. Maxine Peterson moved to New England. Patti Randall, a prosecution witness at Ray Taylor's trial, is living under a new name. Reportedly, she is also happily married with children.

FBI Special Agent Dan Dowd in Ocala has handled the Taylor case for 11 years now, ever since Clay Taylor's federal warrant for unlawful flight to avoid prosecution was sworn out in August of 1980. Dowd says that he is still following new leads in the case, many of them generated by viewers of *Unsolved Mysteries*, which twice has aired segments on the murder.

"I get calls from people who think they've spotted him," says Dowd. "I ask how tall the guy is. They say, 'Maybe six feet.' And I say, 'Forget it.' Remember, this guy is over six feet four inches tall. He can change other things; his weight up or down, or his hair. But he can't change that. He's a big lanky guy."

And obviously a dangerous one, too. Ray Taylor, according to Gerard King, who is now police chief in Wildwood, Florida, in Sumter

County south of Ocala, fears what his younger brother might be capable of, including fratricide, should he consider brother Ray a threat to his continued freedom. Readers should be wary, too. Based on what Patti Randall had to say in her pretrial depositions, Clay Taylor may be responsible for other murders, including the deaths of one or more convenience-store clerks. The FBI, which is offering its usual unspecified reward for information leading to Clay Taylor's apprehension, advises extreme caution in the event anyone encounters the fugitive.

Most Likely

MILTON C. ENGLISH
Binghamton, New York

DATE OF BIRTH: March 24, 1968
HEIGHT: Five feet seven inches
WEIGHT: 145–150 pounds
HAIR: Black
EYES: Brown
DISTINQUISHING MARK: Gold-filled upper right incisor
ALSO KNOWN AS: Melido
REWARD: $500
CONTACT: Detective Joe Cornell
         Binghamton Police Department
         (607) 772-7080

According to OSHA, the Department of Labor's Occupational Safety and Health Administration, the job most likely to get you murdered in the United States is driving a taxi. An OSHA survey shows that taxi drivers are feloniously slain at an annual rate of 3.45 per 100,000 workers. By comparison, the next most dangerous category is "Food Retail," which consists in the main of convenience-store clerks. OSHA says they are murdered at a rate of 2.22 per 100,000. The third riskiest occupation is to be a truck driver, like Dwayne McCorkendale (Section Two, Chapter 4). They sustain 1.62 homicides per 100,000 each year.

Milton English.

Detective Joe Cornell.

Detective Bill Ewing.

A major reason for the high mortality in these jobs is the availability of ready cash and an isolated victim who usually can be set up for quick, low-risk robberies. Cab drivers, like convenience-store clerks and truck drivers, often are sitting ducks.

Such factors were being weighed by three

young men—Anthony Washington, 17, Chaio McBride, 18, and 22-year-old Milton C. English—as they sat together drinking on the warm night of July 9, 1990, in Binghamton, a small town located in south-central New York, near the Pennsylvania border. Washington, McBride, and English had met in an apartment in a southside Binghamton housing project. They considered first that they might call for a pizza and rob the deliverer. Then they changed their minds and decided to stick up a taxicab.

"I don't know how much they figured they were going to get on a Sunday night from a damn cab driver up here," says Binghamton Police Department detective Joe Cornell. "But it wasn't going to be much."

The three instructed the girl in whose apartment they were meeting to call Waylon's Cab Co., and to give the dispatcher another apartment number in the project. They would then intercept the car in the parking lot down below.

It was after midnight when 30-year-old Michael Zembec pulled his cab into the project. Zembec radioed to the Waylon dispatcher that he had picked up three fares, and was proceeding with them to an address on Vestal Ave., about 1½ miles to the west. Milton English and Chaio McBride were in the back of the car. Anthony Washington sat in front with Zembec.

En route, McBride announced that he needed to relieve himself. Zembec pulled over in front of a drugstore, and then sat waiting with the other two, his window rolled down. According to Detective Cornell, when McBride returned he was carrying a length of pipe. With a sign from English, he clubbed Michael Zembec with the pipe, then pushed the cab driver aside as he climbed into the vehicle and took the wheel.

Zembec was not seriously hurt—yet. As McBride punched the gas, Zembec grabbed his radio receiver and yelled to the Waylon dispatcher, "Help me! I'm being robbed!" At that point, Washington and McBride later told the Binghamton police, Milton English leaned over the front seat with a seven-shot .32 and pulled the trigger six times. Incredibly, not one of the rounds hit a vital organ. One of the three thieves then pulled a butcher knife and stabbed Zembec, who died in the car from loss of blood.

Alerted to the trouble by the Waylon Cab Co. dispatcher, the Binghamton police sent several cruisers into the southside of town, looking for Zembec and his cab. They found him about an hour later on Evans Street, a mile or so from the housing project where he'd picked up the three. The cab, which had blown a tire, was empty except for Michael Zembec, who lay dead in the front seat, and Zembec's money, $52, safe in his money bag. The thieves had grabbed his other, empty, money bag when they fled.

A canvass begun that morning turned up witness after witness who'd heard the killers running across a schoolyard east of where the cab was found, then over a creek and up a steep hill toward the housing project. Inquiries among the 200 or so families in the project narrowed the detectives' focus to the girl who had made the call to Waylon's, and soon the names of all three suspects were known.

One of the Binghamton cops, it turned out, was personally acquainted with Anthony

Washington's family. His mother was persuaded that the best course of action was to
bring in her son, which she did three days after the murder. A stakeout on Friday the four-
teenth led to Chaio McBride's capture.

That left Milton English, who is a native of
Panama and therefore should have fingerprints on file at the U.S. Immigration and Nat-
uralization Service, but does not. English,
whose only known employment is as a dish-
washer, lived with his brother in Endicott,
New York, about 2 miles from Binghamton. He
was periodically enrolled as a criminal justice
student at a local junior college.

According to his brother, Milton came home
the Monday of the murder and announced he
was heading down to New York City to visit
their parents. A short time later, Detective
Cornell's partner, Bill Ewing, heard from a
Binghamton girl that Milton English was calling her, collect, from Atlanta, Georgia, where
she believed he was staying with a friend from
the area.

Cornell and Ewing traveled to Atlanta in
September and spent a week looking for English. They distributed fliers in the neighborhood from which the calls to Binghamton had
been made, and found two people that Cornell
is fairly certain had seen their suspect. One remembered him drinking champagne—Milton
English's trademark. The other, an off-duty
cop whom Cornell and Ewing interviewed in
the Atlanta bar where he worked as a bouncer,
described an individual—undoubtedly English—who'd been around just an hour or so
before.

The trail then went cold. Since the autumn

of 1990, the hunt for Milton English has hit several dead ends, and continues to be hampered not only by the lack of fingerprints, but also of any other reliable way to identify him, especially if he is clever enough to have the gold inlay removed from his upper incisor. Should he be taken into custody, Cornell and Ewing say they'll have to rely upon one of English's professors from the community college, a district attorney, to tell them for sure if they have the right man.

Rampage

LARRY DONALD GEORGE
Talladega, Alabama

DATE OF BIRTH: December 19, 1955
HEIGHT: Six feet two inches
WEIGHT: 170–175 pounds
EYES: Brown
HAIR: Black
DISTINGUISHING MARKS: ''Trish'' tattooed on left arm.
REWARD: $10,000
      Alabama Governor's Office
      Murder Fugitive Program
CONTACT: Any FBI office
      (I.O. #5120)

Larry George is, in a word, peculiar. A mama's boy, according to the police, he is fascinated by the occult, says his former wife, Geraldine, who reports that George frequently visits mystics and card readers. Another passion is for guns and military regalia. After he was invited to leave the U.S. Army in 1986, he continued to wear his fatigues and other GI attire, clothing that the unstable George is said to believe lends him a menacing, martial air.

He and the rest of the George children—all girls—were raised near Brewton, Alabama, a tiny burg in the southwestern part of the state,

Larry George.

not far from the Florida border. His father, Ransom George, died when Larry was young. Amanda George, his mother, soon thereafter began to go blind, possibly as a result of the

Detective Tom Bowerman.

severe beatings her husband reportedly administered to Mrs. George.

As her eyesight worsened, she packed up part of her brood, including high school-aged Larry, and moved with them northwest to Talladega, about 50 miles east of Birmingham, where Amanda George enrolled at the Alabama School for the Deaf and Blind, which offered a program designed to help people cope with adult-onset blindness. While his mother was learning to adjust to her new world of darkness, Larry was sent north to live with an older sister in Wilmington, Delaware. He completed high school there in 1974.

For the next four years, he drifted from menial job to menial job, staying for a time with one sister, then another, and often in Talladega with his mother and sisters Gwen and Amanda. In 1978, as he approached his twenty-third birthday with absolutely no prospects in the world, Larry finally joined the Army and became a supply clerk.

The same year, he met Geraldine Simmons of Talladega, and dated her from time to time when he was home on leave. In October 1981, Larry and Geraldine were married. His first post as a married man was Ft. Carson, Colorado. Then the Georges were transferred to an Army base in Germany. There, in 1986, he was discovered asleep at his post. A discharge (not dishonorable) ensued, and the George family soon found themselves back home in Talladega, where Larry's abrupt departure from the military seems to have touched off an equally rapid disintegration of his marriage.

Larry and Geraldine once had dreams; they'd started a family and bought a couple of acres outside of town where they hoped, one day, to build a house. But Larry had severe adjustment problems, principally suspicion and jealousy of his wife, which seem to have been exacerbated by his dismissal from the Army. Shortly after returning to Talladega, Geraldine separated from her husband. "She knew Larry was obsessed and overly possessive about her," says Detective Tom Bowerman of the Talladega police department. "That had always been a problem, but it sort of got out of control."

Geraldine and their children, a 5-year-old girl and her 4-year-old brother, moved into a low-income duplex at the City Court Apartments. She found work at a local Wal-Mart outlet, and entrusted the day care of the kids to her next-door neighbor at the City Court Apartments, Janice Morris, who also was a single mother of two.

Larry George, whose civilian work experience began and ended with day labor, wound up borrowing money from his mother and living in his car. He did complete a course in truck driving, and received his certification by late 1987. As far as the police can tell, however, he could not find steady employ.

Instead, the increasingly obsessed Mr. George began shadowing Geraldine. He asked a cousin, also employed at Wal-Mart, to watch his estranged wife and to report what she was doing. He wanted to know with whom she associated at work, and who her friends were. Larry also harassed Geraldine with telephone calls at work nearly every day.

During January of 1988, he pulled on his fatigues and started surveilling the City Court Apartments, taking extensive notes on the descriptions and license numbers of automobiles as they came and left the complex. The police later recovered a notebook full of these detailed observations, his "hot list" of those individuals, male and female, whom George apparently believed were visiting Geraldine. He also made use of electronic eavesdropping devices, with which he apparently tried to overhear conversations in and around his wife's apartment. Weary of this weird nonsense, Geraldine George filed harassment charges against Larry, who was arrested and questioned about his activities on January 27.

In the early evening of February 12, a Friday, Larry was lurking in his car in the parking lot when Geraldine arrived home from work. She didn't see him in the gloom. After unlocking her apartment door, Mrs. George walked directly next door to Janice Morris's apartment where she told her kids to run on home, that she'd be right along.

Geraldine, Janice, and Janice's live-in boyfriend, Ralph Swain, spoke together for a few minutes. Then Mrs. George walked the few feet back to her place, opened the door and encountered Larry, who had slipped into the apartment in the few moments Geraldine was next door.

He was agitated.

"Why," he asked accusingly, "are you letting those people take care of our kids?"

Mrs. George was having none of it. Without answering, she turned to their young daughter, calmly instructing her to, "go call your grandfather and tell him Larry's here."

As the little girl headed upstairs to make the call, her father went ballistic. He pulled out a 9.mm Luger and chased after her. Geraldine, instantly frightened for everyone's life, ran, screaming, next door. But Larry George wasn't there to harm his children. He raced past his little girl, ripped the upstairs telephone from the wall, and then headed after his wife.

Janice Morris was in her kitchen speaking on the telephone with her mother when Geraldine George ran in, yelling something about Larry. "I've got to go," Morris told her mother.

"Geraldine has just come in and needs me." As Ms. Morris replaced the wall-mounted receiver, Larry George burst through her front door, gun in his hand, and drilled Janice Morris dead with a single shot from his Luger.

Geraldine, meantime, had taken refuge behind a stuffed chair. Her crazed husband found her and fired again, hitting Geraldine in the chest, and evidently believing the shot was fatal. In fact, she would survive, although the bullet penetrated Mrs. George's spine and severed her spinal cord, leaving her paralyzed from the chest down.

The fourth adult in the room, Ralph Swain, tried to escape by bolting upstairs. According to one of the Morris children—who witnessed the bloodbath—Larry George followed Swain up the stairs, grabbed him by the hair, and then blew off the back of his head. George then fled.

For all Larry George's manifest—and manifold—mental problems, the double-murder that night at the City Court Apartments, says Detective Bowerman, were neither the work of a legally insane killer nor crimes of passion. "It was very premeditated murder," Bowerman suggests. "He may not have expected to kill Geraldine's friends, but he certainly went there with a gun."

As further proof that Larry George had thought through what he wanted to do on the night of February 12, 1988, Bowerman explains that there were six duffels of Larry George's Army gear stored with furniture and other family property at a mini-warehouse in Talladega. After hanging around the vicinity for a few days after the crimes (probably to monitor the newspapers to get some idea of what the cops knew) Larry George coolly removed his duffels from the locker and hit the road. He left his car behind, abandoned at the homesite he and Geraldine bought about 12 miles outside of town.

Since then, he's been seen on occasion near his sister Zelda's residence in Brewton, as well as in Wilmington, Delaware, where his mother relocated with her daughters after the killings. The older Mrs. George told the Talladega police she was moving out of town because she feared her boy. "That's the farthest thing from the truth," argues Detective Bowerman. Larry George likes to be near his mama. "Her fear was that with her staying here he would continue to have contact with her and she would be having constant contact with the police. She had to go someplace else, to allow her son a place to visit without being watched by us all the time."

That's why the authorities—including the FBI since 1989—think they have a good chance of catching up with Larry Donald George someday. "We're pretty darn sure he's not going to be far away from his family," says Bowerman.

The most recent news of George came in June of 1989 when a resident of Fincastle, Virginia, just outside Roanoke, told the local sheriff he'd discovered a suspicious-looking campsite near the railroad tracks. The camp was deserted when deputies arrived to investigate, but they did find two of Larry George's duffels there. Lacking much in the way of skill or the resourcefulness necessary to obtain, and maintain, another automobile, Larry George probably is traveling by rail a good deal these days.

Payback

MICHAEL DAVID MITCHELL
Bucks County, Pennsylvania

DATE OF BIRTH: August 21, 1946
HEIGHT: Five feet seven inches
WEIGHT: 170 pounds
HAIR: Brown
EYES: Brown
ALSO KNOWN AS: David Michael Mitchell, Michael J.
Mitchell, Michael Mickey Mitchell
CONTACT: Special Agent Tom Carpenter
FBI
Lansdale, Pa.
(215) 368-6550

Although he is no longer around to defend or to explain himself, it nevertheless seems fair to conclude that 35-year-old John F. Egan III, by trade a house painter and a sometime laborer in Springfield Township in rural Bucks County, Pennsylvania, was one of those feckless wannabes of the drug culture, the sort that doesn't understand until it's too late that when you swim with the bottom feeders they sooner or later will turn and devour you.

Egan's bloody fate was set in motion in November of 1982 when, in partnership with a local drug dealer named John Ward, he reportedly sold several pounds of Ward's ma-

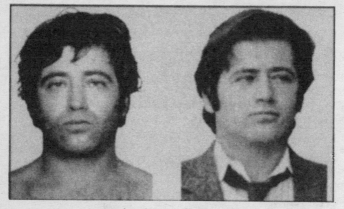

Michael David Mitchell.

rijuana and then pocketed the proceeds, which action irritated John Ward.

It was two years later, the fall of 1984, and Egan still hadn't made good on his Ward peculations when he got himself in deeper by accepting $10,000 worth of marijuana on consignment for sale from Michael David ("Mickey") Mitchell, 38, a strange, violent, and possibly delusional local construction worker who dealt drugs. Later investigation revealed that Mitchell spun grandiose personal fantasies for anyone who'd listen—which often meant no one because of the general fear and dislike in which he was held. "His former friends," says FBI Special Agent Tom Carpenter, "have characterized Mitchell as a BSer and as a wild man whom they would not put anything past."

John Egan soon found himself crosswise with the volatile Mickey Mitchell, too. After Mitchell fronted him the weed, Egan offered

some of it to John Ward as partial payment on
his debt. Ward, however, wouldn't play. He
said the dope was of inferior quality and gave
most of the stuff back. Whatever Egan did with
the rest of the marijuana, or with the profit
from its sale, he did *not* promptly pay the
$10,000 to Mickey Mitchell, who soon made it
clear around Bucks County that he'd stand for
no foot dragging on his drug associate's ar-
rears.

John Egan tried to mollify Mitchell by making periodic, partial payments. By March of
1985, he'd reduced his debt $800. But Mitchell
was not to be nickel-and-dimed. That month he
lured Egan to his house, where Mickey Mitchell stuck the muzzle of his Israeli-made, .9-mm
Uzi submachine gun into the back of Egan's
ear and demanded that Egan sign a promis-
sory note for $9,200. In a curious touch, Mitch-
ell had a notary public on hand to affix an
official seal to the document.

"It shook John up," his common-law wife,
Georgette Scotchell, later testified. Not
enough, however, for Egan to seriously consider his peril. "It bothered me more," Scotchell told the court. "I got a job and started
paying [Mitchell] every week or so."

Even that display of effort and good faith was
not sufficient for Mitchell. After Georgette
Scotchell made two $50 payments, he accosted
Egan (in front of witnesses) in a Bucks County
bar. "Get the money or someone will be getting
you," he snarled. This was not an empty threat,
nor was it the last.

Mitchell kept harassing and menacing Egan
through the spring and early summer of 1985,
until Egan began trying to avoid Mitchell al-

together. As a consequence, it had been several weeks since they'd seen one another when, in the early hours of Saturday, July 20, Egan returned home with his friend, Gregg Thompson, after a night of drinking.

Egan pulled into his driveway and there encountered Mickey Mitchell's blue BMW with Mitchell in it. For some reason—exasperation or possibly a drunk's pot valiance—Egan did not try to run this time. "He'd had enough of Mitchell's taunts," Gregg Thompson would recall under oath.

Egan approached Mitchell's car, and the two soon were shouting at one another. Then shots were heard and John Egan fell to the ground, mortally wounded in his thigh and scrotum. Gregg Thompson looked on as Mickey Mitchell then coolly started up the BMW and gunned it off into the night. "It was a premeditated, cold-blooded, planned murder," Mitchell's prosecutor, Rea B. Mahon, would later assert to his jury. "He wanted to leave a message for everyone in the drug underworld."

The shots from Mitchell's Uzi awakened the sleeping Georgette Scotchell and her friend, Linda Sauter, who was spending the night. Ms. Sauter ran outside, saw Egan sprawled on the ground, and then ran back into the house where she told Ms. Scotchell that her husband had been shot and that she better call an ambulance. Meantime, John Egan had struggled to his feet and stumbled into the house behind Linda Sauter. Teetering in the kitchen before the two terror-struck women, his waist soaked in blood, Egan mumbled, "Mickey Mitchell shot me," and then collapsed onto the floor. John F. Egan III died in the ambulance en route to the nearest hospital emergency room, in Quakertown.

Approximately 12 hours later, at 2:05 on the afternoon of July 20, Mickey Mitchell was arrested at his cabin in Schwenksville. When he exercised his right to make a phone call from the police station, Mitchell dialed home to his live-in girlfriend, Shereen Quattromani. "I've got myself in a lot of trouble here," officers overheard him saying to Quattromani.

On August 1, a Thursday, Pennsylvania District Justice Elizabeth M. Leonard of Nockamixon Township set Mitchell's bond at $1 million. Defense counsel had asked that bond be set at $200,000, and continued to do so at a subsequent hearing on August 15 in Doylestown, before Bucks County President Judge Isaac S. Garb.

At this court session, the Bucks County police testified that Mitchell had once bought an Uzi, but they could not prove he owned the one used to kill John Egan. That weapon was never found. A detective did testify to the discovery of a second weapon, a semiautomatic carbine, which was recovered from Mitchell's house.

"Is it appropriate for hunting?" prosecutor Mahon asked the policeman of the carbine.

"No, it is not," he replied.

When Mitchell's attorney, John C. Kerrigan, intrepidly sought to depict his client as a settled local man, a land-developer with economic interests in the community evidenced by a joint land-ownership venture he had begun with a Donald Simons Marshall, Jr., Rea Mahon responded with evidence that the partnership had lapsed, that the property in question long since had been sold, and that Mr. Marshall was wanted on a hot-check warrant. Mahon further elicited from Mickey Mitchell himself that he had earned no taxable income in 1984, and less than $5,000 so far in 1985.

The zaniest moment of the day came courtesy of the accused, on the stand, when he testified that he was a high-level intelligence operative and had enjoyed a top-secret security clearance in the early 1970s while working undercover in various U.S. embassies around the world. This was a shopworn assertion from Mitchell; anyone who'd sat in a bar with him for more than 10 minutes had heard it. In court, he declined to substantiate his claims, nor would he elaborate on his supposed intelligence work.

Judge Garb reduced Mitchell's bond to $400,000. The money was posted by his family. His murder trial date was set for November 13.

At trial, star witness Georgette Scotchell testified to Mitchell's continuing threats against her family in late 1984 and into 1985. "He said he was going to take my house, myself, my daughter, and my dog if we didn't pay," said Scotchell. "He said he didn't care what our problems were, he wanted his money."

A forensic specialist told the court that bloodstains found on the blue BMW's bumper matched Egan's blood. Another prosecution witness said that a clip of .9-mm ammo, suitable for use in an Uzi, was found atop Mickey Mitchell's bedroom dresser. Still a third witness, Trooper Leon Krebs of the Pennsylvania State Police crime lab in Bethlehem, testified that chemical residues detected on John Egan's jeans showed that he had been shot at close range—"probably three feet from the muzzle, or closer," said Trooper Krebs—a finding consistent with Mitchell shooting Egan from his car seat as they argued.

John Ward interrupted a 12-year prison stretch for interstate transportation of drugs to come to court and relate his business dealings with John Egan and Mickey Mitchell. Ward specifically remembered Mitchell telephoning him about Egan; "Our mutual friend," Mitchell called him. According to what Mitchell told Ward, he said, John Egan had tried to blunt Mitchell's anger by indicating to Mitchell that Ward owed *him* money, not the other way around. Ward set Mitchell straight, he testified.

Defense attorney John Kerrigan presented an alibi defense for his client, a strategy that would exploit confusion in witnesses' recall as to exactly when the shots were fired. Generally, their memories were for sometime between 1:55 A.M. on July 20, and 2:05 A.M. The call to the ambulance service was logged in at 2:06 A.M.

According to certain of Mickey Mitchell's acquaintances, however, it would have been next to impossible for him to have killed John Egan. Why? Because at 2:10 A.M. Mitchell was 16 miles away, at a bar called Apple Jack's. That's what the bartender, William Godell, testified to. Dale Stauffer, Apple Jack's owner, said he saw Mickey Mitchell dancing in his place at about 2:15 A.M.

Naturally, the apparent contradictions in testimony led to considerable discussion in court as to how quickly a person might get from the scene of the crime to the safety of

Apple Jack's bar and its alibi witnesses. One who actually tried the route was Springfield Township police chief Robert L. Bell, who said on the stand that he negotiated the distance in 16 minutes, 37 seconds. "I drove intently," said the chief, "as if I were fleeing someone."

Lawyer Kerrigan, in his closing statement, used the confusion to good effect. He also emphasized for the jurors' edification the fact that John Egan was known to have taken drugs the night he was killed, and that he was legally drunk; Egan's blood alcohol level was .13. As a result, argued Kerrigan, John Egan might have been too addled to correctly identify his assailant.

The eight men and four women chosen to decide Mickey Mitchell's guilt or innocence retired with the case at about noon on Tuesday, November 19. After 10 hours of deliberation, the jury did not find Mitchell guilty of murder in the first degree—which in Pennsylvania as elsewhere requires a specific intent to kill— and instead settled on a conviction for third-degree homicide, in which malice with intent to inflict bodily harm must be present, or willful disregard of the possibility of death. For good measure, the panel also convicted Mitchell on one count of illegal gun possession.

Mickey Mitchell, who was looking at as much as 20 years on the murder charge, plus a mandatory 5-to-10-year sentence on the weapon conviction because the gun was used in the commission of a felony, was allowed to remain free on the $400,000 bond.

This turns out to have been a mistake. On January 27, 1987, the day Mickey Mitchell was scheduled for sentencing, he disappeared. A bench warrant for his arrest immediately was issued. Thirteen days later, the FBI stepped into the case on the strength of a federal "unlawful flight to avoid prosecution" warrant.

The $400,000 bond was declared forfeit, a significant financial reversal for Mitchell's parents, David and Mary Mitchell, whom Mickey's attorney, Charles Kerrigan, later sued for $19,425, the amount Kerrigan claimed that Mitchell owed him at the time of his disappearance.

Painful Memories

KONG CHUNG BOUNNAM
Memphis, Tennessee

DATE OF BIRTH: September 3, 1968
HEIGHT: Five feet four inches
WEIGHT: 125 pounds
EYES: Dark brown
HAIR: Black
DISTINGUISHING MARKS: Tattoo of dragon on upper left arm; female on inner left forearm; cross on index finger; elephant face on left knee; flowers on lower left leg; butterfly on left calf; female on lower left shin; spider and spider web on right foot. Possible bullet scar on upper left groin.
ALSO KNOWN AS: Nam
CONTACT: Any FBI office
         (I.O. #5111)

After 20 years of serving up respectable Cantonese cookery to satisfied Tennesseans, Memphis restaurateur Sheu Chong Lee's Jade East at 3695 Austin Peay had become a local landmark, a busy dinner-only Raleigh-district eatery flanked on one side by an Assembly of God church and, on the other, by the Raleigh branch office of the U.S. Postal Service. "Those were some fine people over there," remembered Jim Nelson, a supervisor at the post office, to reporters William C. Rayne and Lloyd

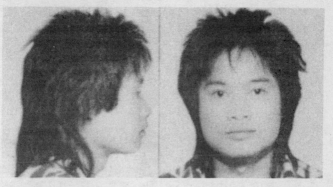

Kong Chung Bounnam.

Holbeck of the *Memphis Commercial Appeal.* "They were always coming in here, and they were so nice. When this facility opened in 1986, they came over with piles of egg rolls and other food as a welcome."

Customarily, Sheu Chong Lee himself was on hand each day to oversee preparation of that night's menu at the 208-seat, family-run restaurant with its distinctive gold-and-red interior, designed to resemble that of an ancient Chinese temple. On October 20, 1987, however, Lee left his No. 3 son, Arthur, aged 24, in charge while he took his wife to a 2:00 P.M. doctor's appointment to have a scald burn on her hand attended to. "I should have been there," Sheu Chong Lee later told the *Commercial Appeal.* "If I had been there, maybe I could have saved my son's life."

Besides operating Jade East, the Lee family's other major business was trading gold and jewelry; Sheu Chong Lee recently had begun amassing both in quantity with the aim of opening his own retail jewelry shop. This information was widely known within Memphis's various, close-knit Asian communities.

At about 1:15 P.M. on October 20, four edgy, gun-wielding Asians of various non-Chinese extractions burst into Jade East's back office, one of them shouting, "Give us the rings!" It was a holdup, and the gang was after the Lee family's gold and jewelry.

Kai Ying Chuey, 75, matriarch of the Lee clan, moved toward the gunmen in the office, as if to talk them out of their foolishness. That is when .45 and .22 caliber gunfire erupted as the panicked gang members began shooting their weapons, wildly.

It was the second such incident of violence in Kai Ying Chuey's life, both motivated by greed. A dozen years earlier her husband, L. M. Chuey, was murdered in the course of a robbery at the Chueys' small Memphis grocery market. Kai Ying had been injured in that theft, too, but recovered and later gave testimony that helped convict her husband's killer. She wouldn't be so fortunate this time.

Of the four family members in the room at the time of the robbery, three were killed; Kai Ying Chuey, her grandson, Arthur Lee, and Arthur's sister-in-law, 23-year-old Amy Lee. The fourth person, a 75-year-old woman whose name has been withheld, also was shot and left for dead. Once the gang departed with their loot—as much as $100,000 worth in all—she fled in terror next door to the post office.

"I was sitting here when this woman came in screaming and crying and pounding on the counter," Jim Nelson recalled. "She didn't speak English. I thought she was saying, 'please,' but later I figured out she was trying to say 'police.' She ran out and I followed her. I ran out of the back of the building and saw her sort of running sideways and gesturing with her hands for us to follow her."

The blood-smeared woman led Nelson to Jade East's rear entrance. "When I got to the back door," he told the *Commercial Appeal* reporters, "it was slightly ajar. I reached for the door and pulled it open slightly and immediately smelled what I thought was gun smoke."

As other workers from the post office came to the door behind him, Jim Nelson slipped inside the Jade East office to investigate further. "I checked the pulses on the first two bodies I came to," he explained, "and there was nothing there. They were both dead. The third was in such bad shape that there was no reason to check."

The third body was Mrs. Chuey.

To solve a triple murder/robbery case beginning with a frightened, non-English-speaking septuagenarian as your only witness is an unenviable investigative challenge. As Sgt. Jackie Hammers of the Memphis Police Department acknowledged at the time, the cops' single thread of hope for quickly identifying the killers seemed extremely fragile. Yet, once she regained her health and poise, the old woman proved to be an excellent witness. With her information, plus tips from several informants, the Memphis cops soon had a handle on the case.

Their first arrest, a few days after the homicides, was that of 18-year-old Duc Phuoc Doan, who initially denied any involvement in the shootings, but later pleaded guilty to second-degree murder and received a 10-year prison sentence. Doan also provided information about the others.

One who came under subsequent scrutiny was 29-year-old Hien Tien Huyn, who had been head cook at Jade East until three weeks before the murders. Huyn left the Lee family's employ, he said, to accept a better paying position. In 1989, Huyn was tried and acquitted for an alleged role in planning the robbery. He was not accused of actually taking part in it.

Another former kitchen employee who was implicated, Heck Van Tran, 21, apparently had quit, too, after Mr. Lee upbraided Tran for making too many egg rolls. Tran later was arrested in Houston, Texas. He was tried and convicted of first-degree murder in 1989, and is now on Death Row in Tennessee.

The key to Tran's successful prosecution, says authorities, was the testimony of a third member of the holdup gang, 18-year-old Hung Van Chung, a Vietnamese who was arrested in Carthage, Missouri, in 1989. Chung adamantly protested his innocence, says Tennessee assistant district attorney general J. Robert Carter, Jr., until a telephone conversation with his mother changed his mind.

In a plea-bargain deal preapproved by the Lee family, Chung pleaded guilty and received three life terms in prison, with no hope of parole for 60 years. He admitted direct, personal responsibility for slaying Amy Lee. In the restaurant office, "she kept getting louder and louder," he told police. "I told her to stay there and I wouldn't do anything to her. She didn't listen to me so I had to shoot her."

He told the Memphis police that the gang

members had been in town for about six months before the murders. Afterward, Chung said, he traveled as "Johnnie" through the populous southeast Asian colonies in Dallas and Houston, Texas, as well as to North Carolina where Chung said he got rid of his murder weapon, a .22 pistol, on an ocean beach.

Chung insisted that the gang had no luck fencing either the Lees' gold or the jewelry they stole. According to him, some anonymous other party ripped off the stolen merchandise in Houston, a story that at least one Memphis homicide detective—who requests that his own identity be withheld—disbelieves. According to this cop, the man most likely to have sold the gold and jewelry and pocketed the profits was Laotian-born Kong Chung Bounnam, the fourth member of the gang.

As his fellow thieves and killers told the story, it was 19-year-old Bounnam who shot Mr. Chuey, after taking a stray bullet himself in his left groin. A subsequent search of Memphis-area hospitals failed to turn up any record of an Asian with a gunshot groin, and the national hunt for Bounnam, assisted by the FBI, also so far has been fruitless. If he is found, say investigators, it'll probably be in some big-city Asian enclave. Bounnam, like the others, has worked as a cook, as well as a laborer in a window-blind factory. With all those tattoos, he should not be difficult to identify.

Sheu Chong Lee kept the Jade East shuttered for three weeks, then reopened for business on a rainy Monday night. Near the front entrance, he placed a small sign that read: In Memory of Kai Ying "Grandma" Chuey, Amy Lee and Arthur Lee. Approximately 70 diners showed up that night, a good crowd.

Soon, however, Sheu Chong Lee began to feel a pall had settled over the Jade East—as if the restaurant itself had died in the murders. "My father's heart wasn't in it anymore," Lee's son Jerry told *Commercial Appeal* reporter Jerry Markon in 1990. "He had too many bad memories of that day. He was afraid to hire people he didn't know well, so we wound up with a bunch of high school kids running the restaurant. Everything just went downhill; the service, the food, the professionalism. My mother cried almost every day. Customers would cry. People just couldn't eat in an atmosphere like that."

In September of 1990, Sheu Chong Lee sold the Jade East for $50,000 to another Chinese family, the Sos. The So family closed and remodeled Jade East, and reopened the restaurant a month later as Treasures of the Orient.

Fatal Encounter

DONALD MICHAEL SANTINI
Bradenton, Florida

DATE OF BIRTH: June 9, 1958
HEIGHT: Six feet one inch
WEIGHT: 160 pounds
EYES: Blue
HAIR: Blond (bleached)
ALSO KNOWN AS: Charles Michael Stevens, Donald Chapman, John Trimble
REWARD: $1,000 from Crimestoppers
CONTACT: Hillsborough County Sheriff's Dept.
(813) 247-8200

"Mrs. Wood," read the Manatee County Sheriff's Office Incident Report, "stated that on October 8, 1983, her husband got mad at her son and began beating him about the head and face. She further stated that he had the boy in a head lock and when she was going to call police he threatened to snap the boy's neck."

Cynthia Ruth Wood, 33, of Bradenton, just south of Tampa and St. Petersburg on Florida's Gulf coast, at last had had enough. For four years she reportedly had endured abuse, intimidation, even extortion, at the hands of her husband, Barry T. D. Wood. As she accused him in a later court filing: "The Husband . . . repeatedly perpetrated acts of physical abuse

261

Cynthia Ruth Wood.

upon the Wife . . . such acts as holding a pillow over the Wife's face in such manner as to cause the Wife to be unable to breathe to the point of becoming semi-conscious, and has struck the Wife on numerous occasions about the face and body with his fists and with numerous weapons, including a 2 × 4 piece of wood. The Husband has struck the minor child of the Wife . . . about the face and head on numerous occasions with his fists, a hammer and, on one occasion, a 2 × 4, for such things as not eating all the meal prepared for him and for failing

Donald Michael Santini.

to do chores about the house. The Husband has a practice of punching said child in the stomach to avoid obvious bruises and other marks. Said child's teachers are aware of the fact that he has appeared in school with bruises and abrasions due to the physical abuse by the husband."

Somehow, Cindy Wood found the courage to risk Barry's wrath by fleeing the horror she described. The day after he allegedly abused 14-year-old Tommy, threatening "to snap the boy's neck," Mrs. Wood drove Tommy and the Woods' two children, 4-year-old Barry, Jr., and Jeanette Trinity, 2, to the Tampa airport, intending to escape with the children back to her native Pennsylvania.

According to reporter Joanne Fiske, who investigated the Wood case for the Bradenton *Herald*, "less than an hour before [her] plane was to depart, an anonymous male caller phoned the airline, claiming someone was kidnapping his two children on the flight to Philadelphia. Another anonymous call, received 25 minutes later, warned of a bomb on the flight. . . . The flight was delayed while the plane was searched. No bomb was found. Meanwhile, Barry Wood arrived at the airport and was questioned as a suspect. . . . More than an hour after her scheduled departure, Mrs. Wood flew with her children to Philadelphia, where she got a job as a child-care worker and tried to start a new life. It was not to be."

In November, Barry Wood filed for divorce from Cindy, charging her with "wrongfully" leaving Florida with their kids. Then he headed north by car to Philadelphia. As his estranged wife later pleaded in her written answer to Wood's divorce petition, on December 21 Barry and his daughter by a previous marriage, Denise, accosted Cindy and their two young children on the sidewalk near a Philadelphia bus stop. Cindy, who would file a criminal complaint as a result of the incident, was pushed to the ground as little Barry and Jeanette were snatched away from her.

Barry Wood returned to Bradenton (familiar to baseball fans as spring training headquarters for the Pittsburgh Pirates) with his children. Cynthia, against her family's advice, followed him back to Florida. Twenty-four days later, she filed a custody petition in Manatee County. "The Wife," read her complaint, "fears for the safety of her children in light of the violent tendencies exhibited by the Husband in the past. The Husband has threatened to do physical harm to the children if the Wife attempts to obtain custody and the Wife fears that the Husband may abscond with the children in an effort to defeat the Wife's custody rights. The Wife requests that a Temporary Restraining Order be issued without notice. . . ."

Cindy Wood was nearly penniless, whereas Barry apparently was anything but. According to Cindy, in 1982 Barry had physically forced her to sign away her share of their real property in Bradenton. "The Wife," she alleged, "executed the Assignment of Agreement for Deed against her will and only after the Husband advised the Wife that he would beat her if she failed to execute said Assignment of Agreement for Deed. Despite the fact that the Wife has provided all payments [for the property], the Wife was paid no sums of money for the assignment and received nothing for her substantial equity in said property."

By Cindy's reckoning, sale of their land and residence in Bradenton had fetched Barry Wood $40,000 with which to finance his side of the custody fight. Mrs. Wood's sole means of income, by contrast, was the position she found in March of 1984 as manager of the Cape Vista Child Care Center in Bradenton.

"I need a lawyer who cares about children as human beings and will take the time and care to prepare my case properly, even if I'm not the richest person in the world," she wrote the following month after a series of disap-

pointments with the free legal counsel she had
been obliged to seek. "I realize that this is not
a simple case and my husband will spend any
amount to spite me. My only concern is for my
children. . . . I feel that the children's rights are
being violated."

Wood fought on. When her husband responded with denials to all her accusations,
and charged in his reply that she was halluci-
nating, Cindy found a psychiatrist who examined her and declared her mentally competent.
Meanwhile, she started to make some headway
in the custody case, beginning with visitation
rights. By early June of 1984, say her friends,
Cindy Wood's outlook had brightened considerably. Plus, her husband was about to stand
trial for his alleged physical abuse of her oldest child, Tommy. On Friday, June 1, 1984,
Cynthia told her niece, Shirley Wood, that a
custody report shortly was due from the Florida Department of Health and Rehabilitative
Services, and that she understood the report
would strongly recommend that she, not Barry,
be given custody of Barry and Jeanette.

Then came her fatal encounter with Donald
Michael Santini.

Santini, a Massachusetts native, grew up in
Texas where *Herald* reporter Joanne Fiske
found Trisha Earley, a onetime friend. Earley
told Fiske that Santini was a lifelong loser. "He
seemed to screw up a lot," said Earley. "He
couldn't keep a job. He reminded me of a little
boy, somewhat naive, lost."

He also had a violent streak. In 1978, while
a 20-year-old U.S. Army private serving in
Frankfurt, Germany, Donald Santini was convicted of rape and sentenced to two years in

the stockade. "He said he was never going to spend time in jail again," Ms. Early told reporter Fiske. "If it came down to killing himself or going back to jail, he said he'd kill himself."

On May 2, 1983, while living in Sugarland, a suburb of Houston, Santini allegedly robbed a convenience store in League City, southeast of Houston. According to Detective Sgt. Pat Bittner of the League City police department, who handled the case, Santini walked into the store in the midafternoon of the second. He grabbed a female clerk by the wrist, shoved a knife in her face, and demanded the store's cash. Santini then fled in a tan Chevy station wagon, his own. The clerk, who was not injured, was able to record his license tag number, which led to his arrest in Sugarland five hours later.

As Trisha Earley related to reporter Fiske, her erstwhile friend confessed to the robbery "after Texas police assured him everything would be all right if he told the truth. . . . He reacted with shock and a sense of betrayal when he was charged with aggravated robbery."

That October, about the time Cindy Wood was fleeing Florida for Pennsylvania with her children, Donald Santini hit the road, too. By the time a Texas judge issued a felony fugitive arrest warrant for him, Santini had made his way to Florida under a new name, Charles Michael Stevens, and had begun work as a janitor at the Gulf Tides Hotel on Longboat Key, an islet directly accessible from Bradenton via a causeway.

True to Ms. Earley's character analysis, Santini managed to lose his janitor's job in less than a month. He was fired on November 14,

1983, after various cleaning supplies and articles of furniture disappeared at the Gulf Tides.

Once again posing as Charles Stevens, he was hired in December as an electrician's helper at Bradenton Electric Co., a position he kept until April. At the start of 1984, he moved in with Pam Kincaid, a single mother and his former coworker at the Gulf Tides. Her residence on 36th Avenue Drive West was but a short distance from Cindy Wood's new workplace, the Cape Vista Child Care Center where, as it turned out, Pam Kincaid's children played while their mother was at work.

Many details of what transpired over the coming weeks have yet to emerge. But it is known that Charles Stevens had begun making payments on a motorcycle owned by Samuel L. Harding of Bradenton. Harding's major miscue was to allow Stevens use of the bike as he paid for it. On April 10, with Pam Kincaid's brother Bob aboard the machine with him, Santini led Florida Highway Patrol Trooper Tim Johnson on a 20-mile chase through Manatee and Sarasota counties at speeds of up to 90 mph. He ran several stoplights and at one point barely missed colliding with a woman and her baby carriage.

"He drove like his life depended on it," Trooper Johnson later told Joanne Fiske, "and now I know why. He had good reason to run." Johnson couldn't catch Santini, but he did get the bike's license number. That night, Manatee deputies arrested Samuel Harding for reckless driving, despite his protests that the man he knew as Charles Stevens was their culprit. Harding spent the night and part of the next day in jail before Trooper Johnson saw him in the lockup and realized the wrong man was behind bars. The following year, Harding sued several of the cops involved in his case for false arrest.

Charles Stevens never was apprehended for the bike incident, even though the Florida Highway Patrol knew from Samuel Harding that he lived with Pam Kincaid. "We don't have the manpower to follow up and stake places out for somebody in violation of a minor misdemeanor," Trooper Johnson explained to the *Herald.* "If we had known it was Santini, we sure would have done everything to get him."

On April 25, Santini-as-Stevens went to work as a receiving clerk at a resort, the Longboat Key Club. "Not long thereafter," reported Fiske, "Mrs. Wood told relatives that a man who came to the day-care center to pick up children had begun asking her out. 'She said he was good-looking with blond hair and big, brown eyes,' recalled Mrs. Wood's niece, Shirley Wood."

It appears that Cindy Wood, a friend of Pam Kincaid, rebuffed these advances, which certainly seem to have been made by Donald Santini. Somehow, her estranged husband, Barry, also became aware of Santini's presence in Bradenton, if not his true identity. In later conversations with the police, Wood would refer to him as Charles Stevens.

More precisely understood is the fact that Charles Stevens eventually moved out of Pam Kincaid's place. On Monday, June 4, 1984, he paid Ms. Kathryn Shipman two weeks' advance rent for a room at 690 Jungle Queen Way on Longboat Key. Ms. Shipman remembered to police that Stevens brought a good many belongings into the room on that Monday, and then left. He did not sleep there Tuesday night, the fifth.

"He was a very quiet person," Kathryn Shipman says today. "He had some nice luggage and a nice leather, or suede, jacket. They looked like they were expensive." Not the sort of gear one buys on a clerk's salary.

That evening, according to Cindy Wood's niece, Shirley Wood, she received a telephone call from her aunt. Cindy said that the man who had been asking her out at the day-care center—she thought he was Bob Kincaid's cousin—now claimed to have information about Barry Wood that might be useful to her in the custody fight. Reluctant as she was to go out with him, said Cindy, she agreed to have dinner with the man that night in order to learn what he knew. According to her son Tommy, a man answering Santini-Stevens's description did come by for his mother about 9:30 that night.

Cindy Wood never was seen alive again.

Kathryn Shipman later reported that her new tenant returned to his room the following morning, June 6. The last she saw of him was about 3:00 that afternoon when he departed, suddenly, leaving much of his personal property behind, including his bottle of peroxide. A later search of his desk at the Longboat Key Club revealed scribbled directions, in Santini's hand, to Cindy Wood's house in Bradenton and a description of her car, as well as its license tag number.

Sometime during that day, say police, Santini also confessed to Pam Kincaid that he had killed Cindy Wood the night before. What other specifics of the crime, and his possible motive for committing it, that he might have shared with Kincaid are not, at this time, publicly known.

Just before one o'clock on the afternoon of the sixth—two hours before Santini-Stevens vanished for good from the room he'd rented just two days before—Shirley Anne Wood called the Manatee Sheriff's Office to report her aunt Cindy was missing, as well as her suspicions that Cindy had met foul play and that her estranged husband Barry, Shirley's uncle, was somehow mixed up in it.

At 5:05 that evening, Barry Wood contacted the sheriff's office himself. Wood told a deputy that his wife would not "hang around with any man answering the description given by Tommy," and then asked repeatedly where Tommy was. The deputy with whom he spoke (identified only as D. Turner in the police log) then went home, only to hear a half hour later that Wood had called him four times at the police station and had left a number for Turner to call back.

"I contacted him," Turner recorded. "He told me that his wife was 'heavy into alcohol and hung out with a whole bunch of men.' He again asked where Tommy was. . . . He also told me that he had hired a detective, and indicated that he knew me, and wanted to work exclusively with me. He said that 'the only man Cindy hung out with that answered the description given by Tommy was Charles Michael Stephens [sic].' He said that Bobby Kincaid was Stephens' cousin."

The next day, the seventh, Cindy's brother, Joseph Wesley of Newtown, Pennsylvania, telephoned the Manatee Sheriff's Office to say he'd just heard from Barry Wood "requesting information on the location of his son, Tommy Wood. Mr. Wesley believes Barry Wood could be responsible for the disappearance of Cindy. . . ."

Barry Wood was back on the phone to deputy Turner on the eighth. "During the interview," according to Turner's notes, "he again started to describe his wife's character and stated that 'she was heavy into drugs and hung out in various bars. . . .'

The record of these contacts continues until the next day when, at about 3:30 in the afternoon, Cynthia Ruth Wood was found. Two women, residents of the Riverview area of Hillsborough County, directly north of Manatee County, were out bicycling in their neighborhood when they came upon Mrs. Wood's lifeless body, floating facedown in a drainage ditch. She was identified from fingerprint records. The subsequent autopsy showed that Cindy Wood had died from strangulation (the authorities will not reveal exactly how), but that she bore no other marks of injury and had not been sexually abused.

Nine days later in Hillsborough County Circuit Court, Judge Paul Elliott signed a first-degree murder warrant for Donald Michael Santini, aka Charles Michael Stevens et al. Santini subsequently has been reported in Kentucky, where a friend raises horses, as well as in California. He remains at large, however, despite a nationwide manhunt and the intense interest of the news media, including the television program, *America's Most Wanted,* which profiled Santini in 1990. As of April 1991, viewers' tips have led to the capture of 148 fugitives featured on *America's Most Wanted*, but no one, as yet, has been able to lead the police to Donald Santini.

Nor are Hillsborough County Sheriff's Office investigators willing to address with specificity a key question in the case—*why* did Donald Santini kill Cindy Wood? Capt. Dave Terry does concede the authorities believe the murder was a paid hit; that someone in the area hired Santini to kill Ms. Wood. But Terry refuses to elaborate. "All that we can say at this point is we've uncovered evidence that leads us to that conclusion," he explains.

Is the victim's husband, Barry, considered among those with sufficient motive to be a suspect in the case? "I can't comment on that at all," answers Capt. Terry.

Barry Wood, as best can be determined, has left the Bradenton area with little Barry and Jeanette. He may be living in Pennsylvania. However, repeated attempts to locate and interview Mr. Wood for his version of events were not successful.

According to Joe Wesley, Cindy's brother, her son Tommy, now 21, lives with an aunt in Pennsylvania.

His mother's fitting elegy, and vindication, was written the week after her murder. On June 14, Martha Hauber, a counselor with the Florida Dept. of Health and Rehabilitative Services, wrote a letter to the Wood divorce case judge, Nick J. Falsone. "Due to the alleged murder of Cynthia R. Wood," observed Ms. Hauber, "we feel it is appropriate to close the above case without writing a report."

Then she continued. "We had found Cynthia R. Wood to be a very warm, capable, devoted mother whose children seemed well adjusted in her home and to have an excellent relationship with her. The relationship between her fourteen-year-old son and the three and five year old children of her second marriage also appeared to be exceptional as they all seemed to enjoy being together so much but they respected each other as individuals rather than being dependent on them."

The coda to Cindy Wood's sad travail was provided by Joanne Fiske in the Bradenton *Herald:*

> Barry Wood wanted his wife's body cremated. Her brothers wanted her to be buried, according to her wishes, near her mother's grave in Pennsylvania. The brothers' attorney, Herbert Berkowitz, obtained an injunction to prevent the coroner from releasing her body to Wood until the matter could be resolved.
>
> "It was just tremendously important to them," Berkowitz said. "They knew she had a terrible relationship with him and it was meaningful to them that they didn't leave her in his grasp."
>
> A judge found that Wood had a greater right to her remains. The family reluctantly agreed to allow Mrs. Wood to be buried in Manatee County as long as she was not cremated.
>
> On Aug. 3 [1984], nearly two months after her body was discovered, Cindy Wood was buried.

Double-wide Homicide

JERRY
Pittsfield, Maine

DATE OF BIRTH: Mid-1950s (est.)
HEIGHT: Approx. five feet ten inches
WEIGHT: Approx. 180 pounds
HAIR: Dirty blond
EYES: Pale blue and memorable
DISTINGUISHING MARKS: Pocked face, crooked teeth
OTHER: Slight southern accent
CONTACT: Detective Dale Lancaster
Maine State Police
(207) 621-1297

Thirty-two-year-old Shirley McAvoy was a mess; depressive (possibly bipolar), alcoholic, recently separated from her husband, Brian, and barred from contact with her two daughters, aged 8 and 12, after several episodes of physically abusing them. Shirley spent most of her days alone with her two dogs, a mixed shepherd-husky puppy, and a long-haired black cockapoo, in her three-bedroom double-wide house trailer on a 2-acre tract in Pittsfield, Maine, about 25 miles due west of Bangor.

When night came, Mrs. McAvoy usually went bar-hopping in Pittsfield and neighboring working-class towns in south-central Maine. "Since her separation," says Maine State Police detective Dale Lancaster, "she hung out in bars a lot. She fancied herself something of a party girl."

Often as not, Shirley dragged home a new friend for breakfast, or spent the night with him. Sex, of course, was often the upshot of these boozy encounters, but it was not necessarily their object—at least not Shirley's. According to friends, Mrs. McAvoy was consumed by thoughts of intercourse, yet she detested the act itself. This particular wrinkle in her psyche, detective Lancaster speculates, may have cost Shirley her life.

On Thursday, August 8, 1990, she invited several friends to a party at her trailer. On hand for the event was a stranger, maybe in his middle thirties, who had riveting pale blue eyes and spoke with a southern accent. His name was Jerry, he told some people, or Don, as others recalled his conversation. "He manufactured different stories about himself," says Lancaster. "He seemed to be what anybody wanted him to be." Jerry was an Air Force mechanic from Virginia, or a mill hand working down the road in Millinocket. All that other witnesses later remembered was that Jerry, or Don, talked of wanting to be a Navy SEAL. He must have seen the movie.

Shirley wasn't much more forthcoming about the guy. She didn't say where she picked him up, only that he'd been staying with her for three days, and that this was *not* a sexual relationship. Jerry was sleeping in a separate bedroom, she said.

The last person to see Shirley McAvoy alive was a process server, who came to her door with some divorce papers from Brian at 5:00

Shirley McAvoy.

P.M. the next day, August 9. The following morning, Saturday, Shirley's neighbors saw Jerry driving away from the double-wide, apparently alone, in Shirley's 1990 red Oldsmobile Cutlass Supreme.

Late that Saturday afternoon, on Boston's crowded Southeast Expressway, a man answering Jerry's description rammed the red Cutlass into a Mercedes 360 driven by a well-known Boston attorney. The accident was little more than a fender-bender. According to what the lawyer later told Maine detectives, Jerry casually and confidently produced insur-

Detective Dale Lancaster.

ance cards from the Olds's glove compartment, and handed them over. Because Massachusetts is a no-fault auto-insurance state, the attorney figured he'd get a repair estimate and then simply send it up to Brian McAvoy, the man he assumed was driving the Oldsmobile. He didn't ask to see Jerry's license, or the vehicle's registration.

On Monday, August 19, 1990, Brian McAvoy received by mail from the Boston lawyer a $1,600 damage repair estimate, the result of a collision with his wife's red Cutlass. Baffled by

Police sketch of the unidentified suspect, Jerry.

the letter, Brian called Shirley for an explanation, but received no answer at the trailer. McAvoy's next call was to the Pittsfield police.

For the next several weeks, the case was treated as a routine missing person matter; the local authorities did not go to any particular length to locate Mrs. McAvoy, whose lifestyle was well known in the community. One reasonable presumption was that Shirley and Jerry had taken off on a trip together, speculation that would prove chillingly accurate.

Then came early October. With Shirley (as well as her dogs) still missing, Brian McAvoy decided to visit her trailer to shut off the water and bleed the trailer's pipes lest an early winter freeze burst them.

Inside the residence, McAvoy sensed something was amiss. When he and Shirley split the previous January, she had impulsively jettisoned all their furniture in favor of new chairs and tables that would not remind her of her former life. Shirley even went so far as to buy new kitchen knives. But Brian had been around enough to be familiar with his estranged wife's new furnishings, and these didn't look right. For one thing, the place seemed altogether too tidy; Shirley didn't keep house that way. He saw that the kitchen curtains now hung in the living room, and that Shirley's wall coatrack had been moved, as had her living-room couch.

Curious about all this, McAvoy walked over and removed one of the coats; there were small dark-red splotches on the wall behind it. Then he slid the couch to its original place, and discovered it had been concealing a red crusted stain, roughly 3 feet long by 2 feet wide. McAvoy called the cops again.

With the discovery of the bloodstains—type O, Shirley's type—in the double-wide, and the consequent presumption of foul play, the Maine State Police came into the case. Detective Lancaster reports that an NCIC check on the Olds revealed it had been stopped for some sort of traffic violation in Florida on August 14, four days after Jerry was last seen in the vehicle in Pittsfield. Further checking placed the car itself in Georgia, after it had been stolen from a parking lot in Florida, repainted, and sold.

In Boston, the attorney with the dented Mercedes provided police a description of the man he thought had been Brian McAvoy; it exactly matched the descriptions of Jerry gathered from Shirley's friends. (Because this lawyer is a key potential witness in the case, his identity is being kept a secret.) A police sketch of the suspect was commissioned and then released to the media.

Shirley McAvoy was found about a month later at 1:15 P.M. on November 20, in a rural area of Spotsylvania, Virginia, near the southbound lanes of Interstate 95 between Washington, D.C. and Richmond. Two hunters, walking in the woods behind an establishment called Todd's Tavern Market, found Shirley wrapped in a bedspread tied at each end with what looked to be cords taken from her venetian blinds. There wasn't enough left of Mrs. McAvoy to establish her cause of death, but it was possible to positively identify her by means of her upper denture, which had S. McAvoy etched into it.

A first-person explanation of why Shirley McAvoy died presumably awaits Jerry's capture, which won't be easy given the paucity of information about him; the Maine authorities do not even have his fingerprints. But failing Jerry's account of the crime, Detective Lancaster opines that Shirley may have gotten drunk with him, sexually aroused her new friend, and then refused him her body. "She might have heated this guy up," says the detective, "and then said, 'No.' And that made him snap."

The Frog Gigger

ALLEN BOYD CURTIS
Largo, Florida

DATE OF BIRTH: August 30, 1953
HEIGHT: Five feet ten inches
WEIGHT: 145 pounds
HAIR: Reddish brown
EYES: Blue
DISTINGUISHING MARKS: One inch-wide chain tattooed around upper right arm. Smaller indistinct tattoo above that. Chest tattoo of skull with "Harley" wings, and caption "Ride to live and live to ride." Many tattoos on left arm.
ALSO KNOWN AS: "Chain"
CONTACT: Largo Police Department
Sgt. Bob Hall, or Sgt. Roy Libengood
(813) 587-6717

Twenty-five-year-old Joseph Valerio of Largo, Florida, a suburb of St. Petersburg, liked to unwind the easy way on weekends. Joe, an appliance repairman, enjoyed going out for a few beers and maybe a few games of pool with friends. That's how Valerio spent the evening of February 6, 1982. He passed several leisurely hours at the ABC Lounge on Missouri Ave. with his younger brother, Dave, also an appliance repairer, and their friend from work, John Pope. Then, at about eleven o'clock, the mellow-but-mostly-sober threesome rose to leave the ABC—innocent of the senseless, ghastly death awaiting Joe Valerio on the dark streets of Largo.

Outside the lounge, Dave Valerio asked the other two to wait while he relieved himself in a deserted section of the parking lot. But just as he was doing so, out of nowhere came a pickup truck driven by Al Curtis, a local tough with a reputation for viciousness. "You shouldn't piss in public!" Curtis yelled at Valerio, and then added a garbled anti-Hispanic slur before speeding on. "I can't remember what it was, but it was uncalled for," the younger Valerio says today.

Dave Valerio quickly finished and ran to join his brother and John Pope in Joe Valerio's 1971 Pontiac. Then they headed down Missouri Ave. in high-speed pursuit of the pickup. In view of what ensued, says Dave Valerio, it is worthwhile to note that Curtis's insult hadn't angered any of them unduly; they weren't really looking for trouble from Al Curtis who, by complete coincidence, also worked as an appliance repairman. Until that moment Curtis was a complete stranger to the Valerios and John Pope. "Joe just speeded up after him," he explains. "He wasn't mad."

Witnesses later told police of a weaving, lurching game of chicken between the two vehicles as they barreled along the avenue. "I just held on for life," an unnamed passenger in Curtis's pickup related to officers. The man said he personally was far too drunk that night "to get involved in anything, much less a war like this."

Sgt. Roy Libengood of the Largo Police Department explains that as the dueling drivers approached the traffic light at Missouri Ave. and East Bay Drive in Largo, Valerio abruptly swerved in front of Curtis's truck, nearly hitting the vehicle, and then skidded to a halt as the light turned red. Al Curtis, now directly behind Valerio, slammed to a stop, too, and then jumped out of his pickup. "I'm going to see what his problem is," said Curtis to his passenger as he headed on foot for Valerio's driver-side door.

Dave Valerio says that Al Curtis had the murder weapon in hand as he approached brother Joe's car window, and that Curtis immediately and without warning thrust the device into his older brother. The police version of the episode differs.

As Sgt. Libengood recounts events, just as Al Curtis came athwart the Pontiac, Joe Valerio whipped open his door, "real hard, hitting Curtis. At that point they started fighting furiously. Curtis was somewhat smaller, and he was getting his butt whipped. At one point, he was covering his face with his hands to defend himself. About this time, the fight moved off to one side where the witnesses couldn't see exactly what happened."

Dave Valerio and John Pope didn't hear anything, either, until Joe Valerio suddenly lurched back into view at his car door, howling in fear and agony. The four-foot handle of a frog gigger jutted grotesquely from his bloody chest. The gigger—some call it a frog sticker—was outfitted with multiple razor-sharp, gafflike prongs used by bullfrog fishermen to impale their prey underwater. The prongs had been plunged deep into Joe Valerio, puncturing his lungs and partially severing his aorta.

Bleeding and screaming, Valerio fell against

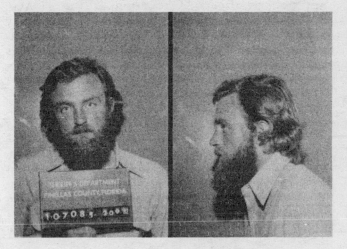

Allen Curtis in 1982.

the Pontiac as he desperately tried to yank the gigger from his chest. According to his horrified passengers, Joe tugged and jerked and finally wrenched the weapon free, only to lose consciousness as he did so.

An emergency medical squad was dispatched to the scene, but Joe Valerio already had lost too much blood. "They tried to revive him," says his brother Dave. "But he never had a chance. He was dead."

Allen Curtis meanwhile jumped back into his pickup. "We need to get the hell out of here!" Curtis shouted to his passenger as he whipped the truck into a U-turn over the Missouri Ave. median strip and gunned the vehicle in the opposite direction. John Pope told police he tried to catch

Curtis as he might appear today.

Tammy Curtis.

A frog gigger.

the pickup's license tag number before it got away, but he couldn't because a small fishing boat in the pickup's bed obscured the plate.

Curtis sought refuge with relatives. He drove the pickup to a brother-in-law's house and hid it there. Another family member, unidentified, spent the rest of the night driving Curtis around in order to forestall his immediate apprehension. By morning, Curtis's father-in-law, Elois Avera, had found a lawyer, William Barja, who delivered the suspect to the county jail.

Bond in the case was first set at $50,000, then reduced to $25,000, which Elois Avera covered by offering his house as collateral. Once out of jail, Allen Curtis hung around Largo long enough to determine that despite his attorney's efforts to negotiate a reduced charge of manslaughter, the vividly gruesome testimony that Dave Valerio and John Pope gave before the grand jury was going to ensure a first-degree murder charge against him, and a high degree of certainty that he'd be convicted.

That's when he and Elois Avera's daughter, Tammy (Curtis's second wife), took it on the lam, possibly into Tennessee. They remain at large.

In the aftermath of the murder and Curtis's bond jump, his father-in-law faced a forfeiture hearing. Mr. Avera testified that neither Al nor Tammy said so much as good-bye when they left, and that he had spent a good portion of his available assets on private investigators he hired to look for the couple. In the end, a judge blocked seizure proceedings against Elois Avera, who subsequently sold his house and left the Largo vicinity. The police have since lost track of him.

Al Curtis's parents both are now dead. Neither his first wife nor his daughter by her, live in Largo. "He has nobody back here anymore," notes Sgt. Libengood. Without the lure of friends and relatives, it is much less likely that Al Curtis would ever hazard capture by a return to Largo. Nearly 11 years after the frog-gigger murder, "he's not going to be the easiest guy to find," concedes the officer.

Vianna/Leslie

VIANNA BRANHAM
East Point, Georgia

DATE OF BIRTH: February 3, 1957
HEIGHT: Five feet three inches
WEIGHT: 135 pounds
EYES: Blue
HAIR: Brown
DISTINGUISHING MARKS: Birthmark on right knee; three small scars on right hip
CONTACT: Supt. Wally Brooks
         Metro Fugitive Squad
         PO Box 370808
         Decatur, GA 30037
         (404) 244-2557
             or
         Special Agent Dave Olcott
         FBI
         275 Peachtree St. N.E.
         Atlanta, Ga 30303
         (404) 521-3900

"When you sat and talked with her, you had no idea of her background," remembers Stockbridge, Georgia, attorney Phillip Lewis Ruppert, of his onetime client, the murderess Vianna Branham. "She could have come from one of the Ivy League colleges."

About the only schooling that Vianna Bran-

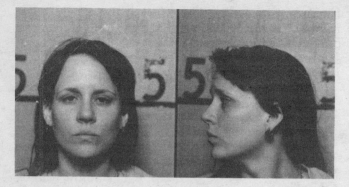

Vianna Branham.

ham in fact ever received as a young woman
was in despair and survival. A chubby little
girl, exceptionally intelligent, outgoing, and af-
fectionate, too, Vianna appears to have been
deeply wounded, emotionally, by violent dis-
cord in her parents' marriage. She was 11
when the Branhams at last split for good, a
domestic rupture that seems to have completed the psychological devastation previously wrought upon the girl. Mrs. Branham left
Vianna to her father, against whom she then
became increasingly rebellious. It wasn't long
before Mr. Branham committed Vianna to a
mental institution. She was released at age 15
in early 1972, and did not look back.

Vianna Branham headed south for New Or-
leans where, just a few weeks later, she earned
the first entry in what was to become Branham's rather lengthy rap sheet; a bust for possession of marijuana in May of 1972. In
September, in Atlanta, and then again the following July in New Orleans, she was arrested

for prostitution. In the autumn of 1973 she was nabbed in her home state, Illinois, on a larceny charge. Two years later she was collared twice again for hooking, once in Atlanta and once in Las Vegas. In April and October of 1977, the New Orleans police busted her two more times on theft beefs. During this period before her twentieth birthday, Vianna also conceived a child fathered by her black pimp.

Given such a personal history, it surprised no one later connected with her case that early 1979 found Vianna Branham still caught in her downward spiral, living as Leslie Branham Brown with her 14-month-old son in the Atlanta suburb of East Point in an apartment house populated by dingbats and misfits, a loose coalition of losers whom Vianna's attorney, Mr. Ruppert, later dismissed as 'Idiots Anonymous.'

Ms. Branham had hooked up with the IAs on her way south after visiting her dying mother in Illinois. Apparently, most members of this pathetic community were drunk or stoned most of the time. When money or dope ran low, say investigators, the group planned and pulled off petty robberies. It was in the course of one such amateur caper that Vianna ("Leslie") Branham stepped over the line.

On Sunday evening, February 11, 1979, she and her neighbor, Sabra Abercrombie, were out cruising around East Point in Abercrombie's Volkswagen when the two women spotted a likely mark, Mrs. Charles Brown, an older woman who was driving home after paying her respects to a recently deceased relative reposing at a local funeral home. Abercrombie and Branham decided to follow her.

At the Brown residence, 2995 Redwine Rd., Mrs. Brown pulled her sedan into the lighted carport. The VW, which she nervously had watched in her rearview mirror on her way home, pulled into the driveway behind Mrs. Brown. Vianna Branham jumped out of the passenger side of the Volkswagen. She approached Mrs. Brown and demanded her purse. Mrs. Brown refused. Branham, according to Mrs. Brown, then fetched her a knock on the head with a .22 handgun, and shot at her, too.

The bullet missed. The women grappled for the purse. Its strap broke. Vianna Branham grabbed the bag and began to run west across the Browns' front yard with it. Meantime, her panicked partner, Sabra Abercrombie, had popped the clutch on her idling VW, killing the motor.

As Abercrombie furiously struggled to restart the car, 56-year-old Charles A. Brown, a Georgia State Department of Health employee, emerged from his front door to see his wife holding herself and screaming in the carport, a strange VW bucking and coughing in his driveway, and a stocky young woman dashing across his lawn with Mrs. Brown's purse.

Astonished but game to see justice done, Charles Brown gave chase. He nearly caught up to the fleeing Branham next door in the driveway belonging to Brown's neighbor, East Point Police Department Capt. J. D. Lynn, when she turned and let Charles Brown have it in the neck with her .22. This shot brought Capt. Lynn from his house. The police officer thought someone was shooting at his dog, or perhaps at his vehicle. Then he saw his neighbor, Mr.

Brown, crumpled and dying in his driveway. At the same moment, Lynn saw, indistinctly, a human figure running quickly east on Redwine toward a vehicle, the VW, which Sabra Abercrombie had restarted and then positioned for a quick getaway at the corner.

The murder weapon, a six-shot revolver with its serial number abraded away, was recovered near Charles Smith's body. His wife's purse rested nearby. The handbag contained a total of $12.00.

Two days later, the cops arrived at Vianna Branham's apartment house door with a search warrant. They arrested her and her neighbor. At the police station, as attorney Phillip Ruppert recalls, Ms. Abercrombie was questioned first. She finally broke under a relentless barrage of questions, but continued to swear that she personally hadn't killed anyone. Abercrombie told the cops an ominous "they" would get her if she told the whole truth of the matter.

Then it was Vianna Branham's turn. Curiously, as her lawyer recalls, the police allowed their suspect to brace herself with a bottle of codeine-based cough medicine before the questioning began. After it did, the interrogation went on for four grueling hours until she finally collapsed into sobs and confessed shooting Mr. Brown. Branham insisted she had not meant to commit the murder, that she pulled the trigger only because Brown kept coming after her. Vianna signed her confession, says Phillip Ruppert, and then was taken by the police to a local McDonald's for lunch that day.

It turns out that a clerical misstep by the cops could have blown the whole case; their search warrant had the wrong address on it, and thus was legally invalid, according to attorney Ruppert, who says the police later altered the address on the document. However, Sabra Abercrombie had proceeded to cut a deal with the prosecutors—testimony against Vianna in return for freedom. Vianna Branham's confession therefore stood, and she was sentenced to life, plus another 10 years for the armed robbery.

The state of Georgia shipped Vianna Branham to its Women's Correctional Institution in rural Milledgeville, about a two-and-one-half-hour drive south from Atlanta. There, having sunk about a low as she could, the 22-year-old mother, thief, prostitute, and killer began a slow but determined campaign to rehabilitate herself.

Vianna, known exclusively as Leslie while at Milledgeville, worked hard and earned a high school GED, or Graduate Equivalency Degree. Then she enrolled in a prison general studies program, operated by Georgia Military College, and was awarded an undergraduate diploma. Next came graduate school equivalency courses from Mercy University. Branham's grades were almost all *A*'s and *B*'s, and she presented no disciplinary problems at all.

Her work schedule was dominated by volunteer time spent down the road at Central State Hospital, at one time the largest mental facility in the United States, housing more than 13,000 patients. When Branham arrived to work there, Central State had shrunk to 2,000 residents, mostly runaways and orphan children. No doubt, the institution struck a chord in her.

Part of her duties was to act as a teacher's aide, reading to mentally impaired kids at Central State. She also did clerical work in the office, and helped supervise the lunchroom and swimming pool. Ms. Lois Irvin, who supervised volunteers at Central State, dictated a note to Branham's file at the prison. "She is patient and forgiving with her charges," the letter reads in part. "She is frequently sought out by students needing help. She has common sense and demonstrates originality and competence." Ms. Irvin added: "She imparts ethically sound and consistent value systems to our children who are frequently confused and angry."

Others who knew Branham while she was a prisoner remember her enormous energy, a decided contrast to the lethargy that so commonly afflicts the incarcerated. Attorney Phillip Ruppert, who visited her several times over the years, says that his client exercised constantly; she was out jogging whenever she had a moment free from her busy schedule. Dr. Eleanor Kates, another of Branham's supervisors at Central State, also recalls Branham's eager energy. "Leslie was the kind that if there was nothing else to do, she'd be dusting the books in the library," says Dr. Kates.

Purposeful "Leslie" Branham, then, was a model prisoner from the start, the mirror opposite of the troubled Vianna Branham who murdered Charles Brown. If her transformation was genuine—and most who knew her as a prisoner insist that it was—then there is some small hope for redemption for a portion of the approximately 700,000 other people behind bars in the United States, and the roughly

70,000 more who are incarcerated (often, rein-carcerated) every year.

Unfortunately for penology, it is at present impossible to say whether Leslie, or Vianna, is toeing the straight and narrow. On May 18, 1987, a few months after her thirtieth birthday and exactly 15 years after she was first ar-rested, Branham slipped off a lawn-cutting tractor she was operating outside the Mil-ledgeville fence, and disappeared. Rumors per-sist that someone on the hospital staff abetted the escape. Inmate Branham would have been eligible for parole in about one year.

Later, Ms. Branham surfaced in New Or-leans, where her son, now a teenager, has been raised by his paternal grandmother. Most re-cently, according to the FBI, Branham tele-phoned a relative to say she was doing fine and holding down a good job.

Stay tuned.

Risita

MARIO TAURO COTO
Hialeah, Florida

DATE OF BIRTH: May 5, 1948
HEIGHT: Five feet eleven inches
WEIGHT: 180 pounds
HAIR: Black
EYES: Brown
DISTINGUISHING MARKS: "Mario" tattooed on left arm.
ALSO KNOWN AS: Julio Jiménez, Alberto Gómez, Raul Estrada
CONTACT: Hialeah Police Department
(305) 769-7700

Havana-born Mario Coto, an ex-con known around south Florida by his Spanish street name, *Risita* ("Little Smile"), is neither a subtle nor a complex person. According to the police, Coto has two favored pastimes—operating high-power speedboats and driving four-wheel-drive vehicles. Also according to the police, Coto pays for his pleasures by plying his two marketable skills—killing people and protecting people from being killed. He finds his clients (and most of his targets) within the illegal drug trade.

On Sunday, May 22, 1977, *Risita* was in his pro-active mode. His objective was a second-floor apartment at 1250 West 30th St. in Hia-

Risita Coto.

leah, the residence for several years of divorced hairdresser María Luisa Pacheco and her son, Bienvenido. Within the past few months, the 35-year-old Mrs. Pacheco had acquired a significant other, a 30-year-old drug thug named Pedro Luis Machado, whose new Cadillac more often than not was parked out in front of the apartment on West 30th. Somehow in the course of affording the new car, Machado seems to have run afoul of a colleague in the drug business—identity unknown—who let a contract for Pedro's erasure to Mario Coto.

Late that Sunday morning, Machado was asleep in María's bed. His brother, Alberto Ramírez, 25, also a resident at 1250 West 30th, was sleeping in another room. Sixteen-year-old Bienvenido Pacheco occupied a third bedroom. His mother, as she later recounted to police, had risen at about ten o'clock. Mrs. Pacheco did some housework, she said, then took out the garbage before disrobing for her shower just before noon.

That's when Mario Coto came calling with his .32 automatic. Edna Buchanan, the *Miami Herald*'s Pulitzer prize-winning police reporter, told her readers on the twenty-fourth that Pedro Luis Machado was shot in the head, throat, and shoulder on Sunday morning in Hialeah, while his brother Alberto took slugs in one eye and one shoulder. Both died of their wounds. Neither Mrs. Pacheco nor her son were harmed.

"The shower María Luisa Pacheco took Sunday morning may have saved her life," wrote Buchanan in one of her trademark crime-story leads.

The first statement Mrs. Pacheco gave Hialeah detectives was that she knew nothing, and had heard nothing, until the killer slammed her front door on his way out. Only then, she claimed, did she emerge dripping wet from her bathroom to discover the carnage.

After eight hours of questioning, however, María Luisa's story changed in several significant ways. Coto, whom she knew only as the drug enforcer, *Risita*, actually confronted Mrs. Pacheco in her shower, she admitted. For undisclosed reasons of his own, she further explained, Mario Coto decided against killing the only living witness to his crimes and contented himself, instead, with giving her his little smile and a stern warning that Mrs. Pacheco better keep her *boca* shut.

María Luisa provided police with a good description of Coto, and mentioned also that she had spotted an Avis car rental agency logo on the keychain the killer was carrying in his hand. Working only from this information, Hialeah police detective Dan Birkenstock was able to locate a Miami Beach Avis Office that had rented Coto (using the alias Julio Jiménez) a car.

He was soon identified, and a murder warrant was issued. But it would be three years before the police caught up to Mario Coto, and even then his capture was a fluke.

It came about on August 8, 1980, another Sunday. Miami police intelligence officers Ozzie Austin and Sergio Piñón, working with Florida Department of Law Enforcement investigator Danny Benítez, had received a tip that fugitive drug dealer and killer, Juan Ramón Pérez-Llamas, was holed up in a Fort Lauderdale neighborhood, which the detectives had put under surveillance. Pérez-Llamas was disdained by the police as a varsity dirtball. Like Mario Coto, he had been loose since 1977 when he jumped a $100,000 bond on a murder beef in his native Puerto Rico. Not surprisingly, Pérez-Llamas and Coto were close associates.

In an act of sheer felicity that evening, Officers Austin and Piñón stopped to make a telephone call in front of a motel at 2909 Vista Amor Drive in Fort Lauderdale. At just that moment Mario Coto, whom they immediately recognized, strolled out of the motel. They arrested him as he climbed into his rented Chevy

Camaro, from which they also confiscated a Mac-10 submachine gun and a .38 automatic. Later in the day the officers visited Coto's apartment where they found a kilogram of cocaine and arrested his wife, María, for possession.

"On the night Coto was arrested, I spoke with him for maybe 15 or 20 minutes," says Hialeah detective Dan Birkenstock. "He's articulate. He's not a dummy. He's very cool, calm, and collected. He was arrested on two counts of first-degree murder, but you would have thought he was in for running a red light. He's a nice dresser."

Outwardly poised as he was, Mario Coto must have taken pause to reconsider his previous decision to spare Mrs. Pacheco's life. Without her eyewitness testimony, the double-murder case against Coto would be weakened considerably. Police conjecture that this is why a gorilla from Carbondale, Illinois, named Marty Tajra suddenly hove into view, making pointed inquiries at the hair salon where María Luisa Pacheco worked. Mrs. Pacheco reported that Tajra—on the street despite two prior convictions for murder—also had come looking for her at her residence.

Hialeah police officers collared Tajra the next day at the beauty salon. He was driving a stolen vehicle, and in it they found a stolen handgun. Although the authorities weren't able to prove Coto had hired Tajra to kill Mrs. Pacheco, they did successfully charge him with car theft. He ultimately was convicted and served 18 months before his release. Mrs. Pacheco was not menaced again.

She was safe because Mario Coto meanwhile

had copped a plea in the two murders. In 1981, he pled guilty to second-degree homicide in both cases and was sentenced to two consecutive life terms in the Florida prison system. Coto's first stop was the maximum security state penitentiary at Raiford, where he was processed in April of 1981. From Raiford he was moved several times over the succeeding years. Coto also picked up a certificate as a trained auto mechanic as he patiently hoped and planned for a chance to escape.

The opportunity came in June of 1985 at the Glades Correctional Institution in Belle Glade, Florida. According to Chester Lambdin, superintendent of the facility, Coto ambled across the prison recreational yard to its perimeter fence one day at about noon. He seems to have had bolt cutters secreted at the fence—nobody who knows is saying how this was accomplished—and used them to cut his way to freedom. A guard later reported seeing a car in the vicinity of the recreational yard that day, and this automobile, recovered some miles away, appears to have been used in the escape.

Risita Coto remains at large. There have been no arrests in connection with his escape from Glades. Since then, he has been more-or-less reliably reported in Puerto Rico, Colombia, and Chicago, where Coto has connections in the local drug trade plus one or more girlfriends. "This guy," says Detective Birkenstock, "is either doing drugs or still killing people. That's the only skill he has."

Anthony Angúlo, a Hialeah detective sergeant who helped investigate the 1977 murders and is now retired from the police force, agrees. "We've been told over the years that

Coto commutes and is in and out of the United States," says Angúlo, who believes that Coto has the money and the smarts to easily pass in and out of the United States on his various drug-related errands without detection. "He's going to come in with proper-looking papers and everything," says Angúlo. "He's not going to be one of these offshore guys."

Dirtballs

WILLIAM JORDAN
Wadesboro, North Carolina

DATE OF BIRTH: September 18, 1942
HEIGHT: Six feet two inches
WEIGHT: 150 pounds
HAIR: Brown
EYES: Blue
DISTINGUISHING MARKS: Scars on chin, left arm, right hand between thumb and forefinger, right leg; discoloration on forehead; large mole near center of forehead. Tattoos of skeleton on right forearm and spider on upper right arm; cross and name "SIBYL" on left forearm; "LOUISE" on left leg.
CONTACT: Tommy Allen, Jr.
Anson County Sheriff
Wadesboro, NC
(709) 694-4188
or
Any FBI office

Our word for a primitive, violence-prone lout, *yahoo*, was coined in 1711 by the satirist, Jonathan Swift, in his *Gulliver's Travels.* "Upon the whole," observes Lemuel Gulliver of these brutish humanoids he encounters in the book, "I never beheld in all my travels so disagreeable an animal, nor one against which I naturally conceived so strong an antipathy." Of course, Swift's Gulliver never met Bill Jordan.

In early March of 1974, while out on parole from the federal prison system for interstate transportation of a stolen automobile, Jordan and his young buddy, 24-year-old Ted Anthony Prevatte, decided to go on a crime spree, "traveling around like a pack of dogs," as their prosecutor later put it. The bearded outlaws hit several residences—including houses occupied by two of Jordan's relatives—in their native Wadesboro and surrounding Anson County, which lie about 50 miles southeast of Charlotte. They stole whatever they could find, including an uncle's car, a shotgun, and several other firearms. Then, with Anson County sheriff's deputies hot on their trail, Jordan and Prevatte sped away out of state.

At about 8 o'clock on the night of March 6, a Wednesday, witnesses saw the suspects 300 miles to the west, at the bar in a Holiday Inn in Lawrenceville, Georgia, a few miles northeast of Atlanta. With them was James A. Rouse, Jr., an assistant principal at East Atlanta High School. Rouse was conspicuously attired that night in slacks, black loafers, and a bright red sport jacket with matching socks. He bought a round of beers, and paid for the three drinks with a $50 bill.

Why James Rouse drove his car, a blue Toyota station wagon, to the Holiday Inn in Lawrenceville that night, rather than attending his evening classes at the University of Georgia as he was supposed to, is not known. Nor can police say how he met up with the fugitives from North Carolina. Rouse's wife in suburban Morrow, Georgia, in Clayton County, just south of

William Jordan
after his arrest.

Ted Anthony Prevatte
on the same day.

Atlanta, and about 25 miles from Lawrenceville, would later report that her husband
called her around 8:30 to say he'd be home "in
a couple hours." At about the same time, according to witnesses, Jordan and Prevatte rose
and strolled out of the Lawrenceville Holiday
Inn bar. Five minutes later, James Rouse followed them outside.

The next afternoon, March 7, Anson County
sheriff's deputy and chief investigator, Tommy
Allen, and fellow deputy Ed Thompson, received a tip that Jordan and Prevatte were back
in the area. The caller reported that the suspects were driving a blue Toyota station wagon
with Georgia plates, and that the vehicle at that
moment was parked outside Jordan's sometime girlfriend's house. The fate of Jordan's
uncle's car, the one he and Prevatte stole in
Anson County during the first phase of their
crime binge, never has been determined.

Allen and Thompson arrived at the address
provided by the tipster; sure enough, they saw
the blue station wagon. Knowing that Jordan
and Prevatte probably were armed, and not
averse to a shoot-out if it came to that, the deputies cautiously approached the house in their
cruiser. As they did, the outlaws burst from
the front door, jumped into the Toyota, and
gunned the vehicle down the street.

The deputies gave chase, exchanging gunfire
with the desperados as they radioed for help.
At one point, Allen and Thompson saw a shiny,
stubby object fly out the Toyota's window, and
noted where it landed. After 15 miles of high-
speed pursuit, Jordan and Prevatte tried to
shake Allen and Thompson by swerving onto a
dirt access road. Instead, they plowed into a

Jordan posing with his guns and James Rouse's auto.

Prevatte's turn.

ditch and the chase was over. Shaken but un-
hurt, the fugitives were handcuffed and taken
into custody.

The Toyota was filled with stolen property,
mostly weapons, but also an instant camera
with which Jordan and Prevatte had taken
photos of one another, posed with a sawed-off
shotgun, in front of the car. The snapshots
were found tucked into the driver's side visor.
The object that was tossed from the Toyota
during the chase turned out to be the same
shotgun, stolen from a county resident during
the suspects' crime spree. Jordan and Prevatte
had been responsible for sawing off its barrel.

Tommy Allen, who is now sheriff of Anson
County, remembers that the recovery of the
altered shotgun raised his suspicion that Jordan and Prevatte were into something much
heavier than housebreaking and theft. In the
Wadesboro jail, when he asked the two how
they had acquired the blue Toyota, the suspects claimed they'd found it parked, keys in
the ignition, on Peachtree St. in Atlanta. Over
the next couple days, Allen made several attempts to alert Georgia authorities that he'd
impounded a suspected stolen vehicle, but
problems with the National Crime Information Center (NCIC) computer system prevented
the information from getting through, he says.

Meanwhile, on Saturday, March 9, at Old Tit-
shaw Lake in Gwinnett County, Georgia, near
Lawrenceville, a woman and her children came
across James A. Rouse, Jr. He was shoeless and
sockless and splayed out dead on the ground,
framed by a pool of his own blood. A single
point-blank shotgun blast virtually had blown
his head away. Near the body, investigators

found the spent shell, which tests later would show had been fired from the sawed-off shotgun recovered after the car chase in Anson County.

Gwinnett County detectives used fingerprints to establish that the dead man was Rouse, but because of the NCIC glitch, says Sheriff Allen, they had no way of knowing about his car or the two men arrested in it. Finally, on Monday, March 11, Tommy Allen in Anson County used a Georgia auto-license directory to figure out where in the state the blue Toyota was registered. Then he called the authorities in Clayton County.

Bingo.

"I thought the guy was going to come through the phone at me!" says Allen of the Clayton County cop's reaction to Allen's news that Anson County, North Carolina, authorities had James Rouse's blue Toyota and were holding two suspects who'd been caught with the vehicle.

Although they would protest their innocence throughout, the evidence against Jordan and Prevatte was overwhelming. Besides the sworn statements of witnesses who placed the pair in the bar at the Holiday Inn with Rouse, authorities connected them with both the murder weapon and the victim's car, the Toyota. Moreover, when he was arrested, Jordan was wearing Rouse's expensive watch.

Furthermore, Tommy Allen was alert enough to notice a deep cut in the web of Bill Jordan's right hand. Jordan tried to pass off the cut as an incidental injury. However, the shotgun used to kill James Rouse had a unique metal barb behind its trigger. Any right-hander, such

The killers cleaned up and heading for trail.

Prosecutor Bryant Huffman with James Rouse's widow (far right).

Sheriff Tommy Allen, Jr.

as Bill Jordan, who fired the weapon would suffer exactly the same cut Tommy Allen noticed on Jordan's hand. This peculiarity helped establish that Jordan did the actual shooting, and the scar is now included with other information on Jordan's rap sheets and wanted posters (see p. 304).

Gwinnett County district attorney Bryant Huff, who was proud of his record in winning death-penalty sentences (Huff was known to sport a hangman's noose-shaped lapel pin), prosecuted the two in separate trials before Judge Reid Merritt in Lawrenceville in June of 1974. Prevatte's jury deliberated 2½ hours be-

Jordan in a 1979 mugshot.

fore finding him guilty. Jordan's panel came back with the same verdict after only an hour and a half. On June 13, Judge Merritt sentenced both men to the Georgia electric chair, and set their execution date as October 4.

The day after sentencing, Jordan and Prevatte were on Death Row at the Wayne Correctional Institution, outside Brunswick, Georgia, just north of the Florida line. By now, both would long since have been executed. In 1972, however, in *Furman* v. *Georgia*, the U.S. Supreme Court had ruled that the death penalty was employed in a "freakish" way so that its use was often "cruel" and "arbitrary."

As a result, Georgia and other states passed new death penalty statutes. In Georgia, one provision of the new state law was that all death sentences be reviewed by the state Supreme Court, which ultimately commuted Jordan and Prevatte's sentences to life terms.

For the next 10 years, Bill Jordan kept his head down and his nose clean. By 1984, he was regarded as trustworthy enough to be allowed into the medium security section at Wayne, and was assigned to a prison farm detail that worked outside the walls. At about seven o'clock on the morning of August 7, 1984, Jordan and another inmate, Kenny Leon Green, were supposed to gas up the prison truck used to transport everyone out to the fields. Jordan and Green took the truck, and then kept on going.

One report places Jordan on a bus in his hometown of Wadesboro a few days later, but that is the only sighting since his escape. His partner, Ted Anthony Prevatte, now 41, remains behind bars. According to the FBI, any hope Prevatte holds for parole is contingent upon Jordan's recapture.

Rogue Cop

ARMANDO GARCÍA
Miami, Florida

DATE OF BIRTH: January 20, 1962
HEIGHT: Five feet nine inches
WEIGHT: 180 pounds
HAIR: Brown
EYES: Brown
DISTINGUISHING MARKS: Burn on left cheek
OTHER: Garcia is left-handed, and has given himself the nickname "Scarface."
CONTACT: Any FBI office
        (I.O. #5057)

There are approximately 15,000 independent police departments in the United States, and at one time or another every one of them has had to cope with questions about their officers' competence or probity. Rarely, however, has a city police force been rocked by the sort of scandal that hit the Miami, Florida, police department in the mid 1980s.

They were known as the Miami River Gang, a score or more rogue cops who saw each day on the street how much money was being made in the illegal drug business, and who decided to cut themselves in on the profits. At first, the dirty cops confined themselves to shaking down small-time cocaine dealers, then selling

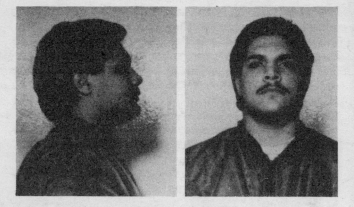

Armando García.

the coke out of their patrol cars, or passing it on to friends and relatives for resale.

In time, however, the gang moved on to bigger scores, extorting snitches and drug wholesalers to turn over their stashes. At last, on a night in July of 1985, several of the cops—including muscular Armando García, a five-year veteran of the Miami police force—raided two vessels moored on the Miami River, and stole from the crafts an astonishing 800 kilos of cocaine, nearly a ton of dope. Three Colombian nationals aboard the two boats were later found drowned in the river.

The blatancy of this and other heists by García and the rest of the gang led to the formation of a unique FBI task force in Miami, a squad of special agents dedicated exclusively to rooting out the corrupt cops. As a result of the Bureau's ensuing two-year investigation, the drug ring was smashed. Ultimately, more than 20 members of the Miami River Gang went to jail. Only two are now at large: fugitive ex-cops Víctor Zapata and Armando García, whom the FBI describes as "extremely dangerous," and for good reason.

García and six other patrolmen were brought to trial together in December of 1986. In a pragmatic decision dictated by circumstances—according to a police source—the local authorities chose not to charge any of them with murder; although homicides clearly had been committed, it was impossible to prove whom among the gang members actually pushed the victims into the river.

The Florida state prosecutors also knew they'd have trouble building sympathy among jurors for slain Colombian drug peddlers. Instead, the Miami River Gang members were all brought up on federal racketeering charges, and were tried in federal court.

Assistant U.S. attorney Patrick Sullivan, who helped to prosecute many of the cops, says that gang members made as much as a million dollars apiece in the drug business. Sometimes, the patrolmen were negligent in how they spent this excess income. Later, certain of their less restrained purchases caused the ex-cops' defense attorneys some trouble in court. In Armando García's case, a threshold of incredulity was met at the disclosure that his fiancée, Gisela Porras-Pita, in 1985 paid $13,000 in cash for a new Datsun 300ZX.

Defense lawyer Sam Rubin gamely put 22-year-old Porras-Pita on the stand and then asked her how she raised such a large amount of cash. Well, said the young woman, she earned some of the money as a seamstress. Just then, a double-rack of Porras-Pita's creations was whisked into the courtroom, occasioning a few sniggers and general amazement in the gallery. On display for the jury's edification was a white lace wedding gown, a purple cocktail dress, a denim outfit, and other items of hand-sewn *couture* from the Porras-Pita collection. In all, García's fiancée testified, her industry with a needle had earned her $5,000 toward the Z car.

The balance of the purchase price, another $8,000, was a gift from her self-employed, truck-driving father, she said. However, although the elder Mr. Porras claimed under oath that inasmuch as he made $56,654 in 1985 he could well afford such a grand present, he also conceded under cross-examination that the family's total net income, after taxes and his expenses, came to less than $18,000 for the year.

The trial ended in a mistrial in January of 1987, which turned out to be only the beginning of Armando García's troubles. Two other defendants in the case, Rodolfo Arias and Luis Batista, changed their pleas to guilty and promised the Feds testimony against their former brother officers in exchange for reduced, 10-year prison terms. Their prospective evidence meant Armando García faced even steeper odds against acquittal when his case came up for retrial.

Meantime, according to FBI Special Agent Gary Hoskins, investigators learned that a full year before, in March of 1986, García and his father, Torribio Dagoberto García, had arranged to pay an itinerent thug named José Martínez $50,000 to permanently silence two *other* prosecution witnesses, Armando Un

Roque and Pedro Ramos. Martínez took the
Garcías' money and then disappeared, only to
resurface a year later as a prosecution witness
against them. "This," says Agent Hoskins of
the complex affair, "was like a movie."

Then the tale grew even more tangled. In May
of 1987, Armando was formally charged in the
aborted murder scheme. At the same time,
lengthy sworn statements provided by Arias
and Batista persuaded U.S. District Judge
Kenneth Ryskamp to revoke García's bond.
Trouble was, no one could find the defendant.
"He indicated to me that he would meet me
tonight and arrange to turn himself in," attorney Rubin told the press. "He did not meet me
so I assume he will turn himself in tomorrow."

That assumption was not well-founded.

With Armando García gone, the Feds turned
their full attention to his dad, Torribio, who,
according to Gary Penrith, special agent in
charge of the FBI office in Newark, New Jersey, is every bit as dangerous as his boy, if not
more so. The elder García, says Penrith, is a
killer and "a member of a large group of individuals who have committed murder and are
known to be armed with automatic weapons."

The reason that a New Jersey-based federal
agent is familiar with Torribio Dagoberto García is that the old man surfaced in northern
New Jersey after fleeing Florida not long after
he, too, was charged with hiring Martínez to
ice Armando Un Roque and Pedro Ramos. Gisela Porras-Pita disappeared from Florida at
about the same time, as well.

In the summer of 1989, the FBI arrested an
Elizabeth, New Jersey, hairdresser, Antonio
Pino, and charged Pino with aiding the fugitive

Garcías. Drucilia Wells, spokesperson for the Newark FBI, says Pino cashed a very large check for Torribio García, and then accompanied Ms. Porras-Pita north into Canada where she boarded a plane for an undisclosed destination in South America and, according to the FBI, a reunion with her fiancé. Antonio Pino later received the equivalent of a suspended sentence for helping the Garciás.

That September, the Bureau's Newark office made a second arrest for aiding the Garcías, that of a Weehauken woman named Angela Ramos. As Gary Penrith tells the story, Torribio García contacted the 53-year-old Ramos, and instructed her to pick up and deliver to him, in Union City, two suitcases of Armando's clothing. These had been spirited north from Miami two years earlier. Ramos later received probation and a fine.

This seems to be the most recent information available as to the Garcías' whereabouts and movements. The FBI will not say if they think Torribio remains in the United States, or if Armando and Gisela are still south of the border. Agent Hoskins of the Bureau office in Miami does report that Armando is a light drinker and recreational drug user, nothing to excess. His only significant addiction is to pumping iron; Armando is sure to be living in the vicinity of a bodybuilding facility. "He's got to be somewhere near a gymnasium," says Hoskins.

"One of the Worst"

Columbus, Georgia

Jim Johnson of Columbus, Georgia, says he knew in an instant that Michael Curry was not the man for his daughter, Ann. This was not a difficult conclusion to reach.

Back in the summer of 1979, soon after Ann Johnson, then 18, and Mike Curry, 21, first met, she rushed home one day to report that her new boyfriend was at nearby Pine Mountain State Park, threatening to shoot himself. Jim Johnson, a retired Army lieutenant colonel, drove out with Ann to the park and managed to dissuade Curry from suicide.

He now deeply regrets his success.

"We did everything we could to discourage any relationship with him whatsoever," says Johnson today. "I saw no future for Ann at all with him."

There was lots of trouble in Mike Curry's life, much of it apparently caused by drug abuse. According to what Johnson claims he later learned from the Columbus police, dope was the reason Curry had been bounced out of the Navy. Stealing (presumably to support his habit) also had cost Mike his job at a Columbus electrician's shop, says Johnson. After another incident in which Curry discharged a weapon in his father's apartment, the police took Mike to the hospital. Later, he was transferred to a local drug clinic called Alchemy, where he spent several months.

Despite her parent's strong misgivings and Mike's unpromising personal history, Ann Johnson married Curry in 1981. He found work as an electrician and maintenance supervisor at the Bradley Center, a private psychiatric hospital. In 1984, the Currys purchased a three-bedroom ranch-style house in a middle-class East Columbus subdivision called Brookview Estates. They appeared to be settling into married life.

Yet behind these outward signs of stability was a tension-wracked marriage that seemed to carom toward an explosion from the outset. Her father says that Ann's diary for 1981 describes the couple's fight over their first child, Erika; Mike wanted the baby aborted. Three years later, he seems to have been similarly opposed to the birth of their son, Ryan. Still according to James Johnson, Mike was upset when Ann became pregnant again in early 1985.

There was never enough money, either. Even though they had two incomes—Ann worked as a night-shift customer service representative for Blue Cross-Blue Shield of Georgia—Mike Curry's unwillingness to live within a budget kept their finances tight and Ann in tears, says her mother, Bernice Johnson.

By 1985, the Currys were talking both bankruptcy and divorce. That August, as Ann neared her term with their third baby, she developed phlebitis, which required 10 days' hospitalization. At the same time, Mike started fooling around with Pam Burt, a married woman he'd met at the Bradley Center.

Thursday, August 29, was literally a dark and stormy day in Columbus. Massive, booming thunderheads rolled across the sky, drenching the countryside below. Ann Curry, whose phlebitis had made it prudent to go on early maternity leave, left her 20-month-old son, Ryan, at his grandmother Johnson's house that morning, while she and 4-year-old Erika drove to Sears in Ann's white Ford Escort station wagon to shop for a small present for Erika to take to a birthday party that evening.

When Ann Curry and her daughter returned to Mrs. Johnson's, a few minutes from their own house, she told her mother that her legs were hurting again, and that she looked forward to going home and resting. Bernice Johnson thought for a moment to offer to keep little Ryan for Ann, but for some reason didn't mention anything. Sometime between 12:30 and 12:45, as Mrs. Johnson remembers, Ann and the two kids left to go home. "It was just another day," Bernice Johnson later told Columbus *Ledger-Enquirer* reporter, Bobbi Miller. "If anything had been troubling her I think she would have mentioned it, or I would've known."

At approximately 3:00 that afternoon, police dispatcher Jimmy Larson in Phenix City, just across the border in Alabama, received an eerie call from a woman whose voice Larson described as husky. She asked the dispatcher if he knew anything about the triple murders in Columbus that day. When Jimmy Larson replied that he did not, the woman said, "I guess my friend must have been joking with me, then."

Around 5:30 P.M., Mike Curry arrived home. The next thing that his neighbor across the street, Eddie Gravel, knew, Mike Curry had dashed over to his house and was attacking him. "He grabbed me," Gravel told reporter Miller, "threw me up against the wall, and said," 'Why did they want to do it? Why did they want to do it?' " Young Gravel, 19, remembered asking Curry who "they" were, and receiving no answer.

Gravel's mother, who thought that Curry was having a heart attack or seizure, called the police. Responding officers described Mike Curry as "belligerent." They wrestled him to the floor, and then cuffed Curry's hands behind his back. "He seemed freaked out," said Jim Bryant, an EMT at the scene.

With Mike Curry subdued, Bryant, his partner Jim Waites and Columbus police officer Bobby McLendon walked across the street to investigate what had upset Curry so. What they discovered, Bryant later told reporter Miller, was "one of the worst."

They found Ann Johnson Curry and little Ryan in the den. Between them on the floor was a curved-blade brush ax with which someone had struck twice at Mrs. Curry, hitting her once in the head and once in the neck. She also had a broken arm, but bore no defensive wounds, characteristic of a struggle, meaning that Ann Curry's killer probably had taken her completely by surprise. The county coroner,

J. Donald Kilgore, later determined that she had bled to death.

Ryan lay dead on the other side of the ax, which had been used to kill him, too. He also bore two wounds, one on his head and one in his chest. Four-year-old Erika was murdered in the adjacent kitchen with a single blow of the ax to her head. Her broken glasses rested nearby on the floor.

The fourth victim was Ann's unborn child. A pathologist was summoned to perform a post-mortem Caesarian section in the hopes of saving the slain woman's infant, but the effort came too late. The child, a perfectly formed boy weighing 5 pounds, 12 ounces, had suffocated in his mother's womb. He was named Tyler and later was taken to Ann Johnson Curry's coffin where the unborn infant was arranged for burial in his mother's arms.

Michael Curry's father, Orval, received a telephone call at about 10 o'clock that night. "Something tragic's happened at Michael's," the caller said.

Assuming that the tragedy had to do with their daughter-in-law's pregnancy, the Currys jumped in their faded blue Mercedes and drove through the rain to Mike and Ann's house, about 2 miles away. When they arrived, all that greeted them was an empty residence cordoned off with yellow police ropes flapping in the night wind. Two doors to the house were posted: "Do not enter—By authority of police department."

Still unaware of what had transpired, but frightened by what they'd found, the Currys got back in their car and drove on to the Johnsons', where Jim and Bernice were dressing for

Ann, Mike, and
Erika Johnson
in 1983.

Bernice Johnson with her grandchildren
in the den where Ann and Ryan were
murdered.

Erika Johnson in July 1985.

Erika and Ryan three days before they were slain.

bed. One look at Orval's worried expression told the Johnsons that something dreadful had occurred—but what? They wouldn't know until they dressed and rushed downtown to police headquarters with Orval and Joyce Curry. On the way, Bernice Johnson had a partial premonition. "I knew on the way down that Ann was dead," she'd later say. "But I hoped the children weren't."

Police Chief Jim Wetherington, summoned from a banquet that night, barely reached headquarters ahead of the Currys and Johnsons. They were quickly shown into his office where Wetherington gave them the news. As the four parents tried to absorb what he was saying, upstairs Mike Curry was being interrogated by detectives behind closed door.

Curry spoke with the detectives for three hours and said nothing to incriminate himself in the slaughter of his wife and children. He gave them permission to take hair, blood, and saliva samples, and promised that night that he'd be available for more questions the next day. Before a second conversation was arranged, however, Orval Curry hired for Mike one of Columbus's most prominent criminal attorneys, Frank Martin, who told his client to say nothing more to the police. In the years since, Michael Curry has hewed religiously to this admonition.

The Columbus police refrained from terming Mike Curry a suspect—their *only* suspect in the case—but no one else with the opportunity or motive to kill Curry's family has ever come to their attention.

Nothing was stolen from the Curry house that day. None of the victims was sexually assaulted. A small window at the back of the den near a door was broken; glass shards were found inside and outside. Yet the door itself appeared untouched. Its dead bolt was locked and a key was in it.

There were no fingerprints on the murder weapon. Serological and microscopic fiber tests also revealed nothing of value. And a canvass of the neighborhood turned up very little. One woman reported seeing a man in a green car pull up in front of the Curry house on the afternoon of the twenty-ninth. The witness said the man honked his horn and then drove off. A letter carrier thought he'd seen a stranger near the house the day before.

Time of death for the four victims—usually difficult to establish—was put at about 2:30 P.M. to 3 P.M. Pam Burt, Curry's lover, told police she saw him at work at the hospital at 1:30, 1:45, and at 4:45 P.M. His supervisor at the Bradley Center recalled walking around the grounds with Curry from about 1:00 to 1:45 that day.

No one, in short, could positively connect Mike Curry to his family's murder, and no one could demonstrate his innocence. An inquest, called to review all the evidence late in 1985, also failed to exonerate Curry, or to produce enough for the local district attorney to indict him.

Mike Curry and his parents termed the investigation and inquest nothing more than an attempt to railroad him. "They convicted me before they even left the house," he complained at the inquest. "You can't do that in a murder investigation. You can't get the facts that fast."

"We've been treated like the guilty ones," Orval Curry later told the press. "The condemning of Mike in the news media and by Ann's family has not been Christian-like."

"We're decent people," allowed Joyce Curry. "This is something that has shocked us and we haven't been allowed to mourn."

Mike Curry collected around $50,000 in life insurance, and moved to St. Petersburg, Florida, in 1987. His companion there was a woman in whose name Ann Curry's Ford Escort was reregistered. Curry's former in-laws, Jim and Bernice Johnson, traced him to Florida, and have tried to keep track of him ever since. They are certain Mike Curry killed their daughter and grandchildren. Most recently, they say, Curry has been living with a woman in a trailer park in Shoals, North Carolina.

As for the mystery call to the Phenix City police dispatcher the afternoon of the murders, Jim and Bernice have issued a special appeal. Four months after the homicides, they wrote a letter to the *Ledger-Enquirer's* editor. "The longer the person who knows the identity of the killer does not talk," it read in part, "the more likely it is that person will be the next victim. . . . The murderer will become bolder. For your own safety—and the others in the community, call the police department."

There is a $35,000 reward in the case. Readers with information should contact Sgt. Rick T. Boren of the Columbus Police Department at (404) 596-7162.

ABOUT THE AUTHORS

Stephen G. Michaud is the author of seven books, five of them with Hugh Aynesworth. Mr. Michaud has also written for *Newsweek*, *Business Week*, *The New York Times Magazine*, *The Smithsonian*, and several other publications. Among his present assignments in the "Telescope" column for *American Way* Magazine.

Hugh Aynesworth is a veteran investigative reporter. Besides his collaborations with Michaud, Mr. Aynesworth has been a correspondent for ABC-TV's "20/20," a bureau chief for *Newsweek*, an editor at several daily newspapers, and a private investigator. He is a foremost authority on the assassination of President John F. Kennedy. Aynesworth currently is a national correspondent for *The Washington Times*.